Technology and the Regulation of Financial Markets

**Lexington Books/Salomon Brothers Center
Series on Financial Institutions and Markets**

The Deregulation of the Banking and Securities Industry
Edited by Lawrence G. Goldberg and Lawrence J. White

Exchange Risk and Exposure
Edited by Richard M. Levich and Clas G. Wihlborg

Securities Activities of Commercial Banks
Edited by Arnold W. Sametz

Mergers and Acquisitions
Edited by Michael Keenan and Lawrence J. White

Crises in the Economic and Financial Structure
Edited by Paul Wachtel

Option Pricing
Edited by Menachem Brenner

Financing and Investing in Hi-Tech
Edited by Fred B. Renwick

The Emerging Financial Industry
Edited by Arnold W. Sametz

Market Making and the Changing Structure
of the Securities Industry
Edited by Yakov Amihud, Thomas S.Y. Ho,
and Robert A. Schwartz

Technology and the Regulation of Financial Markets:
Securities, Futures, and Banking
Edited by Anthony Saunders and
Lawrence J. White

Technology and the Regulation of Financial Markets

Securities, Futures, and Banking

Edited by

Anthony Saunders
Lawrence J. White

New York University,
Graduate School of Business Administration,
Salomon Brothers Center
for the Study of Financial Institutions

Lexington Books
D.C. Heath and Company/Lexington, Massachusetts/Toronto

Library of Congress Cataloging in Publication Data

Main entry under title:
    Technology and the regulation of financial markets.

    (Lexington Books/Salomon Brothers Center series on financial institutions and markets)
        1. Capital market—United States—State supervision—Addresses, essays, lectures.
2. Commodity exchanges—United States—State supervision—Addresses, essays, lectures.
3. Money market—United States—State supervision—Addresses, essays, lectures.
4. Finance—United States—Technological innovations—Addresses, essays, lectures.
I. Saunders, Anthony. II. White, Lawrence J. III. Series.
HG4910.T38   1986   332.1′ 0973   85-45040
ISBN 0-669-11143-0 (alk. paper)

Published simultaneously in Canada
Printed in the United States of America
Casebound International Standard Book Number: 0-669-11143-0
Library of Congress Catalog Card Number: 85-45040

The paper used in this publication meets the minimum requirements of American National
Standard for Information Sciences—Permanence of Paper for Printed Library Materials,
ANSI Z39.48-1984.
∞ TM
The last numbers on the right below indicate the number and date of printing.

10 9 8 7 6 5 4 3 2 1

95 94 93 92 91 90 89 88 87 86

Contents

Preface

Anthony Saunders
Lawrence J. White

On May 13, 1985, the Salomon Brothers Center for the Study of Financial Institutions, Graduate School of Business Administration, New York University, sponsored a conference on "Technology and the Regulation of Financial Markets." The conference participants included government regulators, representatives of the exchanges, individuals from the financial community, and academic researchers. We were the conference directors. We believe that the conference sessions provided an interesting exchange of ideas and viewpoints. This book is the outcome of that conference.

We owe debts of thanks in many directions. Charles B. McQuade, Terrence F. Martell, Frederick S. Hammer, and Robert J. Woldow served as able chairmen and moderators of the sessions. David Marcus provided an interesting luncheon address. Margie Guinyard, Mary Jaffier, William Jones, and Ligija Roze smoothly managed the behind-the-scenes details of arranging the conference. And Arnold W. Sametz, director of the Center, was a constant source of support, encouragement, and valuable advice.

1
Introduction

Anthony Saunders
Lawrence J. White

The past few decades have seen major changes in telecommunications, information, and computer technologies that affect the regulation of financial markets and institutions—in particular, regulation in the areas of securities, futures, and banking. On May 13, 1985, the Salomon Brothers Center for the Study of Financial Institutions held a conference to explore the relationship between technology and the regulation of financial markets. In this introductory chapter we will try to summarize the major themes that emerged from the conference papers and discussion.

Technological change has allowed existing financial transactions to be conducted in a faster and more efficient fashion. And, perhaps more important, it has opened up new ways for participants in financial markets to carry out transactions. It has allowed the creation of new financial services and transactions. Dramatic decreases in the costs and improvements in the quality of telecommunications, computers, and information services have made possible the worldwide trading of some securities; a dazzling array of new securities, options, and futures (and concatenations among them) that would not have been possible two decades ago; the "securitization" (and, hence, easy marketability) of bank assets, such as residential mortgages and automobile loans; and the borrowing, lending, and transferring of funds among banks in phenomenal volume. These are, of course, just a few examples.

At the same time, financial markets have been, and continue to be, among the most heavily regulated sectors in the U.S. economy. An array of federal (and, for banking, state) agencies oversee and regulate the firms and transactions in these markets. Also, for securities and futures, the exchanges themselves serve important oversight and "self-regulatory" roles vis-à-vis their members.

The new methods and new types of financial transactions can alter the structure of financial markets and create new challenges for regulators. To some extent, the new transactions may bypass existing regulatory structures. "Bypass" is a concept that has arisen in the history of most forms of regulation. Sixty years ago, the advent of the motor truck allowed freight shippers to bypass railroads and their regulated rates. Twenty years ago, large financial institutions turned to "the third market" to try to bypass the New York Stock Exchange and its system of fixed brokerage rates. Ten years ago, individuals and small business turned to money market mutual funds in an effort to bypass Regulation Q's limitations on the interest rates that depository institutions could pay. And today, improvements in telecommunications technology are allowing large users to create their own private communications systems and bypass the regulation-induced high fees of the existing local and long-distance telephone companies.

From a policy perspective, the decision as to whether bypass is an unequivocally good thing that ought to be encouraged, a moderately good thing that should simply be brought within the regulatory sphere, or a bad thing that ought to be prevented depends on the judgment about the social value of the regulation involved. If the regulation is protectionist in nature—shielding firms from the rigors of competition or attempting, through enforcement of cross-subsidy schemes, to protect firms or individuals from having to pay the appropriate costs of goods or services purchased—then bypass is generally a good thing. It usually engenders more competition, more innovation, superior products, and prices that are equal to the long-run marginal costs of production.

But where regulation attempts to deal with genuine market failures—monopoly power, externalities (spillover effects of one market participant on another), or problems of incomplete or asymmetric information from market participants—and where it comes reasonably close to a sensible solution to these difficulties, bypass can create new problems. Financial markets are closely interlinked; market participants are tightly enmeshed and dependent on each other, either directly or indirectly, and problems of externalities and informational asymmetries abound. Accordingly, technological innovations that create new risks may also generate greater financial instability and a potential for contagion effects, and new regulatory problems may arise.

Technological change, of course, has occurred in regulation as well as in financial transactions. Computerization, especially, has allowed regulatory agencies and the exchanges to acquire and analyze information far more rapidly and to monitor and regulate more effectively (within their existing frameworks, of course).

Technology and regulation interact in yet another way. The technology of the trading process itself, which takes many forms—the specialist system of the stock exchanges, the dealer system of the over-the-counter market and government securities market, and the open outcry system of the futures exchanges are a few of the possibilities—can affect the ability of regulators to oversee and monitor transactions. A current controversy, for example, centers on futures markets: Are the open-outcry system of trading, the time-stamping of transactions, and effective regulatory surveillance of these markets mutually compatible?

Part I of this book focuses on corporate securities. Charles C. Cox and Bruce A. Kohn discuss responses of the Securities and Exchange Commission (SEC) to applications of new technology to the markets for securities: the use of computerized trading systems, the electronic filing of documents with the SEC, and the internationalization of securities markets. The SEC has been both reactive and proactive in its accommodations to technological change, prodding the market participants to move in directions it believes will spur more competition. Richard O. Scribner focuses on securities market surveillance and enforcement. He describes ways in which the American Stock Exchange and other self-regulatory organizations (SROs) have put new technology to work in monitoring market transactions. But since new technologies have also widened the market opportunities for transactors, they have increased the surveillance challenge for SROs and even for the SEC. Henry F. Minnerop and Hans R. Stoll point out that changes in the technology of securities transacting, combined with the deregulation of brokerage commission rates in 1975, have altered the structure of the securities brokerage industry. The industry has tended to become less vertically integrated, with greater specialization and division into retail-oriented "introducing" firms (whose numbers are growing) and wholesale-oriented back-office firms (whose numbers are declining). The significant legal and regulatory questions created by this new structure have yet to be resolved.

In part II, on futures, Molly G. Bayley discusses the use of new technology by the Commodity Futures Trading Commission (CFTC) in performing its market surveillance role, as well as the need for improved audit trail capabilities that would permit the futures exchanges and the CFTC to reconstruct trades to an accuracy rate of within one minute of actual execution. Further, drawing on the analogy of the development and computerization of the National Association of Securities Dealers Automated Quotation (NASDAQ) system, Bayley suggests that improved technology on the trading floor of the futures exchanges could mean increased competition, depth, liquidity, and credibility for the futures markets, and possibly even a reduced regulatory role for the CFTC. Todd E. Petzel focuses on the self-regulatory role of the futures exchanges and their strong interest in maintaining tight surveillance over market activities, since perceptions of market manipulation are likely to cause the long-run withering of the markets themselves. He also emphasizes that any regulatory efforts to improve audit trail accuracy should consider the cost-benefit ratio: What is gained in exchange for compliance and the added expense, and how is the efficiency of the marketplace affected? Seymour Smidt analyzes the prospects for continued growth and technological change in securities and futures trading. He points out that innovations are easier to develop and incorporate if they can occur piecemeal and if they do not require the involvement of large segments of an industry. In this respect, technological change has occurred more rapidly and will probably continue to do so in securities trading, where small experiments in trading mechanisms can take place outside of existing institutions, than in futures trading, where they cannot.

In part III, on banking, David B. Humphrey focuses on the large increase in large-dollar wire transfers among banks that has accompanied automation of these transfers and on the intraday borrowing of funds that has accompanied these transfers. A failure to settle one or more of these large transactions could have a serious domino or contagion effect on a substantial number of banks, possibly causing bank failures and impeding the smooth operation of the payments system. He also discusses possible remedies for the problem. The seriousness of the problem was underscored in the week before the conference by the Federal Reserve's recommendation that limits be imposed on bank exposures in these markets. William C. Dudley also discusses these large "daylight overdrafts" and possible corrective measures. He points out that, despite their real costs and risks, a price is not charged for these overdrafts and, hence, as with all items for which no price is charged, the market participants have no incentive to economize on their use. Also, because many (or most) banks probably assume that the Federal Reserve would not allow failure to occur, they may be less careful in controlling risk exposure than they should be. Finally, Gregory F. Udell points out that modern technology has endowed depository institutions with the capability of making rapid changes in the risk characteristics of their portfolios and that periodic bank examinations can detect these changes only after they have occurred. He suggests that, in addition to deposit insurance premiums being adjusted for the riskiness of an institution's portfolio, the periodic bank examinations should be retrospective in nature. In this way, examiners could track the riskiness of an institution's portfolio over time and penalize the institution retrospectively for any increase in risk above the level it had indicated to the insuring agency (and on which its insurance premiums had been based).

Comments on these papers are provided by Lee B. Spencer, Robert A. Schwartz, Roger D. Rutz, Stephen Figlewski, Jarl G. Kallberg and Ken Parkinson, and Frederick S. Hammer. We conclude with overviews by Marc L. Berman, Franklin R. Edwards, Laurie S. Goodman, and Edward J. Kane that integrate the experience from the three market areas.

The wide variety of ideas and viewpoints expressed in this book is indicative of the many facets of technology, regulation, and financial markets. It is, we think, a healthy sign of the fruitful interactions between regulators and regulatees and of the vibrancy of those markets.

Part I
Securities Markets

2
Regulatory Implications of Computerized Communications in Securities Markets

Charles C. Cox
Bruce A. Kohn

The utilization of advanced technology in the securities markets has created increased opportunity for competition in recent years and promises to revolutionize these markets in the relatively near future. The Securities and Exchange Commission has encouraged these developments and—with respect to corporate disclosure information filed with the Commission—has sought to position itself at the forefront of technology. These efforts have required the Commission to be flexible in adopting and administering its regulations while still protecting investors. Such flexibility is consistent with the policy of federal securities laws that the Commission not adopt rules that would impose an unnecessary or inappropriate burden on competition.[1]

In applying its authority to deal with technological changes, the Commission has been both reactive and proactive. Sometimes it has had to decide whether to change rules that are barriers to competition—or to approve rule changes by self-regulatory organizations subject to its oversight—in order to let a new competitor or financial product enter the marketplace. In some cases, however, the Commission has actively attempted to affect the structure of the markets. Such intervention may be indirect, such as requiring the dissemination of information to which the market can react, or removal of some other barrier to competition. Finally, in still other cases, the Commission is itself an important enough participant in the dissemination of information that changing its means of receiving, processing, and distributing information can contribute to market changes.

Three developments illustrate the regulatory challenges resulting from the application of technology to the markets for securities: first, the use of computerized trading systems; second, the electronic filing of documents with the

The views expressed herein are those of Commissioner Cox and Mr. Kohn and do not necessarily represent those of other commissioners or the staff of the Securities and Exchange Commission.

SEC; and third, the internationalization of these markets. Automated trading is already widespread and promises to grow. Electronic filing is being developed in the Commission's pilot program known as EDGAR, an acronym for Electronic Data Gathering, Analysis and Retrieval system. Internationalization is of such current interest to the SEC that it recently published releases soliciting comments on two approaches to facilitate multinational offerings[2] and on issues related to the regulation of international trading markets.[3] The descriptions of these developments in this chapter are selective rather than comprehensive, since they are intended only to illustrate the SEC's regulatory reaction to technological changes.

Computerized Trading Systems

Market developments suggest that computerized trading has had a significant effect on competition among marketplaces for the trading of securities. Congress and the SEC have sought to foster such competition through legislation and rules designed to create what is known as a National Market System (NMS).[4] These efforts have been tempered by the wish to avoid disrupting what are already deep and liquid capital markets in the United States.

The Example of NASDAQ

The success of the National Association of Securities Dealers Automated Quotation system (NASDAQ) demonstrates the competitive effects of computerization. NASDAQ links over-the-counter market makers in one computerized system for the most prominent over-the-counter securities. The system was implemented in 1971 as a result of a suggestion made in 1963 in the SEC's Special Study of the Securities Markets.[5] Originally, NASDAQ provided securities brokers with the market makers' current quotations of the prices at which they were willing to purchase and sell securities, but not with the price at which the last sale of a security was effected. The latter capacity was added in 1981, when the Commission adopted a rule requiring last-sale reporting despite resistance from the National Association of Securities Dealers (NASD). This rule was one of the Commission's initiatives resulting from legislation in 1975 that called for the National Market System. Indeed, real-time reporting of securities transactions is the major requirement the SEC has imposed on over-the-counter securities that are broadly enough traded to be designated NMS securities, pursuant to Commission rules. And despite its initial resistance, NASD has since been pleased with the results. As summarized by NASD President Gordon Macklin in 1984, "The National Market System is that rarest of commodities: an enormously successful commercial product originated in a government agency."[6]

A broker with a customer who wants to buy a security quoted on NASDAQ can now acquire virtually instant knowledge of the current market for that security, even though the market makers are dispersed around the country. This has helped the over-the-counter market to compete with the stock exchanges, which historically have consisted of a trading floor where the market information for a listed security is available in one place. Although the largest companies have traditionally used the New York Stock Exchange as the market for their securities, it appears that companies that are eligible for listing on the NYSE are moving there more slowly than they did prior to the existence of NASDAQ and, in some cases, are choosing to remain traded over the counter. One reason for this preference may be the differences in regulations applicable to over-the-counter markets, but whatever the causes, NASDAQ markets seem to be attracting more volume than they previously did. Thus, NASDAQ may be an illustration of the SEC's ability to enhance competition by requiring dissemination of market information. Even so, some observers view the increased viability of the over-the-counter markets as a mixed blessing. In a sense, it has engendered much of the current debate over whether the NYSE should alter its listing standards so that companies can take steps that are designed to deter takeover attempts and that are permitted in the over-the-counter markets.

Other Aspects of the National Market System

The competitive benefits of electronic market linkages led the SEC to advocate a central market system in the early 1970s[7] and led Congress to pass a law in 1975 requiring the creation of the National Market System. In enacting the legislation, Congress made a series of findings about the opportunities created by new technologies, stating, for example, that "new data processing and communications techniques create the opportunity for more efficient and effective market operations."[8] Congress further indicated that it expected some of these benefits to be realized as the result of an improved exchange of information: "The linking of all markets for qualified securities through communication and data processing facilities will foster efficiency, enhance competition, increase the information available to brokers, dealers, and investors, facilitate the offsetting of investors' orders, and contribute to best execution of such orders."[9] The 1975 legislation directed the SEC to facilitate the establishment of a national market system consistent with these and related findings.[10]

Initiatives to implement the goals of the NMS legislation have utilized computer technologies to link the nation's securities markets. Information about current market transactions and quotations is available through a consolidated transaction reporting system and a composite quotation system, respectively. In 1978, moreover, brokers acquired the capacity to route orders from one market center to another when national stock exchanges were linked through what is known as the Intermarket Trading System (ITS). This system apparently originated from an idea advocated in 1976 by representatives of several stock exchanges constituting the National Market Association; the idea led to the development of ITS as an alternative to some SEC proposals inspired by the 1975 NMS legislation.

The Commission was more directly proactive in linking ITS with NASD's Computer Assisted Execution System (CAES), an automated system for trading exchange-listed securities in the OTC market. In 1981 the Commission ordered an electronic linkage between ITS and CAES. CAES has relatively low volume, however, in part because the most heavily traded exchange-listed stocks are not eligible for OTC trading.

NMS initiatives have also fostered the development by some stock exchanges of systems that automatically execute market orders at a price determined by the inside quotes in the consolidated quotation system. These systems are limited to relatively small securities transactions, generally those involving 1,099 or fewer shares. Legislative and regulatory interest apparently combined here to encourage the development of systems that would facilitate the flow of orders.[11]

Options on OTC Securities

Computerized trading systems are also affecting proposals for the trading of standardized options on OTC securities. NASD and five securities exchanges have submitted proposed rule changes to the SEC to permit trading of such options. The Commission has approved such options trading in principle but has indicated that the proposals would have to be modified to make them consistent with the Securities Exchange Act. Under the proposals, a stock would have to be displayed on NASDAQ in order to be eligible for options trading. The stock would also have to meet other requirements, including a minimum public float of 7 million shares and at least 6 thousand beneficial owners of the security.

In its release requesting comments on these proposals, the Commission indicated the importance of information available through NASDAQ to the trading of OTC options. Because options prices are closely related to the prices of the underlying securities, current market information about the underlying securities is important to options pricing. The SEC stated that it "preliminarily believes that the information provided by . . . last sale reporting is sufficiently timely and accurate to support options trading" on the securities proposed to underlie such trading.[12] Thus, the Commission's proactive decision to require last sale reporting of securities displayed on NASDAQ has contributed to the possibility of trading standardized options on OTC securities.

Multiple trading of options also illustrates the relationship between technology and regulation. Multiple trading in this context refers to the trading of standardized options with the same underlying security in more than one marketplace. With a few exceptions, multiple trading of options on equity securities has been prohibited. Instead, options are allocated among the exchanges that currently trade standardized options on exchange-listed stocks. However, the SEC has determined to permit multiple trading of options on nonequity securities and on stock indices. To a substantial extent, the price competition that results from multiple trading is made possible by the ability to link markets electronically. Although there is a tendency for the preponderance of trading volume to move to a primary market, the continued potential for competition that emanates from multiple trading is a check on the prices set in that primary market. In approving OTC stock options in principle, the Commission likewise approved in principle the multiple trading of such options.

The SEC's current role with regard to options on OTC securities is generally reactive. The Commission has neither encouraged nor discouraged the trading of such options and has been dealing instead with the issues raised in response to rules changes proposed by organizations that want to trade them.

Trading of Securities through Personal Computers

As part of its responsibility to facilitate development of the National Market System, the SEC has monitored the development of systems that allow investors to send orders to their brokers through personal computers. Last fall, the Commission issued a release expressing its views on such computer brokerage systems.[13] A second generation of such systems, which now allow the routing of orders to brokers, is being developed to permit the routing of orders directly to an automatic execution system without broker intervention. The SEC noted in its release that these systems raise issues of noncurrent market information for trading decisions, surveillance of trading activity, suitability of customer trades, and system safeguards.

Most computer brokerage systems allow customers, before they trade, to review delayed price information at no additional charge or to obtain current last sale information at an additional charge. In contrast, when a customer places an order by talking with a broker, the broker can check the current price to detect unusual price swings. In the fall 1984 release, the SEC expressed its opinion that broker-dealers operating computer brokerage systems must at least inform their customers that the market information is not current and must explain how to obtain current information. The Commission also suggested possible safeguards against customers' trading without current information. For example, when a customer chooses to review only the delayed price information before trading through the computer, the system could be programmed to compare delayed information to current information and to notify the customer if there is at least a specified percentage difference between delayed and current data. However, the Commission stated that the industry should take the initiative in the area of safeguards.

Surveillance issues arise because of rules that require a broker-dealer to be familiar with its customers and their trading activities and to retain books and records. Broker-dealers may have to make additional efforts to keep informed of such trading activities. Some form of monitoring will be necessary when registered representatives on commission recommend computer-executed trades.

The Commission also expressed the view that, owing to the flexibility that computer systems permit investors, broker-dealers should take care in making their initial determinations about customers' financial qualifications and suitability for large and risky investments. In particular, the Commission noted that to the extent that a broker-dealer provides research and analysis amounting to recommendations of individual securities through a computer system, the broker-dealer may be subject to rules on the suitability of the recommendations for customers placing orders through the system. The Commission also urged system operators to consider safeguards for the prevention of unauthorized access to a customer's account. Another type of safeguard would allow customers to reaffirm orders in order to reduce the risk of executing erroneous instructions.

The SEC's comments on computer brokerage systems thus have been reactive and have indicated its preference for the industry itself to take the initiative in developing solutions to the problems these systems pose. The timeliness of the comments, however, signifies the absence of a regulatory lag in coping with this new application of technology.

EDGAR

The Commission's Electronic Data Gathering, Analysis and Retrieval system[14] represents an effort to become more efficient and effective in the dissemination of information to investors. Every year, the SEC receives close to 6 million pages of documents making disclosures under the federal securities laws. Usually these disclosure documents are prepared on word processors or in some electronic format. Hard copies of them are logged in at the Commission's office in Washington and eventually are copied onto microfiche. Vendors, who compile computerized data bases to facilitate analysis and recall, must manually enter the information into their electronic data bases before it is disseminated to their customers.

EDGAR, which is currently a pilot project, is aimed at three goals: first, to provide investors, securities analysts, and the public with instantaneous access to corporate information in disclosure documents; second, to allow companies to make required filings directly over telephone lines or by magnetic tape or diskette; and third, to enable SEC staff to analyze and process filings more efficiently at computer work stations. The growth of EDGAR is being planned to coincide with the growth of home computers, which number 16 million today and are expected to number over 36 million within the next five years.

Approximately 150 issuers of securities are now voluntarily participating in the pilot, which has the capacity to accommodate up to 1,000 issuers. The Commission would like the number of participants to reach 1,000 by the end of this year; the volunteers range from smaller registrants to larger ones, such as General Motors and Exxon.

The pilot program consists of three phases. The first phase ended with the first filings on September 24, 1984, and implemented the filing of disclosure documents directly over telephone lines or on diskette or magnetic tape. The pilot is currently in its second phase, during which the Commission has enhanced the system by adding internal and external electronic mail through which it sends comment letters and other communications to participating companies. Shortly, full-text search of filings will be added, along with electronic file folder capabilities. The third phase, which began in the spring of 1985, will examine the value of transferring the pilot experience throughout the SEC.

EDGAR also will be used for the purpose of cooperation with other regulatory agencies and self-regulatory organizations. The North American Securities Administrators Association (NASAA) has designated three states—Georgia, Wisconsin, and California—to participate in a pilot. These states are receiving access to the public filings in EDGAR for their blue sky review.

Many of the regulatory issues confronting the Commission to date in the development of EDGAR have resulted from the need to account for the difference between the paper format and the electronic format. Thus, for example, when a filing is made with the SEC by direct electronic transmission, a personal identification number assigned to it by the Commission is accepted as satisfaction for the requirement of a signature.

EDGAR also poses some questions pertaining to the structure of the market for disclosure information. The Commission is weighing the pros and cons of various approaches to managing and financing contracts that are to be let to private vendors who will develop and implement the operational EDGAR system. One question is whether the operational system, with a projected cost of between $50 and $70 million, should be financed through general tax revenues or through end-user fees. The Commission's initial inclination was to go with end-user fees, but a decision has yet to be made. End-user fees probably would be paid to the contractor as part of a cost-sharing arrangement through which the operational contractor would provide the SEC with the equipment to operate EDGAR in exchange for the right to sell the data. The contractor, subject to regulations, could sell the data and accompanying services in both bulk and nonbulk transactions. In the process of implementing this regulatory approach, including determination of the means of calculating fees, the Commission would have to balance the public's need for instantaneous access to the SEC data base with the contractor's need to recover its reasonable—but not excessive—costs.

The financing of the EDGAR system, as well as other issues—such as the monopoly implications of granting an exclusive contract to one vendor to operate the system—must be addressed in the relatively near future. Nevertheless, the Commission's flexibility and its place at the forefront of technology have been demonstrated by its role in the dissemination of corporate information to investors and by the decisions it has already made with respect to EDGAR.

Internationalization of the Securities Markets

The SEC is considering a variety of regulatory issues in response to the growing internationalization of the securities markets. These issues generally fall into two categories. The first category is disclosure and distribution practices for multinational offerings of securities by nongovernmental issuers. The second category is regulation of the trading markets. The Commission is playing a proactive role regarding these subjects: In separate releases, it has solicited comments on regulatory approaches to the first category and possible responses to the second category.

Disclosure and Distribution Practices

In a recently published release,[15] the SEC requested public comments on methods of regulating multinational offerings from nongovernmental issuers. In order to provide a framework for such comments, the Commission described two approaches that might be used for offerings in the United States, the United Kingdom, and Canada, as follows:

> (1) An agreement by the three countries that a prospectus accepted in an issuer's domicile which meets certain standards would be accepted for offerings in each of the participating countries (reciprocal approach); and (2) the development of a common prospectus which would be simultaneously filed with each of the country's respective securities administrators (common prospectus approach).[16]

Canada and the United Kingdom were selected for this proposal because issuers in those countries frequently utilize U.S. capital markets and because their disclosure requirements are closer to U.S. requirements than are those of other countries. Because investment companies present special considerations, the proposal would not apply to them.

The SEC's release noted that the reciprocal approach is less expensive and easier to use than the common prospectus approach. The minimum standards in the United States for using offering documents that meet the requirements of another country might be, for example, that the foreign issuer attach a facing page and a signature page to the documents used in its own country in order to create a registration statement for the United States. Only the appropriate authorities in the issuer's domicile would review the document for adequacy of disclosure. A disadvantage of the reciprocal approach could be that a country's investors would receive less information were the issuer's domicile to require less extensive disclosure than their own home country did.

Under the common prospectus approach, all countries would have the same standards of disclosure. Although the Commission suggested that this approach could be used for public offerings of securities, it recognized that harmonization of disclosure standards for such offerings could also benefit the secondary trading markets: "Uniform financial and corporate information may act as the first step in developing an international data base for use in secondary trading."[17]

Both approaches, of course, pose complications that would have to be addressed. For example, more than three jurisdictions would be involved. Securities regulation in Canada falls under the authority of each of the provinces, not of a federal system, and the states in the United States have their own blue sky regulations that could be inconsistent with the conceptual approaches outlined by the Commission. These and other complications notwithstanding, the reciprocal and common prospectus approaches are part of the SEC's proactive response to the growing internationalization of securities markets being made possible by increasingly sophisticated technology.

Regulation of International Trading Markets

Although debt securities have played a large part in international markets, the equities markets are also becoming increasingly global. For example, at the beginning of 1984, 46 foreign companies' securities, or American Depository Receipts (ADRs) on such companies' stock, were listed on the New York Stock Exchange, 52 were listed on the American Stock Exchange, and 294 were quoted in NASDAQ. *Euromoney* magazine has estimated that 236 multinational companies, including 84 U.S. corporations, are traded daily in international markets.[18]

The SEC has already begun to respond to the internationalization of securities trading. For instance, it has approved rules changes that would permit the Boston Stock Exchange to establish trading links with the Montreal Exchange and that would permit the Canadian Depository for Securities, Ltd., a Canadian clearing agency, to become a member of the National Securities Clearing Corporation in the United States. Assuming that increased international trading is a goal of investors, however, the Commission still faces several major issues, on which it solicited comments in a recent release.[19]

One set of issues relates to market structure. The Commission noted that exchanges trading the same stocks, for example, could increasingly have simultaneous trading of some issues during parts of the day or could instead arrange for consecutive trading. Simultaneous trading of some securities already takes place on the New York and London Stock Exchanges. Additionally, securities firms might increasingly provide around-the-clock trading, perhaps in part by passing positions among branch offices in different parts of the world as the trading day closes in one country and opens in another. This raises the issue of whether, or to what extent, government regulators should attempt to shape the kinds of market structures that develop.

Through a consolidated quotation system, real-time reporting of transactions is available in the United States for widely traded securities. As noted previously, such reporting in the NASDAQ system was the result of the Commission's initiative. If real-time reporting does not develop for many securities that are relatively widely traded in international markets, regulators will again have to decide whether proactively to expand such reporting.

In its release, the Commission also asked for comment on international barriers to entry into the broker-dealer business. Foreign broker-dealers can register relatively easily with the Commission and gain access to U.S. securities markets. However, some other nations and securities markets deter entry into those markets by U.S. firms. Moreover, differing regulatory schemes can act as de facto barriers. As technology permits the securities markets to become more international, regulators become more interested in the effects of these barriers to competition.

Other issues are raised by differences in regulatory schemes for broker-dealers in various countries and by approaches to surveillance for manipulative trading and other practices that threaten the integrity of the securities markets.

Conclusion

The Securities and Exchange Commission is responding to a variety of challenges posed by burgeoning new technologies to regulators of the securities markets. Sometimes the Commission's role is simply to decide whether to approve rules changes proposed by participants in markets affected by those technologies, but at other times its role consists of more actively trying to remove barriers to competition. In some aspects of the markets, such as the Commission's full disclosure program, the SEC is a more direct participant in the dissemination of corporate information. Both domestic and international market developments pose the question of how the Commission can best respond to the effects of new technologies—whether by improving information flow and otherwise reducing barriers to competition or by attempting more actively to shape the securities markets.

Notes

1. Securities Exchange Act of 1934 § 23(a)(2), 15 U.S.C. § 78w(a)(2); see also Securities Act of 1933 § 19(c)(2), 15 U.S.C. § 77s(c)(2).

2. Securities Act Release No. 6568 (Feb. 28, 1985), 50 Fed. Reg. 9287 (7 March 1985).

3. Securities Exchange Act Release No. 21958 (18 April 1985), 50 Fed. Reg. 16302 (25 April 1985).

4. See Securities Exchange Act of 1934 § 11A, 15 U.S.C. § 78k-1, and rules adopted thereunder.

5. *Report of Special Study of the Securities Markets of the Securities and Exchange Commission*, H.R. Doc. No. 95, 88th Cong., 1st Sess., Part 2, at 655-59 (1963).

6. Mr. Macklin's quotation is contained in an NASD press release for July 9, 1984, and is among remarks prepared for a luncheon observing the addition of the 1,000th issue to the list of NMS-designated securities traded through NASDAQ.

7. See, for example, the SEC's statement on the Future Structure of Securities Markets (2 February 1972), 37 Fed. Reg. 5286 (Mar. 14, 1972).

8. Securities Exchange Act § 11A(a)(1)(B), 15 U.S.C. § 78k-1(a)(1)(B).

9. *Id.* § 11A(a)(1)(D), 15 U.S.C. § 78k-1(a)(1)(D).

10. *Id.* § 11A(a)(2), 15 U.S.C. § 78k-1(a)(2).

11. For further discussion of development of the National Market System, see Feller, Fitterman, and Colby, *The National Market System: A Selective Outline of Significant Events 1971-1983* (30 April 1983). Much of the discussion of the National Market System in this chapter is drawn from this outline, which is available by contacting Robert Colby at (202) 272-2857.

12. Securities Exchange Act Release No. 20853 (12 April 1984), 49 Fed. Reg. 15291, 15295 (18 April 1984).

13. Securities Exchange Act Release No. 21383 (9 October 1984), 49 Fed. Reg. 40159 (15 October 1984).

14. This section is drawn from the author's remarks entitled "EDGAR: Truly a Revolution," delivered at the Conference on SEC in Depth: Advanced Reporting and Compliance, sponsored by the SEC Institute, Inc., on December 10, 1984, in Los Angeles.

15. Securities Act Release No. 6568 (28 February 1985), 50 Fed. Reg. 9281 (7 March 1985).

16. Ibid., 9281.

17. Ibid., 9284.

18. *The Corporate List*, Euromoney, May 1984, at 71.

19. Securities Exchange Act Release No. 21958 (18 April 1985), 50 Fed. Reg. 16302 (25 April 1985).

3
The Technological Revolution in Securities Trading: Can Regulation Keep Up?

Richard O. Scribner

My thesis, simply stated, is that securities regulation, which has experienced significant advances in the past decade as a result of technological improvements, is now being confronted with significant obstacles to its effectiveness in a rapidly expanding marketplace whose own growth has been stimulated by technology. The application of modern communications and data processing technology has facilitated the development of derivative products such as options and futures, which in turn has led to the creation of sophisticated trading strategies employing these products and their underlying instruments; it has also accelerated the expansion of intermarket trading of the same securities and cross-market trading of related products. Additionally, technological growth has accelerated the internationalization of securities trading and has made possible the emergence of non-exchange-based, computer-assisted markets such as NASDAQ and Instinet.

By increasing the speed, dispersion, and complexity of the marketplace, these developments have introduced new challenges for the regulator, particularly with respect to market surveillance and enforcement. Although technology will continue to assist in confronting many of these challenges, others, particularly those involving varying governmental and jurisdictional constraints, are more difficult to overcome and call for compensatory readjustments to our existing regulatory framework.

Innovations and Structural Changes Promoted by Technology in the Markets

The technological revolution has greatly enhanced our ability to search out evidence of possible fraud, abuse, and unfairness in the market. But tech-

The author gratefully acknowledges the assistance of Stephen L. Lister, Esq., and Joan F. Berger, Esq., respectively senior vice president and special counsel, Compliance Division, American Stock Exchange, in the preparation of this chapter.

nology does not belong to the regulators alone. It has sped trading; has extended access to the markets, both temporal and geographically; and has assisted in, if not directly given rise to, a plethora of complex derivative products, challenging the ability of market regulators to perform their functions effectively.

Modern communications and data processing technology burst through the boundaries that until the early 1970s had segmented and confined our securities markets in their traditional molds. New technical capabilities have greatly facilitated intermarket trading in the same security between physically separate markets. An order to purchase an Amex listed stock brought to the Amex floor can be electronically shipped via the Intermarket Trading System (ITS) for execution on a regional exchange displaying a lower offering price, and vice versa. Recently, the Amex announced an arrangement whereby, using technology similar to ITS, brokers on the Amex and Toronto Stock Exchange will be able to access the other's market in dually listed stocks. The newspapers have carried reports of discussions aimed at the development of pilot projects between the New York and London Stock Exchanges to trade stocks and other financial instruments, as well as joint methods of reporting stock prices and trading volume.[1] These international linkages will undoubtedly become more prevalent as the process of internationalization accelerates over the next several years. Indeed, the rapidly declining cost of communications is making international linkages increasingly practical.

Whether or not markets are linked by formal agreements, the application of technology (together with relaxation of the rules that once largely confined trading in exchange-listed securities to those markets) is facilitating the growth of "off board" trading. The activities of Jefferies & Co. in trading NYSE stocks when major news announcements occur after the New York close and the increasing talk of twenty-four-hour trading in certain "world class" U.S. equities by dealers in other countries are ready illustrations of a trend that is surely only beginning to manifest itself.

Related to multimarket trading of the same instrument is cross-market trading in related instruments. In addition to the classic example of stock-option trading, trading recently began on the Chicago Board of Trade of futures on an index (the Major Market Index) on which options are traded on the Amex. Similar futures and options trading occurs in the Standard & Poor's 100 and 500 indexes on the Chicago Mercantile and Chicago Board Options Exchanges. Here, too, technology significantly contributed to the development and rapid growth of these latest versions of the derivative product. Without that technology, the recalculation and wide dissemination of the index on the underlying stocks on a minute-by-minute basis would be impossible. For reasons that will be discussed next, these crossovers between options and futures markets, which frequently involve transactions in the underlying stocks as well, pose particularly difficult challenges for the regulators.

Without the computer capability that enabled the Options Clearing Corporation to issue standardized certificateless options, to open and close thousands of options positions on a one-day settlement basis, and to generate automatic exercise notices, exchange-traded stock options as we know them today could never have existed.[3] Similarly, the ability rapidly to analyze options premiums against theoretical pricing models has fueled the growth of professional options trading and has given rise to various combination strategies involving two or more related products, such as conversions and reverse conversions, which are severely testing the capabilities of the single-market, single-product regulators.[4] Witness, for example, the technique called "conversion arbitrage," in which a trader establishes a position consisting of long stock, short calls, and long puts. Instead of a single stock and its overlying call and put, the trader could employ a conversion strategy using several of the heavily weighted stocks in a particular index and calls and puts on that index. These puts and calls could be comprised of securities options, options on futures, and futures, and could be traded on several different options and futures markets. The impact of such positions on the stock and options markets, and the resulting surveillance difficulties, have recently attracted the attention of the press.[5]

Finally, technology supports, if indeed it did not cause, the growth of nonexchange, computer-assisted markets such as NASDAQ and Instinet. Markets of this type hold a very great potential for radically expanding the physical and temporal boundaries of the marketplace and suggest to all of us, even those whose business continues to be centered around a physical trading floor, that the future will belong to those who can most successfully adapt technological opportunities to the changing needs of the marketplace. Electronic markets that include an execution feature should result in enhanced surveillance capabilities insofar as they produce an immediate audit trail identification of the parties to a trade.[6] However, these markets, which are by definition physically dispersed and which greatly extend the number and variety of people having direct access to them, will pose problems with which we have relatively little familiarity.

Technology-Aided Advances in Market Surveillance

Before exploring challenges to regulation created by the expanding marketplace, it will be useful to consider briefly the principal ways in which modern technology has in recent years been harnessed in support of regulation. In addition to aiding in the detection of illegal and unethical activity, contemporary surveillance tools have dramatically increased the regulator's ability to monitor and assess the quality of markets maintained by stock and options market makers and have led to far higher standards of performance.

By way of introduction, it should be noted that the large majority of trading market surveillance is performed by the exchanges and the NASD, although, owing to limitations in jurisdiction, they frequently refer possible violations to the SEC for further investigation. So, although it may not appear so from the newspaper account, the next SEC insider trading case reported in the press, in all probability, will be unearthed by one of the self-regulators.

Each of these self-regulatory organizations, or SROs, has availed itself liberally of the computer's capabilities for capturing, sorting, and analyzing quotation, trade, and clearing data for surveillance and other regulatory purposes.[7] We have come a long way from the not-too-recent past when we simply "watched the tape" and relied on our floor professionals to holler when they thought something was amiss in the market. Today, we employ a battery of on-line systems, post-trade exception reports, and, increasingly, comprehensive audit trails to alert us to possible violations and to assist us in investigations.

One illustration is the Amex's on-line surveillance systems, which are designed to monitor stock and options trading activity as it occurs. Our Stock Watch Alert Terminal (SWAT) provides a sophisticated method of detecting deviations from "normal" volume or price movement in listed equity securities on a real-time basis. SWAT employs a continuously updated data base of historical price and volume information to establish norms for each stock based on its own unique trading characteristics. Activity outside predetermined limits—which are automatically adjusted to reflect overall market conditions and which may be narrowed by an analyst to look even more closely for the first signs of unusual activity when we know an as yet unannounced development is in the offing—is immediately called to the attention of a Stock Watch analyst by an eerie "R2D2" voice issuing from the SWAT terminal. The analyst's next step most likely is to consult an array of news and data recall devices to determine whether publicly reported events may account for the unusual activity. If there is no ready explanation, further inquiries will ensue, typically involving the trading floor and company officials. This is a good place to point out that although computers are indispensable for identifying potential problem situations, there is no substitute for trained, motivated analysts and investigators to turn these leads into enforcement cases.

The Amex's on-line Stock and Options Watch capabilities are best suited to the early identification of a misuse or leakage of nonpublic information—a security surging in price and volume just prior to the announcement of a major corporate development. The workhorses of surveillance, however, are the off-line transaction journals and exception reports that permit an SRO to examine activity in a security in more detail and over a longer time span. At the Amex, these tools are used to surveil possible misuses of nonpublic information, market manipulation, and market-maker misconduct (for instance, failure to maintain fair and orderly markets, trading ahead of the public, violation of the short sale rules, and so on). The availability of computerized exception reports—in which large masses of trading data, often covering long time periods, are sifted against preestablished criteria, or *parameters*, to identify unusual levels or frequency of activity—is especially critical to the proper oversight of the options markets, since the pricing relationships between an option and its underlying equity and the leverage nature of the option contract create significant incentives for abuse. For example, a member is considered to be acting unfairly in relation to other participants in the market when he or she effects a transaction in options while having knowledge of a pending block transaction in the underlying stock; this transgression is called "frontrunning." Another transgression, called both "capping" and "pegging," occurs when a market participant enters orders in the underlying stock to keep its price from rising above (or falling below) the exercise price of his or her position in the underlying option.[8] It would be extremely difficult to surveil all such abuses, involving as they do large numbers of transactions and activities in two different markets, absent the computer's ability to sift through huge quantities of trade data and to identify transactions which, because of their particular juxtaposition, appear to suggest violations. Similarly, to detect various forms of market manipulation, the Amex employs longer-term exception reports such as one identifying firms that over an eight-week period have accounted for an especially large volume of purchases or sales in a security, along with special reports of activities, at or near the close of trading over a period of time, that may be evidence of attempts to "mark a close."

These types of reports, of which only a few have been mentioned, suggest further areas for inquiry by our analysts and investigators. They, alone, rarely catch a violator red-handed. This is particularly true for trades effected by public customers, since we must still depend on the firm that has been identified in our report as having effected the trades to furnish us with the identity of the customer for which it has acted. Since sophisticated persons engaged in fraudulent or manipulative schemes frequently operate in groups and disperse their trading activities among a number of firms to conceal their identities and intentions, the regulator, even one armed with the most advanced technology, faces a stiff challenge.

Until recently, regulators have been frustrated by the absence of comprehensive audit trails. The solution to this problem, again, is being accomplished through the aid of technology. Essentially, the difficulty that the stock and options exchanges faced was their inability to match a particular reported trade with the actual participants to the trade. The reason for this inability, in the simplest case, was that each party to a trade recorded the information essential to complete the trade—security, price, quantity, and contraparty—on his own trade ticket and went on to the next trade. The exchange employee reporting the transaction to the tape, however, owing to the constraints of time and visibility, recorded security, price, and quantity, but not both parties' identities. Because of the large number of trades occurring at similar prices, it became impossible to match reported trades with cleared trades during periods of high volume. This inability precisely to reconstruct the market came to the forefront with the introduction of option trading and the onset of intermarket stock-options violations of the type previously described. By the late 1970s, the options exchanges pioneered techniques to match trade and clearance reports to provide workable transaction audit trails. Similar techniques are now being applied by the NYSE and Amex in their stock markets. Of course, these efforts have been greatly facilitated by the computer's ability to assemble vast amounts of data into manageable formats and have led to the creation of comprehensive stock-option transaction journals and on-line recall systems.[9] One system, first developed by the NYSE as "ISIS" and in its Amex adaptation called "ALIS," permits the generation of individually tailored exception reports from a data base consisting of ninety days' worth of consolidated quote, trade, and clearance information on Amex stocks and options, as well as the NYSE stocks underlying those options.

Challenges to Regulation in the Computer Age

Even this brief set of illustrations clearly shows how technology has fundamentally expanded the scope of our securities markets. The extent of this change is only beginning to be felt. What, then, are the most pressing problems facing the regulatory community in this new and emerging environment? The most serious and intractable problems, which do not, unfortunately, admit merely of technological solutions, arise from the extension of the new markets beyond the jurisdictional boundaries within which the self-regulators and national regulatory authorities have historically worked.

The essential problem is that no single SRO has sufficient surveillance information or broad enough disciplinary jurisdiction fully to regulate conduct affecting its market, nor does the SEC have the information or jurisdiction to regulate conduct occurring beyond our national borders that has consequences in the U.S. securities markets. Moreover, the technology revolution I have been describing is likely to heighten these limitations.

At the level of domestic securities markets, each SRO "knows" only what occurs in its own trading market and enjoys investigative and disciplinary jurisdiction only with respect to its own members, member organizations, and their employees. If this was tolerable during the time of single-product, quasi-monopoly markets, it became intolerable with the advent of derivative products and multimarket trading. To surveil my options market properly, I simply must know what it is that persons trading there are also doing in the underlying stock market. To close this information gap, the eight securities exchanges and the NASD in 1981 formed the Intermarket Surveillance Group (ISG). The ISG provides a means for the SROs to share relevant surveillance data among themselves and with the SEC. It has also established protocols and procedures for conducting coordinated investigations of certain "intermarket violation conditions" and has in general promoted a much higher degree of cooperation among the SROs than previously existed. Similarly, in recent years much closer coordination has taken place between the SROs and the SEC, resulting in several notable enforcement successes.[10] Nonetheless, fundamental weaknesses exist. Since the SROs cannot effectively reach persons outside their respective memberships, it is difficult to conduct comprehensive investigations, and it is necessary to rely on the already scarce resources of the SEC to complete investigations and to take enforcement action against "members of the public" over whom the SROs have no jurisdiction.

The situation becomes even more complex and difficult in the international arena. The classic example, which has had several real-world embodiments in the recent past,[11] involves a foreign national who uses inside information to trade on a U.S. options exchange. The options exchange's surveillance department discovers what it thinks may be insider trading—a large purchase of deep-out-of-the-money call options just prior to the company's announcement of a very favorable development. Upon inquiry of the member firm handling the purchase, the exchange learns that it was made for the account of a foreign bank. Since it has no investigative or disciplinary jurisdiction over the bank, which is not a member or member organization, the exchange turns its findings over to the SEC. But the foreign bank, although it has some jurisdictional presence in the United States because it maintains a branch office in New York, explains to the SEC that it is only acting as agent for a customer in the transaction and that because of a bank secrecy law in its home country, it is unable to divulge any information about the customer, including his (or its) very identity.

The SEC recently has shown great creativity in squeezing cooperation out of foreign financial intermediaries, especially when the intermediary has assets and a franchise in the United States that can be held hostage to their cooperation. Nonetheless, the existence of bank secrecy and "blocking" laws in certain countries have made it nearly impossible to pursue investigations into trading activities conducted through financial intermediaries in these countries. This problem suggests two possible avenues of attack: first, unilateral U.S. action to extend the SEC's enforcement reach, and, second, bilateral or multilateral arrangements with foreign jurisdictions for exceptions to secrecy or blocking statutes in appropriate circumstances. This process is greatly complicated by differences in trading ethics among countries. Conduct that is considered reprehensible in the United States—for example, insider trading—may not be viewed as wrongful somewhere else.

The former enforcement director of the SEC, John Fedders, has authored an imaginative and highly controversial proposal, called "waiver by conduct," which contemplates the enactment by Congress of legislation providing, in essence, that any person who initiates a securities transaction in a U.S. market thereby is automatically deemed to have waived any secrecy law of the country from which the transaction is initiated.[12] It is not the purpose of this chapter to analyze or critique the waiver by conduct concept, which is already receiving a great deal of attention from commentators.[13] It suffices here to note that even this far-reaching proposal only begins to scratch the surface of surveilling and regulating transnational securities transactions. Clearly, vastly expanded cooperation will be required among national law enforcement authorities and market regulators in many countries.

To some extent, the requisite cooperation can be accomplished by formal treaties and by less formal intergovernmental agreements.[14] However, these arrangements involve long and complex negotiations and cover only narrow topics. It may be that our experience with the Intermarket Surveillance Group in the domestic securities market can be employed in an international context. Thus, both governmental and self-regulatory authorities might find it useful to align themselves informally, with a view to systematically sharing such surveillance and other information as they are able to under their own respective laws for combatting fraud and market manipulation. Although such an alignment would not initially address such a matter of concern to U.S. enforcement officials as insider trading, it might form the basis on which international standards could be upgraded over time. Indeed, it might not be unreasonably optimistic to hope that over time real progress could be made toward the development of uniform standards and requirements in at least certain key areas among the principal financial centers.[15] The further spread of market linkages and the extension of multimarket trading in certain "world class" financial instruments will lend further impetus and urgency to such efforts.

A second, and related, challenge arising from the technological revolution is that new persons are arriving on the scene, even in the domestic trading environment, who do not fit within the existing regulatory framework. For one thing, we are now seeing the development of "trading markets" in stocks that are not conducted by exchanges or the NASD. These include Instinet, which maintains electronic facilities for use by subscribing members in trading both listed and over-the-counter stocks. Additionally, several securities firms—Troster Singer Corporation (a subsidiary of Spear, Leeds & Kellogg, a leading specialist firm) is one example—are offering automatic execution services and minimum-size guarantees to brokers who send them over-the-counter business to transact. My purpose is not to criticize these innovations but simply to point out that their operators are not self-regulatory organizations in the statutory sense. For the time being, the exchanges and the NASD will continue to surveil trading in their respective securities that occurs through these facilities, but it is questionable whether that will be fully feasible should they become the principal markets in certain securities. Would not the problem become even more acute should such "markets" spring up offshore? Certainly the technology for such an eventuality is readily available, and the International Futures Exchange, or Intex, located in Bermuda, is even now seeking to establish a worldwide electronic futures trading mechanism.

For another thing, what are the regulatory implications of investors having the ability to trade directly from their own personal computers?[16] Of course, we are a time away from that world; for the immediate future most customers will continue to have access to markets only through "members."[17] But how much incentive or ability will member firms have to interfere with a customer's electronically expressed desire to purchase 100 shares of IBM or Apple or "XYZ," assuming they have reasonable confidence that he or she can pay for it? What then will become of our traditional notion of suitability and of the supervision of salespeople? Imagine the market manipulation or insider trading potential of a person entering orders, perhaps through multiple accounts at banks and brokers, directly from his living room. On the other side, imagine the Big Brother implications of establishing a comprehensive surveillance scheme giving regulators on-line access to customers' trading activities and positions, which might be required to oversee this type of trading environment adequately.

While these last possibilites may seem extreme, their realization, and that of others like them, is not far distant. It is axiomatic that when tools become available, they will be used. The technological tools are there. The only question is, How rapidly will the financial community's ever fertile imagination find dramatically new ways to put them to use? I think it will not be long, and we regulators will have to be equally imaginative and more statesmanlike than we have been in the past in order to keep up.

Notes

1. Intermarket linkages are progressing at an even faster pace in the commodities world. Within the past year, linked trading in select products has commenced, at least on a pilot basis, between the Boston Stock Exchange and the Montreal Exchange, the Chicago Board of Trade (CBOT) and the London International Financial Futures Exchange (itself an electronic trading mechanism centered in London), the Chicago Mercantile and Singapore Monetary Exchanges, New York's Commodity Exchange and the Sydney (Australia) Futures Exchange, and the Philadelphia Stock Exchange and the Hong Kong Futures Exchange. Additionally, discussions are under way for a linkage between the CBOT and the Tokyo Futures Exchange.

2. For a comprehensive discussion of issues raised by the movement toward global trading, see "Request for Comments on Issues Concerning Internationalization of the World Securities Markets," Exchange Act Release No. 34-21958, 18 April 1985. See generally, "World Financial Curbs Eased by Technology and Ideology," *New York Times*, 26 January 1985.

3. Technology has also led to the creation of options trading on over-the-counter securities, a precedent-setting innovation just approved by the SEC on April 16, 1985.

4. A prime example of such theoretical pricing models is the highly regarded Black-Scholes options pricing model, used to estimate the dollar-for-dollar sensitivity of an options price to movements in the price of the underlying security at any time.

5. See, for example, "Is the Tail Wagging the Dog?" *Barrons*, 10 December 1984; "Calls Before, Puts Later," *Barrons*, 18 March 1985; "Meet the Missile," *Barron's*, 15 April 1985; "Futures/Options—Witching Hour for Investors," *New York Times*, 15 April 1985. See also "Index Options Proliferate: A Guide to Calls, Puts and Striking Prices," *Wall Street Journal*, 13 March 1985.

6. At the present time, the vast majority of trades in NASDAQ stocks are completed via the telephone, not through the system itself. Trades in NASDAQ/NMS securities are required to be reported promptly to NASDAQ, but the efficiency of this system, especially in fast markets, has been subjected to question. See, for example, Exchange Act Release No. 34-20902, 30 April 1984. NASDAQ is currently introducing an automatic execution feature on a pilot basis through its small-order execution system. Executions employing the touch screen technology of the Amex's AUTOPER System, and the automatic execution capabilities of the Philadelphia Stock Exchange's PACE System and the Pacific Stock Exchange's SCOREX System, provide instantaneous identification of the parties to a trade but are not currently structured to provide real-time access to this information.

7. Although most of the facilities described herein carry American Stock Exchange names, similar installations exist at other stock and options markets. These distinct facilities are functionally interconnected under the auspices of the Intermarket Surveillance Group, whose purposes and procedures are outlined later in the chapter.

8. A variation on this theme is mini-manipulation, an attempt to influence the short-term price movement in a stock to benefit a previously established options position.

9. The use of automated small-order routing systems like the NYSE's "DOT" and Amex's "PER" further facilitates this process by creating a more accurately timed electronic record of orders and trade reports, showing in the latter case the name of the contra party.

10. See, for example, *SEC v. Warren M. Choset and J. Barris Lepley, Jr.*, No. 83 Civ. 4460 (WCC) (S.D.N.Y. 1983).

11. See, for example, *SEC v. Banca Della Svizzera Italiana*, 92 F.R.D. 111 (S.D.N.Y. 1981), and *SEC v. Certain Unknown Purchasers of the Common Stock of, and Call Options for the Common Stock of, Santa Fe International Corporation*, No. 81 Civ. 6553 (WCC) (S.D.N.Y. 1983).

12. This proposal is embodied in Securities Act Release No. 33-21186 (6 August 1984). For commentary by Mr. Fedders on the subject, see (1) Fedders, *Crime and Secrecy: The Use of Off-Shore Banks and Companies*, Hearing before the Permanent Subcommittee on Investigations of the Senate Committee on Government Operations,

98th Cong., 1st Sess., 134–147, 318 (1983); (2) Fedders, "Preserving the Integrity of the Internationalized Capital Markets," before the Seminar on Litigation of Business Matters in the U.S. and International Legal Assistance, Zurich, Switzerland, 27 September 1983, 18 Int'l Law. 89 (Winter 1984); (3) Fedders, "Foreign Secrecy: A Key to the Lock," *New York Times* (16 October 1983), sect. 3, p. 2; (4) Fedders, Wade, Mann, and Beizer, "Waiver by Conduct—A Possible Response to the Internationalization of the Securities Markets," 6 J. of Comp. Bus. and Cap. Market L. 1 (1984); and (5) Fedders, letters to Senator A.M. D'Amato, chairman of the Subcommittee on Securities of the Senate Committee on Banking, Housing and Urban Affairs, and Representative J.D. Dingell, chairman of the House Committee on Energy and Commerce, 30 March 1984.

13. To date, the policy issues raised by the proposed legislation have been addressed by a total of sixty-five letters of comment. One practical shortcoming of the waiver by conduct approach, which communications technology has perhaps exacerbated, is that layers of intermediaries, each from a different secrecy jurisdiction, can be inserted, thus making it even more difficult to trace the real party in interest.

14. For example, the *1977 Treaty on Mutual Assistance in Criminal Matters Between Switzerland and the U.S.* provides for cooperation between law enforcement authorities regarding investigations and court proceedings involving criminal offenses, including fraud (27 U.S.T. 2019, T.I.A.S. No. 8302). See Greene, "U.S., Switzerland Agree to Prosecute Inside Traders," *Legal Times*, 4 October 1982, at 12, col. 1; Honegger, "Demystification of the Swiss Banking Secrecy and Illumination of the United States—Swiss Memorandum of Understanding," 9 N.C.J. of Int'l L. & Com. Reg. 1 (Winter 1983).

15. On a related front, the SEC recently suggested the possibility of common registration standards for certain offerings to be made in the United States, United Kingdom, and Canada. See Securities Act Release No. 33-6568 (28 February 1985). More comprehensive efforts at "harmonization" have been under way for some time among countries of the European Community.

16. For the SEC's views on this subject, see Exchange Act Release No. 34-21383 (9 October 1984).

17. Instinet currently provides direct market access to numerous institutional clients.

4

Technological Change in the Back Office: Implications for Structure and Regulation of the Securities Industry

Henry F. Minnerop
Hans R. Stoll

> As it is the power of exchanging that gives occasion to the division of labor, so the extent of this division must always be limited by the extent of that power, or, in other words, by the extent of the market. When the market is very small, no person can have any encouragement to dedicate himself entirely to one employment.
> —Adam Smith, *The Wealth of Nations*

The benefits of the division of labor and specialization of functions, outlined by Adam Smith in 1776, and the limits on the division of labor imposed by the size of the market, as noted by Smith in the preceding quotation, provide the basis for our analysis of the changing structure of the securities business. Our thesis is simple: technological change in the securities business has increased the extent of the market. This, combined with deregulation, has made possible increased specialization of certain functions—particularly back-office functions—at reduced costs. Other functions of a brokerage firm—those pertaining to direct customer contact—are less subject to computerization and cost reduction, but even in this area the computer is enabling individual brokers to serve a larger number of customers by collecting and managing data quickly and more efficiently. The result has been a structural change in the securities industry: the development of specialized, wholesale brokerage and data processing firms that provide routine back-office services to other firms and the growth of smaller, customer-oriented firms. This division of labor between back-office functions and customer-

We gratefully acknowledge the assistance of individuals at Bear Stearns & Co., J.C. Bradford & Co., The Chicago Corporation, Merrill Lynch Pierce Fenner & Smith, Inc., the National Securities Clearing Corporation, the New York Stock Exchange, the NASD, and the SEC in clarifying various aspects of the execution, clearing, and settlement process.

contact functions has in turn generated legal and regulatory questions with respect to the responsibility for customers' funds and the requirement to "know your customer."

Division of Labor and Extent of the Market

Efficiencies arising from division of labor and specialization of function lead to declining average costs (ACs) of production at higher output levels, as shown in figure 4–1. According to Smith,[1] these increasing returns to scale are limited by the extent of the market, say, at Q_m. In a small market, many functions are performed by the same person, whereas in a large market, specialization leads "to the increase of dexterity in every particular workman; . . . to the saving of time which is commonly lost in passing from one species of work to another; and . . . to the invention of . . . machines which facilitate and abridge labour."[2]

Stigler points out the implication in Smith's proposition that markets will be monopolized because the producer having the largest market share will also have the lowest average cost of production. But how, then, does one reconcile Smith's proposition with the observed competitiveness of many markets? Stigler resolves this apparent contradiction with the observation that individual firms engage in a variety of activities, with economies of scale existing for some and being exhausted for others. Stigler's point may be illustrated by considering a firm that produces a product or service that requires only two

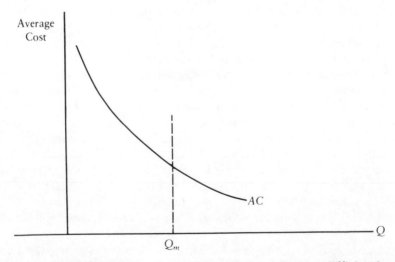

Figure 4–1. Relationship between Labor and Specialization Efficiencies and Average Costs of Production at Higher Output Levels

input activities. For our purposes, activity number one can be thought of as customer contact, and activity number two, as back-office work. Assume also that the optimal size for engaging in activity number one is quite small, say, output Q^1 in figure 4–2, whereas the optimal size for activity number two is quite large, say, output Q^2 in the same figure. The average cost curve for the firm as a whole is then AC, as shown in figure 4–2; and given a market size of Q_m, several competing firms may exist.

As Stigler notes, with an expansion of the market, one might expect firms to spin off activity number two to a single large firm. This firm would possess a natural monopoly, limited, nonetheless, by the ability of other firms to integrate back into activity number two. In other words, Smith and Stigler predict that in an expanding industry, pressures for vertical deintegration exist that tend to increase the number of specialty firms.

Vertical deintegration is limited in a number of ways, however. First, the activity subject to increasing returns to scale may not be important enough to be carried out by a separate firm. Second, the cost of communicating and coordinating with a separate firm may be greater than the cost of carrying out the various functions within a single firm. Third, different activities of a firm may be interdependent in the sense that doing one thing means doing other things better. Fourth, cartel pricing arrangements or regulatory restrictions may be disincentives to unbundling the activities of a firm. Under cartel pricing of one activity, it may be in the interest of a firm to provide other products or services below cost as a means of reducing the price on the first activity. Until recently, the second and fourth factors have been important in limiting

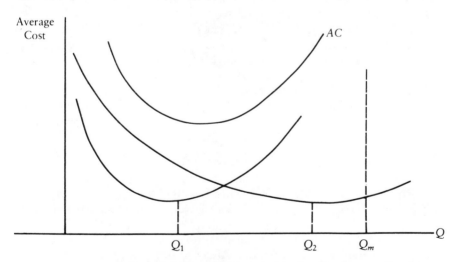

Figure 4–2. Average Cost Curve for Firm Producing Product or Service Requiring Only Two Input Activities

the unbundling of the functions of a securities firm; but with the deregulation of the securities industry and major development in the technology of trading and communicating, the unbundling and rebundling of brokerage firm activities has increased dramatically. Before considering in greater detail the impact of deregulation and technological change, we will outline the principal functions of a securities firm.

Functions of a Securities Firm

A securities firm has traditionally been engaged in one or more of the following activities.

1. *Customer contact.* Direct contact between a customer and an account representative familiar with the customer's needs is an essential activity of most brokerage firms. This activity may involve:

Approving, opening, and monitoring customer accounts.

Establishing the suitability of transactions and activities in the account ("know your customer").

Providing financial planning and investment advice.

Providing information on market prices and market trends.

Receiving and placing customer orders.

Discount brokers provide limited service, emphasizing the receiving and placing of customer orders, whereas full-service brokers emphasize all activities.

2. *Execution of orders.* An order placed by an account representative is sent to a back office and then follows a sometimes circuitous route to execution. Two steps in the process may be distinguished:

Order routing. The order must be routed to the appropriate transaction locale, an exchange, or an over-the-counter dealer. Order routing may depend on whether the order is an odd lot, a round lot, or a larger transaction and on whether it is a limit order or a market order.

Order lock-in. After an order has been routed to an appropriate transaction locale, the transaction must be locked in. The manner in which a transaction is completed will depend on the type of order and on the market in which it takes place. In some cases execution may be completely manual; in other cases, it may be completely automated.

3. *Customer-side confirmation.* After a transaction, the customer is informed as to the terms of the transaction and is billed for monies or securities due. In addition, customer accounts are updated.

4. *Customer-side settlement.* Receiving funds from customers, or delivering funds to them, is a separable activity. The safe-keeping of securities and cash and the payment of dividends and/or interest are closely related activities.

5. *Street-side trade comparison.* The first step in clearing a transaction with the broker for the other side is the comparison of transactions to determine whether the buying and selling side agree on price and quantity. This function is carried out by clearing firms on behalf of their customers.

6. *Street-side settlement.* The second step in the clearing process is the actual settlement of a transaction, which occurs between one and five days after the transaction takes place, depending on the product. This process requires the transfer of funds or securities to the contra-side of the transaction.

7. *Margin lending.* Many securities firms are in the business of lending funds to customers.

8. *Investment research.* Some brokerage firms produce research reports. This activity should be distinguished from the activity of conveying information or providing advice on the basis of research reports prepared by others.

9. *Risk bearing.* Securities firms engaged in market making, block trading, or underwriting are distinguished by their willingness to assume risk in order to facilitate the transactions of their customers. Investment banking firms, for example, purchase securities from an issuer without assurance of the resale price for those securities.[3]

The functions just listed can be grouped into three categories. The first category is the customer-contact function, which frequently depends on face-to-face communication between an account representative and a customer and is therefore highly labor-intensive and not as readily subject to division of labor and specialization of function. Functions two through seven may be grouped into a second category, back-office functions. Our emphasis is on these two categories, which are elements of the transaction process. We place investment research and the risk-bearing function of market makers and underwriters in a separate category because these functions are not directly related to the technology of the transaction process.

Impact of Deregulation on Specialization

The Securities Acts Amendments of 1975 required commission rates to be competitively determined and called for open access to all markets for all qualified broker-dealers. This new regulatory environment has provided a framework in which, for a number of reasons, the unbundling of brokerage activities has become possible.

First, under fixed commission rates, New York Stock Exchange (NYSE) member firms had competed by offering a range of services rather than by cutting official minimum commissions. As a result, each NYSE firm tended to engage in many activities, and this inhibited specialization. With negotiated rates, firms can now efficiently charge only for those services they perform, and this has led firms to concentrate on what they do best. Some firms have failed because of their inability to compete effectively once the minimum commission umbrella was removed.

Second, before 1975, a nonmember firm was required to pay a full commission to a member firm in order to have an order executed on the NYSE on behalf of the nonmember's customer. This made it excessively costly for a nonmember of the NYSE to specialize in any aspect of the brokerage business, such as customer contact, because to do so would require charging the customer more than the fixed minimum commission charged by NYSE members. With the elimination of fixed commission rates, member firms are able to charge nonmember firms only for those back-office services provided, and the separation of back-office and customer-contact functions is facilitated.

Third, the 1975 Securities Acts Amendments called for a national market system extending beyond the floor of the New York Stock Exchange. The recognition that the national market system is a communication system, not a physical location, has made possible an extension of the market and has provided the opportunity for increased specialization of function.

Fourth, the Amendments also called for the development of a national clearance and settlement system that would facilitate the prompt and accurate processing of securities transactions. The Amendments called for the registration of all clearing agencies, securities depositories, and transfer agents and recommended an improvement in the process by which securities are cleared that would, among other things, involve the elimination of the stock certificate. Legislative recognition and support of a national clearance and settlement system has made possible the development of specialized centralized depositories and a single, national stock-clearing corporation, which have dramatically reduced the cost of clearing and settling transactions among broker-dealers.

Impact of Technological Change

Although deregulation has removed obstacles to structural change in the securities industry, technological growth in communications and trading procedures has been the major force for change. The effects of technology have been threefold. First, improvements in communications technology have extended the securities markets in both space and time. Investors are now in a position to trade from any geographical location in the world twenty-four hours a day. In 1792, when twenty-four brokers met under a buttonwood tree to establish the forerunner of the present NYSE, face-to-face communication was the only means of carrying out transactions. Since then, improved communications and the automation of trading have diminished the need for face-to-face communication and may have made obsolete the physical trading floor. Markets in the United States are electronically linked by the Intermarket Trading System (ITS), and brokers in the United States and throughout the world are linked directly to market centers. International links between markets have been established between Boston and Montreal and, in futures markets, between Chicago and Singapore. Discussions to link the NYSE and the London Exchange, Toronto and the AMEX and to create other links are under way. In 1776, Adam Smith noted:

> As by means of water-carriage a more extensive market is opened to every sort of industry than what land carriage alone can afford it, so it is upon the sea-coast, and along the banks of navigable rivers, that industry of every kind naturally begins to subdivide and improve itself.[4]

The rivers of today are the advanced communications links that serve in a similar way to extend the securities market. If Smith was correct, one would expect expansion of the securities market to lead to vertical deintegration of securities firms and increased specialization in providing some of the nine functions of a securities firm listed previously.

Second, the coordination of the activities of separate organizations is now a reality because the same technology that has expanded the market has also provided communications links that connect firms to service organizations, wholesale brokers, or market centers that provide services essential in the transactions process. To an account executive, the difference between executing transactions through the back office of his own firm and establishing himself as an independent broker and executing through the back office of a separate organization is a small one.

Third, technological innovation in the trading and communications process has reduced the costs of trading. This effect is in addition to the effect of the increasing returns to scale that result from the extension of the market, because technology has reduced costs at all levels of output. For example, the efficiency with which transactions are cleared has increased dramatically. Certificates, which used to be sent between brokers, are now immobilized in the Depository Trust Company (DTC), and ownership of certificates is changed by computer book entry. The National Securities Clearing Corporation (NSCC) provides facilities for trade comparison and settlement to its members, the clearing brokers. Computer records of transactions are provided to NSCC by both parties to each transaction, and NSCC compares records to determine that both parties agree on the terms of the transaction. NSCC then calls for payment of a single net cash amount from or to each clearing member and directs the DTC to make appropriate book entry changes in the ownership of each security.

Similar increases in efficiency have occurred in other aspects of the transaction process. For example, the NYSE's designated order turn-around (DOT) system provides for automatic routing of orders to the appropriate specialist post on the floor of exchange, thus bypassing the need for the floor broker. Execution of smaller-size orders has been automated. For example, derivative pricing systems, such as PACE on the Philadelphia Exchange, SCOREX on the Pacific Coast Exchange, or MAX on the Midwest Exchange, provide for automatic execution of an order on the basis of the next price on a principal market, usually the New York Stock Exchange. The NASD has introduced the Small Order Execution System (SOES) that provides for automatic execution of orders of up to 500 shares at the best bid or ask price of dealers. Confirmation is automated and immediate, and trade comparison and settlement are accomplished by computer hookup to the clearing corporation. Finally, the accounting process—the preparation of confirmations and monthly statements—has also been automated and is frequently provided by independent service organizations.

Types of Clearing Arrangements

The computerization of (a) the order routing and execution process, (b) the clearing and settlement process, and (c) the confirmation and accounting process has provided opportunities for specialized firms that are willing to make the necessary capital investment in computers and software to provide these services to other brokers. Today, almost all of the nine functions of a securities firm can be performed by different entities: Customer contact can be provided by an independent broker who purchases a variety of services from other entities. Orders can be routed and executed through another broker, and confirmations can be prepared with the help of a separate service organization. Clearing of transactions can be carried out through yet another clearing firm that specializes in computerizing records of transactions and in clearing through the NSCC. Margin lending can be provided by a separate entity such as a bank. Investment research is frequently purchased from a separate organization. The activity of risk bearing, including underwriting, is also increasingly specialized and concentrated as the need for capital to meet the liquidity needs of institutional investors has grown. The emphasis in this chapter, however, to repeat, is not on the risk-bearing function or on the investment research function provided by securities firms.

The functions other than risk bearing and investment research are typically allocated between an introducing firm that specializes in retail contact with customers and a clearing/carrying firm that specializes in some or all of the back-office functions two through seven listed previously. A clearing arrangement may be on an omnibus basis or on a fully disclosed basis. Under an omnibus account arrangement, the clearing firm executes and settles transactions for the account of the introducing firm and in the latter's name. The clearing firm is not advised of the identity of the customer for whom the introducing firm is acting. Accordingly, confirmations of transactions and statements are provided by the clearing firm only to the introducing firm. The introducing firm, in turn, furnishes its customers directly with individual confirmations and statements, perhaps using an independent service organization to prepare them.

A variety of arrangements are possible between an introducing and clearing firm. Most frequently, the clearing firm performs functions five and six, street-side trade comparison and street-side settlement. Function two, execution of orders, is also frequently carried out by the clearing firm. The question of who bears responsibility for the safekeeping of securities and the holding of cash (function four) is an important area of negotiation between the introducing and clearing firm. Since the firm that has authority to hold customer cash may have free credit balances available, the size of the fee charged by a clearing firm for its services will depend on whether it or the introducing firm holds customer cash. Another matter of negotiation between introducing and clearing firm is responsibility for margin lending. Both omnibus and fully disclosed accounts may be on either a margin or a cash basis. If they are on a margin basis, the clearing broker has authority to lend funds or securities to customers. Since these activities are profitable, the fee charged will tend to be lower if this function is allocated to the clearing broker. Finally, the clearing broker may have responsibility for customer-side confirmation (function three). In a fully disclosed introducing arrangement, the introducing firm—that is, the retail firm—is responsible only for customer contact. All other functions are carried out by a firm that is responsible for carrying and clearing customer accounts.

Structural Change: The Evidence

Despite considerable publicity about brokerage firm mergers and the consolidation of the securities industry, the evidence in tables 4–1 and 4–2 indicates that the total number of brokerage firms has increased since the midseventies. Furthermore, the structure of the securities industry has changed in a way consistent with Stigler's prediction. Fully disclosed introducing firms, which deal directly with customers and for which economies of scale are limited, have grown dramatically in number. NASD member firms in this category grew from 499 in 1974 to 1,694 in 1984, as shown in table 4–1. During this same period the number of NASD member firms clearing and carrying customer accounts declined from 1,461 in 1974 to 1,236 in 1984. The decline in the number of carrying firms probably understates the amount of specializa-

Table 4–1
NASD Member Firms Classified by Type of Activity, 1974–1984

Year	Carrying[a]	Fully Disclosed Introducing[b]	Total Brokerage	Other Firms[c]	Total
1974	1,461	499	1,960	1,267	3,227
1975	1,392	564	1,956	1,059	3,015
1976	1,374	614	1,988	936	2,924
1977	1,336	685	2,021	808	2,829
1978	1,292	760	2,052	779	2,831
1979	1,212	824	2,036	787	2,823
1980	1,191	970	2,098	883	2,981
1981	1,189	1,007	2,196	1,091	3,287
1982	1,164	1,097	2,261	1,478	3,739
1983	1,212	1,397	2,609	2,157	4,766
1984	1,236	1,694	2,930	2,865	5,795

Source: Provided by the National Association of Securities Dealers.

[a]This category includes firms that execute, clear, confirm, or carry customer accounts. The majority of firms hold customer funds and are subject to SEC Rule 15c3-3, which requires them to maintain a special reserve bank account. Some firms do not hold customer funds and have a partial exemption (section (k)(2)(A)) from the rule.

[b]These firms do not execute, clear, confirm, or carry accounts or hold cash. They satisfy exemption (k)(2)(b) of Rule 15c3-3.

[c]These firms offer special products (such as direct participation programs), sell mutual funds, or sell insurance.

tion in back-office functions, because many of these firms do not perform all back-office functions. The trends evident in table 4–1 for all NASD members are repeated in table 4–2 for New York Stock Exchange member firms. Even among NYSE members, whom one assumes to be broadly based, there is evidence of specialization by retail-oriented introducing firms and a decline in the number of firms carrying out back-office functions.

The data in table 4–1 may overstate the growth in the number of independent NASD introducing firms, since some of these firms are likely to be

Table 4–2
NYSE Member Firms Classified by Type of Activity, Selected Years

Year	Total Firms	Firms Dealing with Public Total	Carrying	Introducing
1972	558	496	346	150
1975	494	404	264	140
1977	473	364	225	139
1981	604	390	217	173
1982	617	387	214	173
1983	639	412	218	194

Source: NYSE 1984 *Fact Book,* p. 61. Reprinted with permission.

subsidiaries of other brokerage firms or other financial institutions. On the other hand, table 4–1 is likely to understate the growth in introducing firms because it omits all bank brokerage activities not registered with the SEC. Since most bank brokerage activities are not registered with the SEC, the number of introducing firms is understated by the number of banks providing an introducing function. Coler and Ratner (1983) estimated the number of bank discount brokerage operations at 2,000. Even if this number is an over-statement, it implies that, on balance, the number of introducing firms shown in table 4–1 is understated. Thus, if we take into account all brokers, not only those registered with the SEC, the trend toward a division between wholesale brokerage firms and retail firms becomes even more evident; and the expansion in the total number of brokerage firms becomes significant.

Regulatory and Legal Issues

When the functions of a brokerage firm are subdivided and contracted out, and when the link between two customers trading with each other involves an ever greater number of participants, several legal and regulatory issues arise: Who is responsible if a transaction fails to be completed? To whom does the customer look in case of a break in the transactions link and a failure of one party to perform? Do SEC capital requirements apply to the introducing firm or to the clearing firm? Is a customer always insured by the Securities Investor Protection Corporation (SIPC), even if his account is with an introducing firm that does nothing more than take his order? Is the introducing firm to be viewed as an agent of the clearing firm, which implies a responsibility of the clearing firm for the actions of the introducing firm? Or is the introducing firm to be viewed as the (knowledgeable) customer of the clearing firm?

The Securities and Exchange Commission has recognized the existence of clearing arrangements and has made adjustments in the relevant regulatory requirements to take account of these arrangements. These adjustments generally provide for more lenient capital requirements for an introducing firm, since the firm is not carrying cash or securities of public customers on its books. Introducing firms are also exempt from the reserve requirements under Rule 15c3-3 of the Securities Act. This exemption applies when the introducing firm holds no customer funds or securities and promptly transmits all customer funds and securities to the clearing firm that carries the accounts of customers. For the purposes of insurance under the SIPC, a customer of an introducing firm whose account is cleared and carried by another firm that is an SIPC member is viewed as a customer of that SIPC member.

Considerable controversy has been generated by legal suits brought by customers of introducing firms whose accounts have been mismanaged in some way and who have sought redress not only from the introducing firm but also from the clearing and carrying firm. Such suits typically arise when the introducing firm has become insolvent or is otherwise unable to respond fully to the damages claimed. Cases in this area tend to focus on the separate identities of the clearing and introducing firms and argue that the introducing firm is under the control of the clearing firm or that, at a minimum, the clearing firm has knowledge of the activities of the introducing firm and therefore is responsible for its activities. We turn now to some examples of case law that illustrate some of the legal issues brought about by these clearing arrangements. NYSE Rule 382 and Rule 405 as amended in 1982 are then considered. Rule 382 specifies certain requirements that must be met in clearing arrangements and provides guidelines on the areas in which agreement must be reached in a clearing arrangement.

Case Law

Pre–1982 case and administrative law, a summary of which is contained in the appendix to this chapter, has long recognized that introducing and clearing firms are generally separate entities, subject independently to the same legal and regulatory requirements.[5] Their arrangements with each other are contractual in nature.[6] In *Hawkins v. Merrill Lynch, Pierce, Fenner & Beane*,[7] the court rejected the contention that the clearing firm is the principal of the introducing firm and further stated that the customers are "charged by law with knowledge of the meaning of the relationship of correspondent and carrying broker."

Prior to new NYSE Rule 382, customers were not required to be notified of the existence of the contractual relationship and the specific allocation of functions between the two firms. Moreover, the two firms often blurred the formal lines of separation as a practical matter. Thus in *Hawkins*, the clearing firm closely advised the introducing firm on how to handle inquiries from the SEC to avoid capital requirements associated with handling customer funds and generally directed important facets of the introducing firm's business, leading the court to find that the clearing firm controlled de facto the introducing firm within the meaning of the Securities Exchange Act of 1934. Accordingly, the clearing firm was found liable to the introducing firm's customers for the fraudulent conversion of their funds by the introducing firm.

A lawsuit currently pending in federal court raises issues that perhaps illustrate in an extreme fashion the financial exposure faced by a clearing firm where the introducing firm has become insolvent: *Margaret Hall Foundation, Inc. v. Atlantic Financial Management, Inc.*[8] Although this suit was filed after new NYSE Rule 382 became effective in 1982, the underlying events occurred prior to adoption of the rule.

The various complaints in *Atlantic Financial* were filed by the investment advisory clients of a Boston-based investment advisor whom plaintiffs fully authorized to manage their funds in discretionary accounts in line with their investment objectives. The advisory agreement disclosed that all transactions would be channeled through the adviser's affiliated broker-dealer. Pursuant to a fully disclosed clearing agreement, a New York–based firm thereafter executed and cleared most of the transactions and mailed confirmations and monthly statements directly to the plaintiffs. These confirmations and statements indicated that the accounts were executed and cleared by that firm; no other contact occurred between the plaintiffs and the clearing firm.

The adviser directed the purchase of a substantial number of allegedly speculative oil stocks, concentrating the purchases primarily in one oil company. In time, the price of these stocks declined sharply, leading to large losses. Although the confirmations and monthly statements reflected all purchases (and the resulting concentration), the complaints charged the clearing broker with failing, in effect, to supervise the adviser and the introducing firm and with failing to warn plaintiffs of the alleged mishandling of their funds through unsuitable and concentrated investments. The complaints also alleged that the clearing firm should have become aware of, and then prevented, trading by the introducing firm for its own account in the same oil stocks; this trading was alleged to be in conflict with the investments made for plaintiffs.

The *Atlantic Management* cases are currently in the pretrial stage; all questions of liability are yet to be adjudicated. However, the court has denied a pretrial motion by the clearing firm, which sought to be dismissed from the proceedings as a matter of law. The latter argued that it had simply acted as execution and clearing firm and had fulfilled those duties properly. In denying the motion, the court stated that the complaints alleged there was a "close working relationship" between the introducing firm and the clearing firm that went beyond the usual parameters of clearing relationships. Specifically, the court noted allegations in the complaints that (*a*) the clearing firm sublet office space to the introducing firm; (*b*) the introducing firm used the good name of the clearing firm to generate business; (*c*) the clearing firm promoted the same oil stocks; and, finally, (*d*) the plaintiffs perceived the clearing firm as their broker because they had received confirmations and statements directly from it.[9] The court's opinion did not analyze why these allegations justified the characterization of a "close working relationship." Indeed, the court demonstrated no understanding of the nature of clearing relationships in general and devoted no attention to examining the economically constructive division of function implicit in such relationships. Some of the difficulties posed by this case may be reduced by the adoption of NYSE Rule 382, but to date no court has discussed that rule in any reported decision that we are aware of.

Rule 382

The regulation of clearing or carrying agreements entered the modern era in 1982, when the SEC approved the proposed amendments of NYSE Rule 382 and 405. Under Rule 382, as amended, the NYSE requires that clearing agreements involving a member firm allocate the various responsibilities associated with a securities transaction between the introducing firm and the carrying firm. At a minimum, seven areas of responsibility must be allocated under Rule 382. They are:

1. Opening, approving, and monitoring of accounts.
2. Extension of credit.
3. Maintenance of books and records.
4. Receipt and delivery of funds and securities.
5. Safeguarding of funds and securities.
6. Confirmations and statements.
7. Acceptance of orders and executions of transactions.

Moreover, the customer must be informed of this allocation in writing.

The NYSE acknowledged that the primary purpose of Rule 382 was to clarify existing procedures for allocating responsibilities in clearing relationships, but it also emphasized the exclusivity of the rule with respect to other provisions of the NYSE constitution and rules: New Rule 382 is the "exclusive Exchange rule which concerns itself with the [carrying or clearing] relationship."[10] In particular, Rule 382 has preempted Rule 405—the "know your customer" rule—in the context of the carrying agreements that allocate know-your-customer responsibilities to introducing firms (as virtually all carrying agreements do). Thus, a carrying firm has no responsibilities under Rule 405 (unless such responsibilities are contractually allocated to it), even though the language of that rule requires "every member organization . . . to (1) use due diligence to learn the essential facts relative to . . . every cash or margin account accepted or carried . . . and every person holding power of attorney over any account accepted or carried by [any member] organization." The customer of the introducing firm must be notified in writing of the allocation of responsibilities between firms. The ramifications of Rule 382 and its exclusivity go beyond the NYSE regulatory framework: They enhance the carrying broker's ability to defend against actions by customers of the introducing firm in which allegations of fraud or of aiding and abetting in fraud on the part of the carrying firm are made. Such actions often allege that the carrying firm knew or should have known of the fraudulent activities and that its inaction with respect to the fraud itself constituted fraud. Under amended Rule 382, the carrying firm can now show, first, that it had no duty to "know" the customer, and, second, by inference, that it is not required to maintain or examine customer data beyond what is necessary—normally only the name and address of the customer—to discharge its functions under the carrying agreement. The voluminous transaction data generated by clearing firms should not have to be analyzed by them to determine the suitability of transactions, the existence of churning, and so forth. If the carrying broker follows a practice now permitted under Rule 382, he will not, for example, keep any data on file enabling him to determine the suitability of transactions even through hindsight. Many clearing brokers, no doubt out of habit, may still take in all kinds of customer-related data and store them someplace, never to look at them again unless a document request is served in a lack-of-suitability claim. It is wiser to avoid the collection of such data in the first place.

Conclusions and Broader Implications

Stigler notes that growing industries will tend to be characterized by vertical deintegration and greater division of labor as the extension of the market makes specialization possible. Increased specialization is certainly not observed in all aspects of the securities industry, and a number of securities firms have adopted a policy of full-line service, but evidence on the provision of back-office functions in the securities industry does indicate that increased specialization is occurring therein, accompanied by a significant expansion of retail brokerage firms. Stigler's predictions are driven by an analysis of the costs of producing services, and these predictions do seem relevant to the back-office functions of the securities industry, in which technological change has not only extended the market but has also produced significant cost reductions. Demand-side considerations, such as customer demand for one-stop shopping and convenience, reduce the desirability of specialization and have caused certain firms to provide customers with a portfolio of services; but even these firms will frequently contract out back-office functions with specialized clearing and carrying firms.

The separation of wholesale and retail functions in the brokerage industry can also be observed in other financial institutions, particularly banking. As in the securities industry, deregulation and technological change in communications and automation have widened banking markets and have increased the optimal size of banks engaged in wholesale banking activities. On the other hand, many customer-contact functions are still best served by a banker who is familiar with his or her locality. Again, as in the securities industry, a variety of arrangements are evolving to link many relatively small retail banks with a few relatively large wholesale banks. Whether these arrangements will take the form of traditional correspondent banking relationships, be based on franchising concepts popular in other industries, or use other methods of networking banks is yet to be determined. However, in the new, less regulated environment, any arrangements that are developed will respond to the forces of technological change and will reflect competitive pressures to produce financial services most economically.

Significant legal and regulatory issues arise when component tasks in the delivery of financial services are subcontracted. These issues have to do with determining who is ultimately responsible to the customer and how the financial integrity of the financial system can best be assured as it grows increasingly complex. NYSE Rule 382 has clarified the basis for dividing responsibility in brokerage clearing arrangements, but legal disputes are likely to continue, particularly when a customer has a complaint against a poorly capitalized or insolvent introducing firm, the accounts of which are carried by a well-capitalized clearing and carrying firm. Similarly, questions of the adequacy of capital requirements of brokers and banks in our increasingly automated and interlinked financial system are likely to continue to be an important concern of regulatory authorities.

Notes

1. Adam Smith, *The Wealth of Nations*, ed. E. Cannan.
2. Ibid., Book I, chap. 1, 7.
3. The distribution function of an investment banking firm involves activities, such as customer contact, already considered.
4. *The Wealth of Nations*, Book I, chap. 3, 18.
5. See generally 17 C.F.R. 240. 153 (1983).
6. See, for example, *In the Matter of D.H. Blair & Co.*, 44 S.F.C. 320, 328 (1970).
7. 85 F. Supp. 104, 121 (W.D. Ark. 1949).
8. 572 F. Supp. 1475 (D. Mass. 1983).
9. Ibid., 1480–81.
10. NYSE Information Memo, No. 82-18, dated 5 March 1982.

References

Coler, Mark and Ellis Ratner. "Discount Brokerage Is Here to Stay, and Banks Can Win at the Game If They Play Smart and Define Their Goods," *American Banker* (September 12, 1983):20–23.
Smith, Adam. 1776. *The Wealth of Nations*. Edited by E. Cannan.
Stigler, George J. 1951. "The Division of Labor Is Limited by the Extent of the Market," *Journal of Political Economy* (June):185–93.

Appendix:
Case and Administrative Law
and Commentaries Dealing with
Clearing Arrangements

The following is a chronological listing of cases and SEC proceedings involving clearing arrangements:

1. *Hawkins v. Merrill Lynch, Pierce, Fenner & Beane*, 85 F. Supp. 104 (W.D. Ark. 1949). After a bench trial, judgment was rendered against the clearing firm. The court found that although the introducing firm was not the agent of the carrying firm, the latter exercised de facto control over the former. Hence the customers could recover directly against the clearing firm for the theft of their funds by the introducing broker.

2. *In the Matter of Merrill Lynch, Pierce, Fenner & Beane*, CCH [1948–52] § 76,065 (SEC 1950). The same facts pertained here as in *Hawkins*, leading to admonitions against the clearing broker, which undertook to restructure its clearing relationships.

3. *Livingston v. Weiss, Voisin, Cannon, Inc.*, 294 F. Supp. 676 (D.N.J. 1968). On a motion to dismiss, the court ruled in favor of the clearing firm, which had no alleged involvement with or responsibility for the securities recommendations to the customer. The court left standing those claims alleging violations of margin regulations.

4. *In the Matter of D.H. Blair & Co.*, 44 S.E.C. 320 (1970). The Commission noted that "arrangements between clearing and correspondent firms are a matter of contract between them, so long as the public customers' interests are not jeopardized," 44 S.E.C. at 328; it further noted in the same decision that a carrying firm has no general responsibility of supervision over an introducing firm; idem, "But where, as here, the record shows that personnel of the clearing firm were aware of serious irregularities in an account, it seems to us both reasonable and in the public interest to impose on that firm an independent duty of inquiry and take prompt steps to terminate any participation in activity violative of the federal securities laws."

5. *Faturik v. Woodmere Securities, Inc.*, 442 F. Supp. 943 (S.D.N.Y. 1977). On a motion to dismiss, the court ruled against the clearing firm upon allegations of a "close relationship" with the introducing firm and the pres-

ence of churning in the introduced account, allegedly known or subject to inquiry by the carrying firm under NYSE Rule 405. The court held that the plaintiff had stated a primary claim under NYSE Rule 405 and a secondary aiding and abetting claim with respect to the introducer's alleged 10b-5 fraud. The court pointed out, however, that if the clearing firm could show at trial that it had acted merely in a clerical capacity and as an order taker (that is, as clearing broker), then the requisite control relationship with the introducer would be missing to establish liability under Rule 10b-5.

6. *Schenck v. Bear, Stearns & Co.*, 484 F. Supp. 937 (S.D.N.Y. 1979). After a bench trial, judgment was rendered in favor of the clearing firm, which had liquidated the customer's margin account. The court specifically rejected the argument that the carrying firm was the general principal of the introducing firm, even though in the matter of obtaining the customer's signature to the margin agreement, the introducing firm had acted as agent for that limited purpose.

7. *Baty v. Pressman, Frohlich & Frost, Inc.*, CCH [1979] Fed. Sec. L. Rep. § 96, 897 (S.D.N.Y. 1979). Summary judgment was granted in favor of the clearing broker upon finding no involvement or responsibility in violative conduct of the introducing firm, as alleged by customer. In contrast, in the same case and on similar facts, the court denied the summary judgment motion of NYSE against the same plaintiff, citing the Exchange's statutory duty under section 6 of the 1934 act to enforce its rules with respect to member conduct. *Baty v. Pressman, Frohlich & Frost, Inc.*, CCH [1979] Fed. Sec. L. Rep. § 96, 896 (S.D.N.Y. 1979).

8. *Cothren v. Donaldson, Lufkin, & Jenrette Securities Corporation*, 82 Civ. 363 (E.D. Tex. August 31, 1982) (unreported slip opinion). On a motion to dismiss, the court ruled against the clearing firm on allegations of agency and control. The court does *not* mention NYSE Rules 382 and 405, as amended on March 5, 1982.

9. *Boylan v. Securities and Exchange Commission*, 24 S.E.C. Docket 449 (1981), *aff'd*, No. 82-7111 (9th Cir. March 7, 1982). The SEC sanctioned the introducing firm for failure to advise the clearing firm pursuant to clearing agreement of the introduced customer's past history of nonpayment in connection with cash d-v-p accounts when cleared by prior carrying firms. This omission was held to be a material violation of Rule 10b-5.

10. *Margaret Hall Foundation, Inc. v. Atlantic Financial Management, Inc.*, 572 F. Supp. 1475 (D. Mass. 1983). On a motion to dismiss, the court ruled against the clearing firm on allegations of directly participating in Rule 10b-5 violations and aiding and abetting such violations by the introducing firm and investment adviser. The court does not mention NYSE Rules 382 and 405, as amended on March 5, 1982, although the impact of those rules was briefed. Indeed, the court cites no authority of any kind in support of its rulings. 572 F. Supp. at 1480–1481.

11. *Baratta v. S.D. Cohen & Co..* 81 Civ. 0004 (S.D.N.Y. July 1984). This was an unreported bench decision enforcing the indemnity provision in the clearing contract requiring the introducing firm to pay attorney's fees of the clearing firm in a suit by a customer who alleged misconduct by both introducing and clearing firms. The court, however, denied the clearing firm's claim for attorney's fees in enforcing that provision.

The following is a list of articles and comments relating to the clearing relationship:

1. Charles H. Meyer, *The Law of Stockbrokers and Stock Exchanges*, § 124 (1931); discusses the historical basis of corresponding relationships.

2. Wolfson, Phillips, and Russo, *Regulation of Brokers, Dealers and Securities Markets* (Warren, Gorham & Lamont, 1977 ed.), § 9.03; deals with margin regulations in introduced accounts.

3. S. Goldberg, *Fraudulent Broker-Dealer Practices*, § 7.5 (1978); takes the view that introducing firms are, in reality, part of the clearing firm's branch office system and that, accordingly, clearing agreements are a devious scheme to protect clearing firms.

4. H.F. Minnerop, *Clearing Arrangements*, Securities Industry Association, "Compliance and Legal Seminar Outlines," April 29–May 2, 1984, 778–801.

5. W.J. Fitzpatrick and R.T. Carman, *An Analysis of the Business and Legal Relationship Between Introducing and Carrying Brokers*, 40 Bus. Law. 47 (1984); takes the position that clearing and introducing brokers' responsibilities to third parties should be defined and limited to the function and responsibilities allocated in the carrying agreement.

6. *Regulation of Agents and Introducing Brokers in the Commodities Future Industry*, Association of the Bar of the City of New York, *The Record* 39, no. 7 (Dec. 1984):554–92. This is a report prepared by the Committee on Commodities Regulation of the Association of the Bar of the City of New York, contrasting inter alia CFTC and SEC regulation of introducing and clearing brokers.

There are a number of relevant court decisions and SEC proceedings dealing with the duty of brokers vis-à-vis customers whose accounts are managed by investment advisers:

1. *Rolf v. Blyth, Eastman Dillon & Co., Inc.,* 570 F.2d 38 (2d Cir. 1978), amended in CCH [1978 Decisions] Fed. Sec. L. Rep. § 96,525 (2d Cir. 1978), *cert. den.,* 439 U.S. 1078 (1978), holding, inter alia, broker-dealer liable as aider and abettor to the customer's investment adviser. The court amended its original opinion to note that in garden-variety cases involving managed accounts, the executing broker is not liable to the customer.

2. *Kaufman v. Merrill Lynch, Pierce, Fenner & Smith*, Civil Action B.76-227 (D. Md. 1980), entering a directed verdict in favor of a broker who had simply executed on instructions of the customers' investment adviser.

3. *In the Matter of Merrill Lynch, Pierce, Fenner & Smith Incorporated*, CCH [1982 Tr. Binder] Fed. Sec. L. Rep. § 83,258 (1982), on same facts as in *Kaufman*, noting in a 21(a) report that SEC "believes that the situation described . . . suggests problems . . . [that] may subject the broker-dealer to liability for aiding and abetting." The report refers to various stale data in the broker's custody which, if examined, may have triggered concern that unsuitable securities were being ordered by the adviser. Merrill Lynch agreed to review and implement certain internal procedures.

4. *Cumis Ins. Society, Inc. v. E.F. Hutton & Co.*, 457 F. Supp. 1380 (S.D.N.Y. 1978), holding that NYSE Rule 405 does not require the broker to investigate the manner in which the investment adviser invests funds of the "adviser's customers"; idem at 1390, "This duty would be more than burdensome; it would be ethically unsound."

5. *Rasmussen v. Thompson & McKinnon, Auchincloss, Kohlmeyer, Inc.*, 608 F.2d 175 (5th Cir. 1979), holding that the broker was not liable to the customer for investments ordered by his investment adviser.

6. *Cannizzaro v. Bache, Halsey Stuart Shields, Incorporated*, 51 F.R.D. 719 (S.D.N.Y. 1979). Relying on *Faturik*, the court denied motions for summary judgment or dismissal of aiding and abetting claims against two clearing brokers. The court found that allegations that the clearing brokers knew of the introducing firm's violation of the federal securities laws and assisted in the violation by "clearing" orders constituted an adequate "threshold showing" of a factual dispute concerning the clearing broker's role, entitling the plaintiffs to "at least limited discovery" to support their claim.

Finally, there are several miscellaneous cases of interest:

1. *Buttrey v. Merrill Lynch, Pierce, Fenner & Smith Inc.*, 410 F.2d 135 (7th Cir.), *cert. den.*, 396 U.S. 839 (1969), affirming denial of a motion for summary judgment and holding that the broker may have a duty under Rule 405 to know its customer, an Indiana broker-dealer in insurance stocks. The dealer had converted his customer funds, using them to trade in his own proprietary account with Merrill Lynch, which was alleged to be on notice of that broker's propensity to act wrongfully, having received a number of checks from him that were returned for insufficient funds.

2. *Robinson v. Merrill Lynch, Pierce, Fenner & Smith Inc.*, 337 F. Supp. 107 (N.D. Ala. 1971), *aff'd per curiam*, 453 F.2d 417 (5th Cir. 1972), holding that a commodities broker was not a general fiduciary or agent of the customer required to provide market information to its customer but was only an agent in connection with the specific steps involved in executing orders.

3. *Canizaro v. Kohlmeyer & Co.*, 370 F. Supp. 282 (E.D. La. 1974), *aff'd per curiam*, 512 F.2d 484 (5th Cir. 1975), stating that a broker "who neither solicits the order nor recommends the securities, but who has merely received and executed a purchase order, has a minimal duty, if any at all, to investigate the purchase and disclose material facts to a customer." 370 F. Supp. at 289.

4. *U.S.F. & G. Co. v. Royal Nat. Bank of New York*, 545 F.2d 1330 (2d Cir. 1976), holding that Merrill Lynch had acted "in good faith" under UCC in selling bonds (that turned out to be stolen from E.F. Hutton) for the account of Royal National's disclosed customer. The court held that Merrill Lynch had a right to rely on Royal National's procedures and had no independent duty to investigate under Rule 405 in the absence of irregularities known to it.

5. *Brown v. Royce Brokerage, Inc.*, 632 F.2d 652 (5th Cir. 1980), holding that a broker who merely executed a transaction that was recommended to the plaintiff by another broker owed no duty with respect to the recommendation.

6. *Sherman v. Sokoloff*, 570 F. Supp. 1266 (S.D.N.Y. 1983), granting a motion for summary judgment by a commission merchant that had carried a partnership commodity futures account. The court held that the carrying FCM firm had no duty to supervise an unaffiliated registered floor broker who was the plaintiff's partner with respect to the partnership account and who traded the account.

Comment

Lee B. Spencer, Jr.

My focus will be on the role of the government and, in particular, of the Securities and Exchange Commission with regard to technology and the regulation of financial markets. I write from whatever experience I may have gained as a former director of the Division of Corporation Finance of the SEC.

In the past, some may have viewed the government as vast and all-knowing. Given the political events of recent years, it is no longer so vast, and, I will venture, it has never been all-knowing. Should the government, and the SEC in particular, be a natural leader of change? Economists, as I understand it, might particularly advocate this role in cases of "market failure." Yet, at least in certain respects, there are distinct limits to this endeavor. I believe the phrase "government failure versus market failure" is too strong a characterization, but this phrase illustrates my sense of governmental limitations, particularly with respect to technological change.

Commissioner Cox discussed the role of the SEC as both "proactive" and "reactive." That is to say that in some cases the SEC will take the initiative, and in other cases it will respond to initiatives taken by others. I would suggest that the decision whether to act one way or the other in the area of technology is influenced by some of the factors I am about to describe. My context will be the EDGAR program mentioned by Commissioner Cox and the area of internationalization of the securities markets mentioned both by Commissioner Cox and by Richard Scribner. A proper consideration of the role of the SEC also depends on an assessment of the strength of the need to act in order to fulfill regulatory goals established by Congress, as well as a consideration of whether or not the agency is already involved in the activity in question.

The four limitations that I would mention are as follows: (*a*) knowledge, (*b*) political consensus, (*c*) scope of authority, and (*d*) money (in the sense of funding available to the governmental unit); these factors can and do interrelate. There also can be other limitations.

With respect to knowledge as it relates to technology and, more particularly, to the EDGAR program and related technological change, I might note that an SEC colleague recently referred to SEC computers as being "at the cutting edge of 1953 technology." This may be understandable in that the SEC is an agency currently and historically predominated by lawyers. In recent years, its computer system has been largely designed for internal use (payroll, and so forth). The limited availability of funds certainly is another factor.

The agency decision to contract the EDGAR function to outside professionals was probably a correct one, but it can lead to other difficulties. One such difficulty lies in limitation (*b*) just mentioned: political consensus. With respect to EDGAR, a private contractor, through its access to the dissemination of all the SEC's valuable disclosure data, may be granted monopoly powers. The process of granting such power is not a simple one, and it can evoke strong pressures from other potential contractors. These pressures can be translated into the political arena; there is some evidence that Congress was so approached in the context of the EDGAR program.

Problems of political consensus can also exist in the area of internationalization. The SEC is faced with the issue of what disclosure should be required of foreign issuers seeking to sell their securities in the United States. Typically, much less disclosure is required for foreign companies abroad than for issuers in the United States.

U.S. policy toward foreign investment is normally expressed by the concept of "neutrality." But what *is* neutrality in this context? On the one hand, one could say that a U.S. investor needs the same information about a foreign company as he does about a U.S. company to make an investment decision. Therefore, the same information should be required from both. On the other hand, one could say that a U.S. investor should have an equal opportunity to buy U.S. and foreign investments and, since foreign companies may not sell their securities in the United States without a relaxation of U.S. standards, these standards should be reduced for them. This dispute has never fully been resolved.

As to the scope of authority as a limitation, I might use the example of internationalization with regard to the United States, the United Kingdom, and Canada. Of these three countries, the United States alone has regulation at the federal level, but there is also disparate regulation in most of the fifty states. The United Kingdom has its own regulation, which tends to be much more "self-regulatory" than in the United States. In Canada, there are ten provinces, each with its own securities regulations. And this is only to mention three countries.

The availability of funds is a very real limitation. At least at the SEC, the limitation is certainly acute in terms of the acquisition of computer hardware and software, and funds are almost nonexistent for research and development.

This limitation poses a problem in the international area because, as a very practical matter, there is a paucity of funding for necessary travel of U.S. personnel abroad to engage in discussion with foreign regulators. The same limitation presumably applies to travel by foreign regulators.

Turning then to the role of the SEC regarding EDGAR and internalization in the framework discussed previously, I would suggest that both areas are important to the SEC's current mission and that some active involvement is therefore appropriate. As to EDGAR, given the SEC's limitations in this area in both funds and experience, I believe the Commission was correct not only to have assigned the project to independent contractors but also to have done it on a pilot basis. Considering the observations I made on political consensus, I believe that while the Commission can do what it does best (deal with filing of documents and internal analysis), it must move with care concerning the third function—dissemination of information—because of its competitive consequences. It must develop and create a consensus in this process.

In the area of internationalization, it must be recognized that the SEC cannot move by itself. There is no framework for agreement among various regulatory authorities at home and abroad, nor is there a centralized source of knowledge about the requirements of various countries. I would think the proper first step would be to set a structure in place internationally, by committee and otherwise, that could achieve requisite funding, a pooling of information, and, finally a consensus among those involved for further action.

Comment

Robert A. Schwartz

Charles Cox and Bruce Kohn conclude their chapter by saying: "Both domestic and international market developments pose the question of how the Commission can best respond to the effect of new technologies—whether by improving information flow and otherwise reducing barriers to competition or by attempting more actively to shape the securities markets." I shall try to provide some answers to this question.

Chapters 1, 2, and 3 discuss the technological and economic changes that have occurred in recent years in securities markets. The dramatic expansion of technology has been accompanied by structural changes that challenge regulators far more than they have been challenged before. Can the regulatory challenge be met solely by "improving information flow and otherwise reducing barriers to competition"? I believe not.

Regulation is called for because of what economists term "market failure." There is no market failure when the free, unimpeded meeting of buyers and sellers in the marketplace results in a price that clears all orders, leaves no traders unsatisfied, and allows for no further, mutually beneficial redistribution of resources. With only one exception—no externalities—trading in frictionless, stable, and competitive markets gives the desired results. Unfortunately, trading in the securities markets is not a cost-free process; the markets are not stable; and the competitiveness of the markets has been questioned. All in all, the securities markets certainly do not give us perfect-world results.

Imperfect and asymmetric information is a major cause of market failure. Since the Securities Acts of 1933 and 1934, the major regulatory focus has been on controlling the abuse of position by professionals and insiders and guarding against the manipulation of prices, volume, and information by traders. After many years of enforcing a fair and honest market, the SEC has gained much experience, and for a while it seemed that the task, although as important as ever, had become less pressing as a policy issue. This is no longer the case. Ironically, the very equipment that makes "old line" enforcement easier, has, in the hands of the market participants, resulted in new ways of doing things, and hence new headaches for the regulators. Each of the three chapters makes this point. In response, the Commission should continue to seek improvements in the flow of information—to themselves as well as to the marketplace. But will this, by itself, be enough? I do not think so.

Monopolistic power is another major cause of market failure. In the 1970s, regulatory attention expanded to include the competitive structure of the markets. The era of fixed commissions ended; the quasi-monopoly position of certain market makers has been substantially eroded; entry into market centers has been eased; and the various market centers are now linked electronically. Consequently, further strengthening of competition between dealers and market centers is no longer the crucial issue that it once was. With regard to this one, perhaps the SEC can now relax a bit.

The uncertainty of buyers and sellers concerning transaction prices can also lead to market failure. Regulatory attention has more recently turned to the quality of prices established in the markets. Price discovery is of clear importance in the futures markets, and the quality of price discovery has been an important regulatory consideration for the Commodity Futures Trading Commission (CFTC).

Trading is an action that requires strategy; the prices given by a trading system are affected by the games that traders play; the games that are played and the quality of prices have been profoundly affected by the new electronic technology. Are we now getting better prices from our trading sytems? Perhaps, but we cannot be sure; an appropriate way of measuring the quality of prices has not been advanced in the literature. The issue needs to be given more attention by the SEC—and by others.

An orderly flow of traffic requires an orderly system of traffic lights. Similarly, for all real world markets, rules must be set by which trades are made and prices established. Poor rules are another cause of market failure. Because the new technology has changed the games that traders play, several of the rules by which trading is conducted should be reassessed. For instance, intermarket linkages make the exchanges far more vulnerable to competition from nonexchange market makers during delayed openings and trading halts following the release of major news. Is this a desirable outcome, or does it lead to a suboptimal suspension of trading? The enhanced competition from the NASD market has pressured the exchanges to allow the listing of more than one class of stock. Who should be responsible—the SROs or the SEC—for determining whether such a change would be desirable and for imposing any regulatory restriction that might be called for? Other complex issues exist concerning insider trading, international trading, and the direct access of public traders to the trading arenas via personal computers; the SEC should take a more active role in affecting the shape of the securities markets with regard to all of these issues.

The failure of the markets to expedite the development and adoption of new technology is one further source of market failure. Despite all the change we have seen, the pace of change may in fact be too slow. Moreover, if it were not for the pressure that in the past has been brought by the regulators, we might not have achieved the changes of the past decade. (Cox and Kohn make this quite clear.)

We are all a bit myopic in our view of technological change, and traders get locked into a technology. Much of the new computer technology is an electronic way of doing something better (or at lower cost) that has already been done in the past. ITS replaces the telephone; the NYSE's DOT, the AMEX's AUTOPER, and the OTC's SOES have substituted capital for labor in small-order routing and trade execution. These new systems, however, have not changed the basic structure of our trading arrangements. Despite all the electronics on and about the trading floor, we still have a lot of paper and a lot of noise, and most trades continue to be negotiated in direct, one-on-one contact between traders. We do not yet have an electronic trade execution system to which traders could comfortably submit large, hard-to-handle orders.

What if a continuous market trading arrangement is not an efficient regime for a computerized system? What if the adverse market impact of large orders were smaller; if the ability of the regulators to supervise the market were superior; if the quality of price discovery would be enhanced; and if the cost of trading would be lower in an electronic system that, for instance, batched orders over brief intervals of time for periodic execution at a single price? There is nothing inherent in the unregulated market that ensures that such a computerized system would be discovered or that, if discovered, it would ever be instituted.

As Smidt has pointed out,[1] we are in many respects locked into the old way of doing things. We are locked into our current trading arrangements much as we are locked into the configuration of the keys on a typewriter, or into the distance between the tracks on our railway lines. Nothing leads us to expect that the current way of doing business is indeed the very best way, and nothing assures us that global improvements in the system will in fact be made. On the contrary, the impetus for large-scale, imaginative change is not very powerful, and the resistance to such change is great. If the SEC—or any other force in the industry—were to step forward and fill the void, we could all benefit.

Note

1. Seymour Smidt, "Can You Get There from Here?" in *Market Making and the Changing Structure of the Securities Industry*, ed. Y. Amihud, T.Ho, and R. Schwartz (Lexington, Mass.: Lexington Books, 1985).

Part II
Futures Markets

5
Technology Meets Regulation

Molly G. Bayley

Technology is rapidly changing the commodities markets into a worldwide, twenty-four-hour electronic marketplace. In the process, the Commodity Futures Trading Commission (CFTC) has been required to rely more heavily on technology to fulfill its regulatory responsibilities. While the short-term effect of this new technology has been to increase the need for regulatory monitoring, the long-term effect could well be a more efficient marketplace, with perhaps less need for the type of regulation both the Commission and the exchanges perform today or more need for different types of supervision or regulation. Before discussing the future of technology in the commodities markets and the possible role of the CFTC, let me first explain how technology has already had an impact on the Commission's regulatory responsibilities and how the Commission currently relies on automation to keep pace with an industry which has undergone phenomenal growth.

The technological revolution has brought significant change to the futures industry. Without the technological advances of the last several years, international linkages between markets—the CME/SIMEX link and the link proposed between the COMEX and the Sydney Futures Exchange are two examples—would not be possible. Technological advances speed quotations, volume information, and clearing data around the globe and enable traders in any corner of the world effectively to trade futures twenty-four hours a day. A recent article in a trade publication described a COMEX trader who, after many years on the floor, now trades out of his home.[1] Thanks to computer terminals through which he can monitor the markets worldwide, and to a telephone that links him to the floor of the exchange, he can trade just as efficiently at home as he did during twenty years on the floor. And, as an added advantage, he can take his entire operation with him when he goes on an extended vacation.

The Commodity Futures Trading Commission, as a matter of policy, disclaims responsibility for any private publication by any of its employees. The views expressed herein are those of the author and do not necessarily reflect the views of the Commission or of the author's colleagues on the staff of the Commission.

From the Commission's point of view, these technological changes have added an additional level of complexity to the job of regulation. Let me give three examples.

In the case of the international linkage between the Chicago Mercantile Exchange (CME) and the Singapore International Monetary Exchange, Ltd. (SIMEX), the Commission went to great lengths to obtain adequate assurance from all parties involved, including the Monetary Authority of Singapore, that the ability of the Commission to oversee the trading on CME would not be impeded by the linkage. Further, extensive agreements were entered into by the CME and SIMEX to exchange information relating to market and trade practice surveillance as needed. These agreements ensure that the Commission routinely receives reports from the CME on the operation of the linkage.

Another example is the proliferation in the use of computerized trading strategies. Because such models may rely on similar programs and because of their widespread use, they can trigger trading activity that may be sufficient to affect the price of a futures contract. Such activity raises questions of aggregation[2] and other surveillance concerns for the Commission. This activity is particularly troublesome when the market experiences a sharp move in an upward or downward direction and computerized trading programs generate activity that further accentuates the price move. Discovering the origins of price moves and trading activity that cannot be explained by underlying supply and demand factors requires legwork on the part of the surveillance staff.

A third example is the growth of intermarket arbitrage. Computers can monitor rapid changes in prices simultaneously in an unlimited number of commodities and options and can perform the numerous calculations necessary to track changes in values of hedges, spreads, straddles, and numerous other trading strategies. With the introduction of related and derivative products on competing exchanges, the instantaneous dissemination of market information has enabled arbitrageurs worldwide to monitor the markets for aberrations between similar or related products. On the positive side, arbitrage trading reduces spreads and contributes significantly to the efficiency of the markets. However, it also presents additional challenges to the regulators of those markets. The Commission must be knowledgeable about the markets it oversees as well as all related markets. In addition, before a particular contract is approved, the Commission must determine that the terms and conditions of the contract are compatible with those of other similar or related contracts on other markets so that a trader cannot gain an unfair advantage by trading one contract over another. Subsequently, the Commission must be willing actively to share data with other regulators—both governmental and self-regulatory—having primary responsibility for surveillance in those markets. While this is easy to state as a general policy, it has the potential to break down in actual practice simply because no one regulator or exchange possesses the total picture of the activity involved. Activity which may have triggered an inquiry had it occurred in only one market may not appear unusual if it takes place in several markets. Thus, the regulatory burden is made more complex by the need to develop sophisticated, coordinated surveillance systems between markets.

Fortunately, technology has given the Commission the tools needed to deal with its increasingly complex regulatory responsibilities. Within the agency, automation already is, and will increasingly be, essential to carrying out our regulatory activities. The following is a brief description of the Commission's automated data collection and information system and how it supports market surveillance, economic reviews and studies, and enforcement activities.

The Commission employs a combination of mainframe and microcomputer technology. The mainframe computer in Chicago is a National Advanced Systems AS-5000, a medium-scale general purpose computer with 8 megabytes of memory. Its central processing unit supports high-speed communications access over dedicated communication lines to Washington and to regional offices where Commission staff members have access to the data through terminals. The Commission's microcomputers include a Zilog System 8000 supermicrocomputer, a number of IBM PCs, and an Apple McIntosh. The Zilog supermicrocomputer is located in Washington and, at the moment, is dedicated to handling registration for floor brokers and leverage transaction merchants and their associated persons. As part of the registration processing, magnetic tape input from the SEC is run on the Zilog for fitness checks on potential registrants.

The Commission's market surveillance program is designed to detect and prevent threats of price manipulation, congestion, or other major market disruptions caused by a few large positions or by a small number of traders controlling cash and/or futures positions. In conjunction with the exchanges, CFTC's market surveillance staff monitors, on a daily basis, all active futures and options contracts, activities of large traders, key price relationships, and relevant supply and demand factors. The inherent philosophy of the market surveillance program is to prevent significant market problems, particularly as they relate to contract expirations, deliveries, and contract performance.

The market surveillance program is supported by an extensive data collection system that provides critical information to the surveillance staff on a timely basis. All commodities brokers, known as futures commission merchants (FCMs), and exchange clearing members provide daily reports to the Commission that list the positions of all traders above specified levels. These reports are received each morning and cover the prior day's activity. In addition, exchanges with options programs submit weekly large trader information in machine-readable form. The data from the futures reports are entered immediately into the Commission's computer, which then aggregates all related accounts at all FCMs and prepares detailed listings. Staff economists examine these listings of large traders' positions in every actively traded futures market every day to identify any positions that could pose a threat of manipulation. The Commission has a significant advantage over the individual contract markets in that it brings together position information from all markets; as a result, the staff can review a trader's activity in all markets in a particular commodity—such as gold—and in related commodities—such as Treasury bonds and Treasury bills—and it can monitor a trader's total exposure across all exchanges.

These large trader reports are augmented by other data received from futures exchanges, individual traders, and other sources. Each day, exchanges file reports with the Commission in machine-readable form that show the aggregate open positions and daily trading, by house and customer accounts, of each clearing member in each delivery month of each futures contract and by the expiration date, option type, and strike price of each option. These reports identify the clearing members responsible for any concentration of open positions or trading activity on any day. Each exchange also provides daily machine-readable reports for futures and options which contain prices, trading volume, open interest, and deliveries or exercises. The surveillance staff also collects data on cash prices and supply-and-demand information for each commodity from a wide variety of sources.

When a potential problem arises, these routinely collected data are supplemented with information obtained through special request. The market surveillance staff frequently telephones individual traders, cash market sources, FCMs, and clearing members to obtain more detailed information about futures and cash market activities.

These market surveillance activities are coordinated with officials of the commodity exchanges where the contracts are traded. The CFTC looks to the exchanges as the first line of defense in dealing with market problems, because exchanges can deal very quickly with their member firms to alleviate problems. The Commission's automated analyses and other information help both the Commission and the exchanges to assess more accurately the extent and seriousness of a potential problem and to determine what action, if any, should be taken.

The surveillance economists are dependent in the first instance upon the timely submission of data from FCMs, clearing members, exchanges, and individual traders, and, second, upon the timely crunching of the data by the Commission's computer to identify potential problem areas requiring more thorough review.

In addition to their reliance on the AS-5000 for daily reviews, the surveillance economists rely on the computer to assist in special reviews, such as the study of soybean futures trading that was completed in November 1984. The Commission directed this study as part of its heightened surveillance of the grain markets beginning in the summer of 1983 and also because of the numerous complaints and inquiries from farm organizations, members of the public, and the Congress regarding the volatile and declining price trend of soybeans during the fall of 1983 and early 1984. The study depended on extensive computer analyses of individual clearing members' daily positions and trades, individual traders' daily positions, prices, and open interest data. It is safe to say that without the ability to analyze these data by computer, such a detailed study of daily data covering a period of nearly four months could not have been completed. It is also important to point out, however, that the conclusions of the soybean study were hindered by the absence of complete and accurate data for the adequate reconstruction of intraday trades during the period in question.

Since data on the time of execution of trades are not readily available in the Commission's data base, the reconstruction of the sequence of trading, or audit trail, during a study or investigation is a time-consuming and laborious manual process. In some cases, such a reconstruction is not even possible. To address this problem, the Commission recently requested comments on ways to improve exchange audit trail capabilities. The Commission's objective is to have each contract market develop its own trade reconstruction system compatible with its accounting and record-keeping systems and its own trading environment. Each such system would have to meet the performance standard of enabling the reconstruction of trades to an accuracy rate of within one minute of actual execution. With this expanded capability of reconstructing the sequence of trading, the Market Surveillance staff would be able to conduct quick reviews of intraday market activity when concerns are raised of market manipulation or other illicit trading activity such as wash trades, trading ahead of a customer's order, cross trading, and so forth.

Other economists in the Division of Economic Analysis utilize the Commission's data base of futures and options prices for conducting economic analyses. These analyses may entail a review of historical price and volume data to determine how a proposed rule may affect the market in a particular future or option or to evaluate the effect or efficacy of an existing rule. The Commission also relied on computerized analyses in all three of its recently completed studies required by Congress: the insider trading study, the interagency study of futures and options markets, and the large livestock hedger study.

Attorneys in the Division of Enforcement also use computer analyses of the Commission's data in their investigations. In addition, the Division of Enforcement and Office of Proceedings are developing a data base of the names of persons who have violated the Commodity Exchange Act. It is anticipated that a bulletin will be produced from the data base that will be made available to states and other agencies who work with the Commission on enforcing the commodities laws.

As the futures markets expand and automation plays a greater role, the Commission's capability to monitor and oversee those markets must grow commensurately. As a result, the Commission is currently developing a five-year ADP plan that will provide the framework for expansion and upgrading of its automation capabilities over the next several years. In keeping with this plan, the staff will undoubtedly recommend that the Commission move to require that all data submitted by contract markets and FCMs be submitted on machine-readable tapes or be transmitted directly to the Commission's computer via a computer-to-computer interface. Surveillance economists will rely increasingly on sophisticated computer programs and desk-top terminals to identify those options and futures requiring special surveillance attention, and the Commission staff will make increased use of microcomputers to access and analyze data contained in the Commission's data base in trade practice investigations. In addition, the audit trail proposal and possibly on-line clearing and a single clearing entity for futures transactions would help by reducing the regulatory burden on both the Commission and the exchanges. I will explain how these developments could be beneficial.

The Commission believes that its audit trail proposal will reduce the amount of time required to conduct routine trade practice surveillance and to investigate specific complaints. The recording of trade sequences should assist the Commission and the exchanges in assuring farmers, other commercial participants, and public traders, as well as floor traders, that executions in the futures markets are as fair as possible. The availability of such data will enable both the exchanges and the Commission to respond quickly to inquiries regarding trade executions and public concerns over illegal trading activities or possible manipulation in active markets. Delays in responding to such inquiries are harmful because they create the impression that something is being hidden. With the existence of audit trail data, there will be less need to request voluminous records from FCMs in order to respond to complaints or review potential problems. The response to most inquiries will be achieved by a simple review of the exchange data base. This in turn could reduce the burden on the Commission, since both the FCMs and their customers will have the ability to resolve complaints about the quality of execution by referring to the time of execution of each trade recorded in the exchange's records. The Commission believes that the very presence of an improved audit trail will provide a formidable deterrent to those contemplating trade practice abuses. The recording of the time of execution thus will have the effect of reducing the amount of regulatory resources needed to respond to inquiries and to oversee trade practices on the floor and could eliminate the need for future regulations aimed at preventing such trade practice abuses as trading ahead of a customer's order.

Two other developments—both in the clearing area—could reduce the burden of regulation as well. Implementation of an on-line clearing capability by the clearinghouses could result in a lessening of regulatory requirements and an increased ability on the part of each clearinghouse to monitor the financial health of its members. Trades would be matched as they occurred, thereby allowing outtrade reports to be produced and resolved during the day. This would enable the clearinghouse to monitor more accurately and in a more timely fashion the financial stability of its members—a critical function in the futures markets, where margins are only good faith deposits. Position limits, price limits, and capital requirements are currently established (among other reasons) to protect the clearinghouse and its members from default by an individual firm or customer. On-line clearing and automated programs, which make immediate use of up-to-the-minute position information, would enable clearinghouses to apply such position limits and capital requirements individually and on an intraday basis. This would be preferable to the current practice of applying, across the board, more onerous uniform standards to all members. Another development in the clearing area, which could have a positive impact, is the formation of a single clearing entity. While a combined clearinghouse could have many beneficial effects for exchange members, from the Commission's point of view it would simplify oversight and eliminate the need for the Commission to act as coordinator between clearinghouses, which becomes critical at the time of a market crisis. Of course, these benefits have to be weighed against concerns about the concentration of positions and capital in a single entity.

Can technology be employed further to allow the free competitive market forces to function even better than they do today, so that regulation can be reduced? This question was posed by Lee A. Pickard, then director of the Division of Market Regulation at the Securities and Exchange Commission, in a speech on "Electronic Data Processing and the Securities Markets" before the American Bar Association National Institute in May of 1976. The same question was raised at a conference at the CFTC on Automation in the Futures Industry in June 1977 by Susan Levenson of IBM. The issue of whether competition can substitute for regulation continues to be a valid question eight years later. To answer it, I would like to discuss the development of the NASDAQ market: the automated over-the-counter market for securities.

Prior to the debut of NASDAQ in 1971, dealers in over-the-counter securities executed transactions by contacting each other by phone or through direct wires that linked the major OTC dealers with the largest retail brokers. No information was available on trading volume for over-the-counter securities, and the only price information available was sketchy and at least one day old by the time it appeared in the so-called pink sheets. The advent of NASDAQ provided a computerized network through which over-the-counter dealers or market makers nationwide could indicate the prices at which they were willing to buy and sell the securities in which they made markets. Purchase and sales volume was reported by market makers to NASDAQ, and for the first time ever, up-to-the-minute quotation data and end-of-day volume data were published on over-the-counter securities.

Before the start-up of NASDAQ, over-the-counter dealers expressed doomsday fears that NASDAQ would reduce liquidity and put small dealers out of business by providing complete and accurate up-to-the-minute price information that would allow customers to single out the firm offering the best prices. What the dealers did not realize was that availability of accurate price information would increase understanding and confidence in the OTC markets, stimulate volume in NASDAQ securities, and increase profits manyfold for all over-the-counter dealers. The increased information turned out to be good advertising and good public relations.

In 1979 another significant development took place that had a similar impact on the NASDAQ market. The NASDAQ National Market System debuted in that year and, with it, actual transaction reporting in a selected group of NASDAQ securities. Again, market makers opposed this new reporting requirement. They stated they were too busy to report their transactions within ninety seconds of execution, and they were fearful that dissemination of actual transaction data would reduce liquidity and hinder their ability to position and dispose of large blocks of stocks. The dissemination of real time transaction data in National Market System stocks, however, has actually had a positive rather than a negative effect on the market. Volume has increased in NMS securities as a result of the availability of last sale data. And, along with increased liquidity, trade reporting has given NMS companies increased legitimacy in the eyes of the public despite the fact that they were already among the largest corporations in America prior to their listing on the National Market System.

One additional development in the NASDAQ market debuted in December of 1984. A small-order execution system was introduced, which enables brokers to enter orders up to 500 shares into NASDAQ and have them automatically executed against the best quote displayed at that point in time. Market makers were again fearful of this latest development because they believed that large market makers would dominate the market and capture all of the order flow. In fact, this newest development has not reduced competition but has enhanced it, by providing the smaller market maker with an equal opportunity to compete for order flow. Most important, however, the small order execution system has reduced clerical burden on the market maker and has enabled him to focus on trading those larger blocks of stock that require his expertise.

These developments, all of which resulted from the application of increasingly sophisticated technology to the over-the-counter market, have engendered more competition, visibility, and liquidity in the NASDAQ market. Taken as a whole, they probably explain why NASDAQ is the fastest growing stock market in the world.

Multiple competing dealers, the dissemination of quotation and transaction data, and increased liquidity have all enabled the NASDAQ market to operate with a minimum of constraining trade practice regulations. Instead, the market is safeguarded by a sophisticated computerized surveillance capability that takes advantage of the technology of the electronic marketplace. This suggests that less regulation is possible where technology is employed to the maximum extent possible to improve access to the market, increase competition, and improve the dissemination of market information.

Can the same technology be applied to the commodities markets? Of all the securities markets, the over-the-counter market is the most analogous in structure to a commodities market. The nationwide network of multiple market makers is the counterpart to the competing brokers and traders in a pit on the floor of a futures exchange. In both cases, fierce competition between dealers substitutes for the regulations that are imposed on the specialist on the floor of a securities exchange.

The new International Futures Exchange, or Intex, a corporation located in Bermuda selling contracts internationally, is the first fully automated futures market with many of the same features as NASDAQ. Intex connects brokers and traders worldwide into a computer system that matches bids and offers for futures instantaneously, confirms prices at which the trades are executed on the computer screen or printer of the trader or broker, and maintains a public book of all bids and offers that go unfilled. The automatic execution capability of Intex locks in the price, time, and counterparties to each trade, thus creating an audit trail and, according to Intex, virtually eliminating outtrades.

As in NASDAQ, Intex provides brokers and dealers located anywhere with access to the market and the ability to compete on an equal basis. Intex proclaims itself to be the answer to the growing congestion on exchange floors, the costly rise in errors in order executions, and the industry's shrinking profitability. From Intex's point of view, the only major problem it has encountered to date has been the futures industry's resistance to automation.

Today, the futures markets are faced with some of the same fears and decisions confronted by the over-the-counter market in the late 1960s. As occurred with NASDAQ, the introduction of technology to the trading floor could mean increased competition, depth, liquidity, and credibility for the futures markets and a reduced regulatory role for the CFTC.

Notes

1. "Comex Trading Routine Demanding; Mintz Finds Office at Home Ideal," *American Metal Market* (January 9, 1985):3.
2. All futures positions that a trader directly or indirectly controls and positions traded pursuant to an expressed or implied agreement or understanding must be combined (aggregated) as if they were held by a single person.

6
Self-Regulation and Futures Markets: Benefits from Technology Gains

Todd E. Petzel

T he most obvious and dramatic change in the futures industry over recent years has been the explosive growth in the volume and range of participants in futures markets. Paralleling that broadening scope has been a quieter revolution in technological advances that has allowed the exchanges to handle efficiently more contracts and transactions than were dreamed possible just two decades ago. With this growth has come added demands to maintain the trading integrity of the marketplace. Fortunately, the same technology that has allowed us to process the additional business has also allowed the exchanges to maintain their high self-regulatory standards.

Self-regulation will be the dominant theme in this chapter because it is the cornerstone of our trade. An often forgotten fact is that prior to the creation of the Commodity Futures Trading Commission (CFTC) in 1974, only exchanges trading domestic agricultural products had a federal government regulator to back up or oversee their own self-regulatory efforts. Nonregulated organizations, like the Coffee, Sugar, & Cocoa Exchange, maintained their marketplaces by devoting considerable resources to regulatory areas because of their own self-interest. Since the CFTC umbrella has been opened to cover all futures markets, the incentives of the exchanges have not changed. As the volume, number of contracts, and complexity of the markets have increased, the exchanges have been most active in improving their ability to monitor the marketplace.

Exchange regulation falls into two broad categories: surveillance and compliance, which can be thought of as macro- and micro-regulation, respectively. The function of market surveillance is to protect against manipulative behavior in the marketplace, while compliance monitors the actual trading activity to insure that the exchange rules designed to maintain fair trading

The views expressed in this chapter are those of the author and do not necessarily reflect those of the Coffee, Sugar, & Cocoa Exchange, Inc.

are being observed. The focus of each activity varies, so each will be treated separately.

Manipulation involves trading with the specific intent to cause an artificial price in the marketplace. Manipulation is not only illegal; it is, more important, against Exchange rules. A market that is prone to manipulation is one that serves few in the trade well and will likely fade from lack of use. Even the impression that the market favors one side over the other can seriously damage the trading environment.

The two key elements of manipulation—specific intent and artificiality of price—keep lawyers busy determining potential legal ramifications of any situation. Fortunately, that is not the direction of today's discussion. These two elements simply define the areas of exchange focus in order to gauge the status of their markets.

A trader's position must be monitored closely in order to hypothesize about his intent. To that end we collect daily position data from the clearing members for all accounts carrying positions above a minimum reporting level. These data are then compiled into a consistent record forming a snapshot of a given day's position. If an account has positions at six different clearing members, the computer will recognize this and will aggregate these data for surveillance purposes. Even in relatively small markets, like coffee or cocoa, the complexity of a position can be a high, and without the recent computer advances in storage and processing, timely analysis of these positions would be impossible. As it stands now in our Exchange, we expect to have a complete picture of any day's position before the market's close on the following day; that is, there is at most a one-day lag between the event and our complete knowledge of it.

The steps just described are very similar for most of the exchanges and the Commission's efforts in market surveillance. My understanding is that there is some variance in the capabilities of the hardware and software configurations currently used, but by and large daily surveillance is at hand or is attainable. What should be emphasized here is that without gains in efficiency by the member firms in processing accounts, the exchanges could never receive the data in a timely enough fashion to enable market surveillance to work as well as it does. We have been the beneficiaries of the modernization of the back office. The next major breakthrough in market surveillance will be in the automatic transfer of position data to the exchanges at the time the firm closes its books each night. Instead of having a one-day lag in building the position, the machines will "talk" together overnight so that the market surveillance analyst will have an overview of the position before the opening bell. Currently, we spend about 75 percent of our efforts building the position and only 25 percent analyzing it, but it is obviously only the analysis that provides insight into the trader's intent. This next technological jump will have a great impact on our efficiency.

Once the position is built, the analysis begins to identify trading patterns. This goes beyond looking at individual accounts and extends into seeing whether a pattern might exist across apparently unrelated parties. We do not sit around trying to manufacture conspiracies in this business, but traders have been known to trade in concert. If such activity exists as an attempt to distort the market, the probability of detection is much higher now with our automated procedures than it was previously.

The second avenue of manipulation is the artificial price, and in this regard technology has made only the slightest impact. In markets such as coffee, cocoa, and sugar, it is vitally important to have good information on foreign markets and deliverable supplies. Today's communication networks are superior to their predecessors, but not so much so that our knowledge or understanding of the price structure is radically different. It is, and will continue to be, a virtually impossible task to stand over a market and declare, "That price is artificial." The technological gains in this area will continue to allow information to enter the marketplace more quickly and will make the price discovery process more efficient. However, surprises in supply or demand will never be avoided in a market, for if that point were reached, there would be no purpose for the futures market to exist. We can only continue to strive for careful analysis of each market on a case-by-case basis to see that the contract is meeting its purpose as an accurate price discovery and risk allocation mechanism.

Technological improvements of the past decade have been much more important in the area of compliance than in surveillance, because the focus is necessarily on more minute detail. Market surveillance is primarily interested in the position, or open interest, at any given time and not on all the myriad trades that occurred to produce that open interest. Very good market surveillance can be maintained by looking at the open position on a regular basis, and it is only because of recent technological progress that daily analysis has become cost-effective. Any greater frequency of analysis is beyond our current imagination and, more essentially, would add little to our understanding.

Compliance is quite different. As the volume of trading grows, so does the difficulty of verifying that Exchange floor trading rules are being maintained. The technological improvements that have allowed the brokers and futures commission merchants to handle the ever-growing flow of business have also allowed clearinghouses and exchanges to process and monitor the trades. Without the rapid advances we have observed over the past several years, the exchanges would have been sorely pressed to maintain their trading environments.

Certain features of futures trading are common across all exchanges, but there are significant differences that quickly limit any meaningful discussion of compliance. At the majority of the exchanges using the traditional open outcry system, wide differences exist in the intensity of the trading activity. Coffee and sugar are traded historically at a rate leading to 10 to 20 percent of open interest being turned over daily. Gold, soybeans, or Treasury bonds may average a daily volume of about half their open interest, and the S&P 500 contract regularly trades the equivalent of its open interest every day. Each market faces different compliance issues, but there is the common thread that without the significant recent technological improvements allowing high-speed processing of massive quantities of data, the exchanges would be severely hampered in their ability to police their rules.

I did not personally have the advantage of observing firsthand this period of great change, but it is my impression that the ability of exchanges to monitor trades has more than kept up with the growth in business. We have seen compliance cases brought up that would have been impossible to detect in any trading environment prior to the institution of computer systems such as Coffee, Sugar & Cocoa's MIS. Yet, when the information on the trading record is less than perfectly complete, there is still the question of what more can be done.

Some observers point to a system like that of INTEX, the Bermuda-based, fully automated trading exchange, as the ideal solution. The advantage of going through a computer is that a precise real time record of each trade is made. There can be no violation of the myriad floor trading rules because, by definition, there is no floor. However, the information-discovery process of the open outcry system is subordinated by the INTEX world. It really does make a difference whether one or ten people are willing to reply to your bid, but this is lost in the depersonalized system. Upstairs and downstairs traders alike have all stressed to me the importance of this informational aspect of the open outcry system. Further, full automation does not solve all customer/broker issues. One knows that equivalent orders on the computer will be executed in the sequence they are received, but if a broker handles multiple customers, there is no guarantee that the input sequence will be accurate.

The jury is still out on this boldest technological step, but early experience suggests that the marginal gains from making the trading record perfectly precise have not outweighed the costs. If the gold traders in London, New York, and Chicago had felt very dissatisfied with the current compliance situation, INTEX would have captured a significant share of those markets. But this has not been the case, and the focus of the gold market participants has been on improving the open outcry markets, not on abandoning them.

Today's catchphrase is "one-minute time stamping." However, the emphasis should be on the accuracy of the audit trail, rather than on the desirability of using technology to create an audit trail, albeit an imprecise one. Here the temptation has been to grasp technology for its own sake and to argue that any step in the direction of real-time trade recording is justified.

The fallacies of this limited view are numerous. The key questions should always be, What do I gain in compliance for the added expense? and, How have I changed the efficiency of the marketplace by taking these steps?

A floor broker's job is not an easy one. There are few occupations that combine the intensity and the financial liability of this position. It is highly competitive and at the same time requires great cooperation from the floor community. I have observed a floor broker who had a market order to buy 50 lots and who executed that order by handling six or seven distinct transactions in less than a minute. Upon completion of the order, the broker confirmed and recorded each transaction with each of the opposite brokers. Would that broker's customer have been better served if the broker had been forced to stop after each transaction to record the time? Would the market as a whole have been more efficient? My conclusion is that compliance should not ignore critical issues of trading efficiency.

Exchanges are continually striving to utilize emerging technology for the purpose of maintaining a high degree of compliance with the rules. Alternatives are being explored that would take the existing sequential trade data of the brokers and apply computer sort and match algorithms to reconstruct an accurate audit trail quickly. The emphasis of the exchanges may differ from that of outsiders, since the exchanges place a great value on not imposing extra burdens on their trading populations. However, the objective will be the long-standing one of providing an efficient forum where traders can impartially and fairly express their market views.

Technological gains in futures market regulation have been dramatic over the past fifteen years and promise to continue in that vein. Market surveillance and compliance tools have grown in response to the added demands of the marketplace. These tools will continue to evolve as the users evaluate the costs and benefits of the new technology, and it is ultimately these users who will dictate the direction of tomorrow's technology.

7
Productivity, Technological Change, and Futures Trading

Seymour Smidt

Productivity increases, the major source of growth in real income per capita in the United States, also have major effects on the relative sizes of various industries.[1] An industry can contribute to increased productivity both through introducing new products for other industries and through producing its own output more efficiently. In the long run, changes in the relative price of an industry's output will be determined by the relative rate of productivity change in that industry and by trends in the prices of its main inputs. Since the real cost of labor tends to rise faster than the real cost of most other inputs, the output of labor-intensive production processes can be expected to suffer from above-average cost increases unless these processes can also be accompanied by above-average rates of productivity improvement.

Productivity and Industry Growth Rates

Usually, new products provide more economical or more effective methods of satisfying needs; this is how they increase the productivity of the buyers. An industry that is successful in introducing new products contributes in this way to the productivity of its customers and to its own rate of growth.

An industry can also contribute to overall productivity by becoming more efficient. Agriculture is an industry whose productivity has been increasing at an above-average rate for most of this century, resulting in a decline in the real price of agricultural products. Unfortunately for farmers, the demand for agricultural products, especially food, is generally price-inelastic and only moderately income-elastic. (An exception may be products for which the market is worldwide.) As a result, the prices of agricultural products have declined more than the consumption of those products has increased, and the proportion of per capita GNP going to the agricultural sector has decreased. The rapid increases in productivity and the inelastic demand for its output are largely responsible for the chronic surpluses and economically depressed state of the agricultural sector.

The computer industry is an example of a sector with a very high rate of productivity increase that faces a very price-elastic demand. Both agriculture and the computer industry are experiencing declining prices for their products because of high rates of productivity change, but agriculture, facing inelastic demand, is shrinking and is chronically depressed, while the computer industry, facing very elastic demand, is growing and prosperous.

Application to the Futures Industry

Futures trading evolved during the nineteenth century as a refinement of forward trading in the grain trade. Futures trading constituted a cost-reducing innovation for the grain trade. Hedging is most usefully thought of as a futures transaction undertaken as a temporary substitute for a subsequent cash transaction. Futures trading is attractive to hedgers because it represents a cost-savings means for commercial users to adjust to changing economic conditions. To be an effective hedging vehicle, a futures contract transaction must be substantially less costly than the alternative cash transaction.

New Products

In the post–World War II era, the most dramatic growth in the futures industry has come about through the introduction of new products. By developing new products that were applicable to industries that were not traditional users of futures and by vigorously promoting these new products, the futures industry has made an important contribution to its own growth and to increased productivity in other industries. Initially, new product development seemed to be an "entrepreneurial" function within the futures industry. It has now developed to the point where it is a bureaucratic function; some exchanges have well-staffed departments whose major function is new-product development.

Apparently, futures exchanges are optimistic about the prospects for their growth, since many have recently expanded their physical plant and some have included in their expansion the capability of substantial additional expansion. With respect to the prospects for growth resulting from new products, it is helpful to divide the growth potential into two components. One component is the growing use of futures products by industries that are already being served to some extent; the second component is the development of new products for industries that are not now using any type of futures-based product.

The most outstanding success of the futures industry in the postwar era has been the development of products for use by the financial sector—for example, interest rate, stock index, and foreign currency futures. There are still many investment managers who could profitably use financial futures but who are not yet taking advantage of this opportunity. Financial futures represent a large but finite source of growth for the futures industry. Probably more products have been introduced (or are in the process of development) than can ultimately survive to serve the financial sector. But product experimentation is useful.

The potential for additional growth from extending the concept of futures contracts to new industries is much less clear. There are some products under development, such as those based on the CPI, that may prove to be useful to the manufacturing sector. If so, this is an immense new market.

Price Elasticity of Demand

A very important question for the futures industry is whether the demand for its services is price-elastic or inelastic. If demand is inelastic, productivity changes in the industry may not be too important in determining future demand. As a general rule, demand functions are inelastic if the price is low enough and elastic if the price is high enough. Most important, the existence of good substitutes makes demand more elastic, and, conversely, the absence of same makes demand less elastic.

For hedgers, cash transactions are substitutes for futures transactions. In commodity contracts, product heterogeneity and other factors tend to make futures contracts—even in relatively small futures markets—inexpensive relative to cash transactions. In the case of financial futures, the underlying "cash" market is usually a securities market of some kind, with relatively low transaction costs. Therefore, I believe the demand for financial futures transactions is very sensitive to differences in costs between futures transactions and the underlying securities transactions.

Technological Change

Next I turn to some of the factors that determine the rate of technological change in the futures industry and, particularly, to comparisons of the rates of technological change in futures and in securities. The futures industry produces brokerage services and trading services to support its products. Brokerage services are typically paid for by commissions, and trading services are paid for by the realized bid-asked spread. The conditions determining the rates of technological change in these two activities are quite different.

Brokerage Services. Brokerage services (I include here clearing and settlement) have been subject to relatively rapid technological change as a result of the mechanization and computerization of office operations. The pressure for cost reduction in this area has been increased substantially by the introduction of competitive brokerage commission rates. Some kinds of cost reductions can be introduced by individual Futures Commission Merchants (FCMs) and clearing firms. Theoretically, the clearing and settlement procedures determined by the individual exchanges set limits on what can be accomplished by individual firms. My impression is that the costs of these back-office operations have been declining rapidly in both the futures and securities industries.

As compared to the securities industry, the futures industry has some intrinsic advantages and possibly some disadvantages. I think the main advantage is that most futures contract positions are settled by offset, while most securities positions are settled by delivery. Offsetting is less expensive. The question of size economies with respect to clearing and settlement is less clear. Are the most important economies related to total transactions in all securities, or to the average number of transactions per security?[2] Total trading in securities is greater than total trading in financial futures; but the average volume per security is lower than the average volume per futures contract. If the most important size economies are related to total transactions, the securities industry may have the edge. If the appropriate measure is the volume of transactions in one instrument, then the futures industry may be better off.

Trading Services. On the trading side, there does not appear to have been any substantial technological change in the futures industry. Trading in futures exchange pits is carried out in much the same way today as it was twenty years ago. By contrast, there have been some major innovations in trading techniques in the securities industry. Block trading and NASDAQ are two outstanding examples. Both of these systems have apparently resulted in substantial cost reductions. We have no good evidence on the magnitude of the costs of trading in the futures industry; some recent evidence for the securities industry suggests that trading costs are equal to half the quoted spread.[3] If the same relationship applies in the futures industry, then trading costs might equal between one-third and one-half of the total transaction costs. The proportion is probably higher for hedgers than for small speculators; for the latter, brokerage costs are relatively more significant.

Are there any general explanations for the noticeable absence of technological change from the futures market trading process? I think so. While the situation is complex, at least part of the explanation is related to the degree of control that futures exchanges exert over the location of trading in the futures contracts that they sponsor. The comparison with stock exchanges is informative. The owners of common stock have the right to buy or sell that stock wherever they want. Stock exchanges might like to limit trading to exchange floors, and have sometimes tried to do so; they have never succeeded. While most trading still takes place on the stock exchange floor, experiments with other forms of trading are possible, and some have succeeded. By contrast, futures contracts cannot be traded except under conditions specified by the sponsoring exchange. This has to do with the nature of the futures contract. If I tried to sell you my rights and obligations under a futures contract off the floor of the sponsoring exchange, the clearing corporation would not "accept" the trade. I would still be responsible to the clearing house, and you would not.

In general, futures exchanges permit trading only by open outcry on the floor of the sponsoring exchange during regular trading hours. This limitation makes it costly to experiment with modified trading procedures, as will be explained.

Most technological change occurs as the result of experimentation:[4] someone gets a new idea and tries it. Most such experiments fail. Sometimes the idea can be modified and a new experiment attempted. A few experiments eventually succeed; the successful ideas are adopted, and the unsuccessful ones are dropped.

In part, the costs of an experiment that fails are proportional to the scope of the operations on which the test is made; the benefits are proportional to the scope of the operations to which the successful idea can be applied. When experiments can be performed on a small part of the operations to which they might ultimately be applicable, it is economical to test ideas that are expected to be bad, provided there is at least some chance that the ideas may be good. When experiments can be performed only on the whole operation to which they are applicable, it may not be economical to test ideas that are expected to be good if the costs of a mistake are large compared to the possible benefits. Since all trading must take place on the floor of an exchange, any change in trading procedures must be applied to the whole trading process. Apart from any other consideration, this makes it expensive to learn by experimenting.

The idea of "trading by computer" is a good example. It is not a new idea. Eight years ago, on June 15, 1977, the Commodity Futures Trading Commission sponsored a conference on "Automation in the Futures Industry" in response to a congressional mandate passed a few years earlier that it "determine the feasibility of trading by computer."[5] The conference chairman charitably concluded that "there was no broad consensus on . . . the crucial questions." There were two main factions: the futures trading professionals were generally agreed that trading by computer wouldn't work; the outsiders, mainly economists and computer experts, felt that it could work.[6] Under this system, the best way to get a test of the concept is for those who believe in it to start a new exchange, as some of them have attempted to do.

One step that would lower the cost of experimenting with alternative trading mechanisms would be to allow FCMs more freedom to develop "in-house" trading systems. Arbitrage between the in-house system and the trading pit would be necessary to keep prices more or less in line and to transmit trading imbalances from the computerized system to the floor, and vice versa. If individual brokerage firms were able to experiment with computer-assisted trading systems, it would be possible to gain experience about various methods of operating such systems without committing the whole exchange community to a radical change in the face of uncertain results.

In summary, the futures industry has been substantially more inventive than the securities industry in developing new products. Its success in this area serves to lower the operating costs of the firms who use these new products. But the futures industry has been substantially less inventive than the securities industry in developing innovative trading mechanisms. In part these differences reflect variations in the regulatory environment. In the securities industry, regulators have been reluctant to give exchanges a monopoly on the right to trade a given security. So experimentation with trading methods is relatively easy. In the futures industry, exchanges have great freedom to compete by introducing new products; but the regulators have tended to allow exchanges to maintain a monopoly on the right to trade a contract which they have developed. This stimulates competition in developing new products but inhibits the development of new trading mechanisms.

Notes

1. William J. Baumol, "Macroeconomics of Unbalanced Growth," *American Economic Review* 57 (June, 1967):415–26.

2. These are both economies of scale. If there were economies of scope, then clearing and settling more securities on a given clearing system would lead to a reduction in unit costs. There is no reason to expect such scope economies with respect to clearing and settlement. For some pairs of securities, for example, futures and options on the same or closely related underlying securities, there may be economies of scope in trading.

3. Hans R. Stoll, *The New York Stock Exchange Specialist System: An Economic Analysis* (New York: New York University, Graduate School of Business, Salomon Brothers Center for the Study of Financial Institutions, 1985).

4. William L. Silber, "Innovation, Competition and New Contract Design in Futures Markets," *Journal of Futures Markets* (Summer 1981):123–55.

5. See section 18 of the Commodity Futures Act of 1974.

6. For two representative viewpoints, see Leo Melamed, "The Mechanics of a Commodity Futures Exchange: A Critique of Automation of the Transaction Process," *Hofstra Law Review* 6, no. 1 (Fall 1977):149–72, and Joseph M. Burns, "Electronic Trading in Futures Markets," *Financial Analysts Journal* (January/February 1982):33–41.

Comment

Roger D. Rutz

My comments will take the form of observations on major, recurring themes present in chapters 5, 6, and 7. These themes are: (*a*) the growth of futures trading; (*b*) additional regulations that may be needed because of this growth; and (*c*) technological innovation.

The Growth of Futures Trading

Academic tradition dictates that futures markets be viewed as price discovery and risk-transfer mechanisms. While I agree that these are economic attributes of futures markets, price discovery and hedging are the economic outcomes of a more fundamental centralized trading process.

Lester Telser has written that futures markets facilitate trade among strangers, which in my view is why futures markets are so successful. Most exchanges accomplish this by virtually eliminating any concerns about credit risk and by keeping transaction costs extremely low. Thus, exchanges are able to provide facilities where hedging and price discovery take place more efficiently than anywhere else.

Professor Smidt suggests in his chapter that the government has provided members of futures exchanges with pseudo-monopoly power by which exchanges are able to prevent outside competition coming from technological innovation. He points out that stock exchanges face considerable competition from outside forces because stock does not have to be traded on an exchange. However, a stock issue itself is not a proprietary product but is issued by an independent corporation. The corporation decides which exchange or trading system—for instance, NASDAQ—on which to trade its stock.

Futures contracts are promises, that is, contractual obligations, whereas securities are assets or forms representing ownership. Thus, futures exchanges, by devoting substantial resources to product innovation, design new futures products in which the exchange has a proprietary interest. In addition, exchange clearinghouses provide the all-important guarantee as party to every trade. For example, because the Board of Trade Clearing Corporation will not accept a trade from just anybody, only from those who have been approved to clear trades, it has a sixty-year record of absolute integrity in which no one has ever lost money owing to a contractual default. Exchange clearinghouses desire to "know their customers," and while this may inhibit unfettered competition, it does so with a more important objective in mind—market integrity.

Futures exchanges are far from being insulated, however, from outside competition. Futures and options exchanges are in fierce competition with each other in the area of product development. Forward and over-the-counter markets also come to mind as significant competition to futures exchanges. It is important to remember that futures exchanges are really centralized institutional arrangements for forward markets, albeit with one very important difference—the clearinghouse guarantee.

Arguments can be made that the phenomenal growth of futures trading is the result of new products and that these new products have stimulated technological innovation. Ms. Bayley points out the importance of computer-driven trading strategies and the existence of active intermarket arbitrage. I believe that intermarket arbitrage is perhaps the most significant development to have occurred in futures markets during the past decade. Technological innovation may in fact have been the driving force behind many new products, and if not the driving force, certainly one of the primary reasons that many new financial products have succeeded. Much of this success has been fostered because of computerized models that indicate potentially profitable intermarket arbitrage opportunities. Arbitrage and hedging, which are made easier with computer models, have made futures prices very efficient, so much so that when Treasury bond futures close at 3:00 p.m. Eastern time, the bid-ask spread in the cash market widens from 1/32 to 3/ or 4/32 of a point.

Market Regulation

The second major theme of the three chapters is market regulation. As Mr. Petzel correctly notes, exchanges established rules and regulations long before the government became involved. The reason is that it is in the best interest of the exchanges to ensure that trading in the markets is both fair and efficient. In fact, the Commodity Futures Trading Commission Act of 1974 incorporated many rules and regulations already on the books of various exchanges. As futures markets have grown, surveillance has become more important.

One of the major regulatory issues of the day is trading practices on the floor. In recognition of this concern, the Board of Trade, in conjunction with the Clearing Corporation, has developed a state-of-the-art Trade Practice Investigation system. This system uses interactive computer programs to enable staff to reconstruct trades to detect any trading abuses. Many additional programs are being developed for market surveillance and to ensure compliance with exchange rules. For example, the Clearing Corporation has developed sophisticated simulation models to determine the risks of positions held by clearing members and their customers.

These sophisticated programs are possible because the exchange and Clearing Corporation have invested millions of dollars in hardware and software. For example, the Clearing Corporation has two large IBM mainframe central processors. The system has on-line disc storage of 40,000 megabytes and is capable of processing 7 million instructions per second. Despite this large investment in systems and programming development, the Board of Trade is able to match, process, and guarantee trades at a cost approximating four cents per contract cleared—the lowest cost in the industry.

The Board of Trade and the CFTC are in complete agreement on the need for enhanced audit trails. We disagree, however, with the CFTC's approach, which would require one-minute time-stamping. The Board of Trade is developing a new system known as TRAC (Trade Reconstruction Analysis by Computer). TRAC will merge trade register data, that is, cleared trades, with time and sales data, which specify the price at which trades occur to the nearest second. Not only is this system designed to achieve greater accuracy than the CFTC's one-minute time-stamping approach; it does so at a far lower cost to the marketplace in terms of the efficiency of trade execution.

A recent study by Professors Sanford Grossman and Merton Miller from the University of Chicago estimates that the costs of the CFTC's one-minute time-stamping proposal would exceed any benefits by at least 100 to 1,000 times.[1]

Technological Innovation

The final theme of the three chapters is the impact of technological innovation on futures trading. This innovation may be categorized into three main areas: (1) computerized execution systems; (2) international linkages and twenty-four-hour trading; and (3) the clearing process.

Computerized Execution Systems

The futures industry has witnessed a significant innovation recently with the formation of INTEX, a completely computerized futures exchange located in Bermuda. If the existing open outcry, auction-type markets on exchange floors are indeed antiquated, then INTEX should be a roaring success. Results so far indicate that volume on INTEX is far below expectations. While the theory behind INTEX may be sound, in practice, it has not been an overwhelming success. I believe that Mr. Petzel is correct when he implies that the informational dynamics of an open-outcry, public auction–type market system outweigh potential gains, if any, emanating from a computerized execution system.

In that respect, a fairly recent innovation by the Chicago Board of Trade deserves some discussion. The Board of Trade has developed an on-line, real-time computerized trading vehicle known as the CBOT Market Profile. The exchange provides to various vendors and their subscribers data on volume, price, and exact time of trades for all commodities. These data summarize in an easy-to-use format much of the information available on the floor of the exchange. Thus, except for sight and sound, this so-called liquidity data bank provides virtually all of the relevant information from the exchange floor to the outside public for use in formulating trading strategies. In fact, its development was spurred by one member, and subsequently paid for by the exchange, so that members could trade the markets without being on the floor. And since these data are available to anyone, the CBOT has essentially opened up the floor to the outside world.

International Linkages and Twenty-Four-Hour Trading

The mutual-offset trading system developed by the Chicago Mercantile Exchange and Singapore is a significant innovation to bring markets to the rest of the world and to open up trading hours during non-U.S. business hours. COMEX and the Sydney Futures Exchange are developing a similar linkage.

The Chicago Board of Trade has yet to proceed in that direction for two fundamental reasons: cost and risk. While I have no information, the CME and COMEX may have spent millions of dollars to develop the links. Current trading volume in Singapore suggests that any return may be a long time in coming. Second, the CME has opened up its markets to foreign entities that may pose risks to CME members if a large default occurred. Foreign entities and institutions may not have the same long-standing tradition of ensuring market integrity as do the U.S.-based members of the CME.

The CBOT has invested hundreds of millions of dollars in its building, trading floors, computer systems, and telecommunications. It could be described as a factory for the provision of transactional services. This factory is currently open only about eight hours a day. The CBOT's strategy is to develop international products to be traded in the United States. In addition, if demand exists for trading existing products during foreign business hours, the exchange could simply "flip the switch" and remain open twenty-four hours. I would suggest that the costs of existing telecommunications facilities and paying a "shift" differential to open up during nonregular business hours are far lower than opening up new "plants" overseas. This may be particularly true in providing local floor traders to generate the all-important market liquidity necessary to efficient futures trading. In addition, the United States is well known overseas as the safe haven for investments and trading in fair and efficient markets. Time will tell which strategy proves more successful.

The Clearing Process

The final area in future technological innovation is the clearing process. The Board of Trade Clearing Corporation, for example, is the only clearing organization in the industry with an on-line, trade-data entry system, currently consisting of 200 remote terminals. Other clearing members submit data via computer-to-computer links. At present, more than 80 percent of trade data enter the Clearing Corporation via these two methods. By January 1, 1986, all clearing members at the Board of Trade must submit data on-line or through computer hookups. This will make the clearing process much more efficient. Ms. Bayley raised the issue of continuous clearing and the possibility of common clearing.

Although the Board of Trade system will accept data at any time, there is no requirement that trade data be input throughout the trading day. The Exchange and Clearing Corporation are reviewing the desirability of imposing deadlines for data input throughout the trading day. Continuous, on-line clearing would enhance the ability of the Exchange and Clearing Corporation to conduct market surveillance and assess the risk of positions. I expect this innovation to come about in the not-so-distant future.

While the futures industry is often chided for its many different clearing organizations, as compared to the securities and options market, this is really an unfair criticism. Although the NSCC, for example, processes most securities transactions, it does so through a network of computer links with a number of other independent clearing organizations. In addition, while OCC clears all options traded on organized exchanges, it does not match trades. Each options exchange must invest in expensive systems and personnel to conduct the trade-matching process. Clearing organizations in the futures industry both match *and* clear trades. Thus, objective observation suggests that clearing in securities and options markets is almost as disparate as clearing in futures markets.

Common or centralized clearing in futures is often viewed as desirable, but the issues involved are complex and varied. Thus, I find it useful to differentiate the two distinct functions that clearing organizations perform. One is the processing function, that is, the computer-driven matching and clearing process. There is really no centralized clearing organization in the futures or options markets by this definition.

The second function of a clearing organization is taking on the fiduciary liability or guarantee as party to every trade. Whether a centralized guarantee would be beneficial depends on arguments related to the diversification of risk. Currently, a default on one exchange does not directly affect the integrity of another exchange. There are many significant political implications in asking members of one exchange to guarantee contracts on other exchanges.

Another argument advanced in favor of common clearing is the centralization of position information, which is assumed to provide a better indication of a firm's risk exposure. However, this argument is fallacious. Many clearing member firms have full-line securities, futures, and cash-market activities, including over-the-counter forward and option transactions. Recent experience indicates that repo and reverse-repo transactions have posed substantial risks to banks and securities firms, many of which also clear futures trades. To consolidate all information about the risks of a firm's total exchange and cash positions would require a monolithic organization or agency. Such an effort is best left up to self-regulatory organizations. In fact, the Board of Trade and CME already consolidate such information, which represents 75 to 80 percent of the industry. Exchange-initiated efforts are ongoing to further this consolidation of position information.

Some important arguments have also been made that a centralized, bureaucratic clearing organization becomes an entity unto itself that is not responsive to the needs of exchanges and their members or members firms. Finally, the efficiency of the clearing process at one exchange may provide a competitive edge over other exchanges. In the final analysis, however, any discussion of common clearing must differentiate the matching and clearing process from the fiduciary responsibility borne by each clearing organization.

Note

1. Sanford J. Grossman and Merton H. Miller, *A Preliminary Study of the Economic Costs and Benefits of Implementing the CFTC's One-Minute Time Bracketing Proposal*, Chicago Board of Trade (25 April 1985).

Comment

Stephen Figlewski

The chapters in this section and the previous one have raised a number of issues regarding the impact of new technology on the operation and regulation of financial markets. What I would like to do first is to try to classify these developments into four main areas in which technological improvement has taken place. Then I would like to take up an important point raised by Seymour Smidt: that the futures exchanges have not been able so far to apply technology to increase productivity substantially in the trading pit. I will describe an idea for a technological solution to some of the practical and regulatory issues raised by the trading mechanism in a futures market.

Probably the most important area in which technology, especially in the form of computerization, has affected the financial markets is record keeping. It was less than twenty years ago that the increase in paperwork associated with higher trading volume made it necessary to close the stock exchange one day a week to let the firms' back offices catch up. Today, 80 million shares is regarded as a rather dull day in the market, but the computerized back office is now able to keep up easily.

As Molly Bayley pointed out, computerization of records has greatly expanded the ability of regulators to perform their surveillance function, using reports that are provided by the exchanges in machine-readable form; this ability will be further enhanced by the transmission of data from the exchange computers to the CFTC and other regulatory bodies by direct computer interface. She also mentioned that computers are used (and are necessary) to look for suspicious trading patterns that might be occurring in several markets simultaneously.

A second area in which technology has transformed the financial markets is communications. The speed and volume of information flow has grown enormously in recent years. Traders, including those on the floor of the exchange, have immediate access to a vast quantity of information on computer screens showing prices in different markets, latest news reports, computer analysis of their positions and potential trading opportunities, and more, all continuously updated. This has greatly increased the integration of financial markets, as well as their informational efficiency. In some ways, it has also made such trading abuses as "front running" more difficult, since it is now necessary to run in front of news that travels faster than ever between markets and by a variety of channels.

Communications technology has also transformed order transmission into the marketplace. For example, on some exchanges, orders are transmitted electronically directly to the specialist's trading post, where they can be filled simply by touching a touch-sensitive screen. More rapid order handling results in better execution for the public customer, and quite possibly in greater market liquidity, since the time it takes for order flow to respond to price changes has been cut.

Increased integration of financial markets made possible by improved communications technology has expanded both informal linkages between markets, through intermarket arbitrage, and formal ties, as in the case of the CME-SIMEX link, as well as the NASDAQ system. Both Bayley and Scribner alluded to some of the thorny regulatory issues raised by these linkages, especially when an international dimension is involved.

The third major area in which computer technology has transformed the financial markets is computation, that is, sheer numbers crunching. As markets proliferate and as financial instruments become increasingly complex, the need to perform complicated mathematical analysis rapidly has made computer technology indispensable. This is especially true for futures and options markets. Anyone who has ever had to compute an option value by hand, using the Black-Scholes formula, knows how important it is to have a good computer. And virtually all professional traders do have access to a good computer, as do the specialists, exchanges, and clearinghouses that need to determine appropriate hedge ratios for their inventory, evaluate the risk on market makers' positions, compute required margin, and so on.

Stock index futures and options depend on the availability of values for the underlying index calculated at frequent intervals. Current regulation requires that an index underlying any stock index product must be computed and disseminated at least every minute. This clearly requires a computer.

One point that was raised in the previous chapters had to do with the impact of computerized trading strategies on the behavior of market prices. The argument was that such strategies would tend to signal trades simultaneously, which would destabilize prices or at least give the appearance of coordinated trading. My belief, which is supported by Todd Petzel's story about how technical trading charts were banned from the floors of futures exchanges during the 1920s because of the same fear, is that there is nothing about the use of a computerized strategy per se that would increase the likelihood of this problem occurring. Trend followers and other traders using standard trading techniques will always tend to trade in similar ways at particular times. Whether or not this destabilizes market prices is a question that people can vehemently debate, but there is no necessary connection to computerized trading.

Several of the speakers have referred to the NASDAQ system, along with its offshoot, the NASDAQ National Market System, as a perfect example of how technology can transform the mechanics of trading in a financial market. The new Bermuda-based INTEX market is an attempt to apply the same type of technology to a futures market. It offers participants the opportunity to trade comfortably from their offices or homes. It allows a complete audit trail and automatic time-stamping of orders. It completely eliminates outtrades. And yet, it does not seem to have taken the world by storm. Futures traders, in particular, seem to favor the face-to-face (and body-to-body) contact of the trading pit and will be very reluctant to give it up in favor of a remote computer terminal. One reason for this preference is that a trader who is actually present in the trading pit gains a great deal of information that would be lost in a system run entirely by computer. In particular, by seeing the response in the pit to bids and offers, a floor trader can make an estimate of the quantities available and can also gauge the degree of urgency with which his fellows wish to trade. Thus, as Seymour Smidt observed, technological change in the actual trading process has yet to arrive in the futures markets, even though it has already revolutionized the over-the-counter market for stocks.

Meanwhile, there are forces at work that may soon dictate significant changes in futures trading procedures. One is the regulation proposed by the CFTC that would require futures exchanges to improve the audit trail to the point that each transaction could be pinned down to within a one-minute time interval. This has been called one-minute time stamping. The second force is the sheer congestion in some of the larger pits, like Treasury bonds and S&P futures. Congestion makes it more difficult to get orders and even traders into the pit, and, because traders cannot really trade with someone on the other side of the pit, it can essentially fragment the market into smaller groups that are in physical proximity to each other but that trade among themselves.

After thinking about these problems for some time, a possible solution occurred to me in the form of a technological advance in the trading process. When I mentioned it to Todd Petzel and Terry Martell, they did not laugh me out of the room, so I am going to offer it here.

At present, a floor trader records his trades on a paper trading card. He must write down the quantity bought or sold, the contract month, the price, the counterparty he traded with, and in some cases the counterparty's clearing firm. Under present regulation, these cards are gathered every half hour. Since it is not uncommon for an active trader to make five or more trades in rapid succession in the course of filling a single order, the requirement that each trade be time stamped to the minute is regarded as both onerous and counterproductive in terms of getting the best execution for public customers.

What I have in mind is a device that is a cross between a pocket computer and a cordless telephone that would serve as an "electronic trading card" linked directly into the exchange's computer. A trader would carry the device and use it in place of a paper card for recording trades. In general, computers are faster and more accurate than people, so a well-designed system involving an electronic trading card ought to be no more burdensome than the current arrangement. The device could perform the following functions, among others: it could record trades, receive orders directly from a broker's firm, report back filled orders, remember limit orders, keep track of the trader's position, and receive communications from the central computer regarding outtrades and other problems.

A trading system involving an electronic trading card would have a number of desirable features. It would permit a continuous audit trail, with automatic time stamping of trades to the nearest nanosecond. It would allow instantaneous trade checking as trades were reported into the main computer. This would permit outtrades to be spotted immediately and to be corrected before prices had a chance to move too far. It would allow more rapid transmission of orders into the pit, since they would be flashed directly to the trader's electronic device rather than be carried in by hand. It would make accurate price reporting easier because it would not rely on the skill of human reporters. It would provide traders, their firms, and the regulatory authorities with the possibility of continuously monitoring traders' positions during the day rather than after the close of the next day, as is presently the case. And finally, not the least important feature of the system is that it would reduce the incidence of stab wounds from errant writing implements in the pit.

In reference to Seymour Smidt's point about the difficulty of introducing a change that would require the entire exchange to alter its procedures at once, this system could be phased in gradually, starting with a pilot program run by a single clearing firm. In the end, it might even provide a way to reduce congestion by effectively expanding the number of participants via electronic linkage, without increasing the number of people in the pit.

With regard to the technical requirements of such a system, it seems clear that the rate of data flow would be substantially slower than for a mobile telephone, for example; so the necessary technology already exists. Implementing the technology would be simply a matter of cost. That cost may be prohibitive at present, but we have seen the costs of computer technology drop while its capabilities have been consistently enlarged over the years, so it may not be long before the electronic trading card is cost-effective. In fact, I will venture the prediction that the futures exchanges will be using systems like it in no more than ten years—and sooner if the CFTC sticks to its one-minute time stamping requirement.

Part III
Banking Markets

8
Payments Finality and Risk of Settlement Failure

David B. Humphrey

T he technology associated with the automation of processing large-dollar wire transfer payments has permitted very rapid growth in these payments without real-time balance controls or limitations (Association of Reserve City Bankers). The lack of such limitations has meant that banks that participate on these networks are able, in effect, to "borrow" funds intraday at a zero interest cost. Such intraday borrowing has been termed a *daylight overdraft*. The risks created by daylight overdrafts are the primary focus of this chapter and have been described in general terms by Rosborough and Urkowitz, Stevens, and Smoot, and in theoretical terms by Frankel and Marquardt.

Daylight overdrafts occur frequently—on a daily basis at a given set of large U.S. banks—and are not due just to random computer downtime or other problems having to do with the processing of payments. Overdrafts at institutions often exceed $1 billion and, for certain large banks, also exceed their total capital position (Humphrey). The concern is that if there were a failure to settle one or more of these large debt debit daylight exposures, the smooth operation of the payments system and financial markets would be significantly disrupted. I shall present evidence to support this contention in the form of results from a settlement-failure simulation exercise performed by Federal Reserve staff. This will be followed by a discussion of payments finality as one way to reduce the risk of settlement failure. Other "solutions" to this problem have been described elsewhere (Association of Reserve City Bankers and Humphrey) and include bilateral net credit limits and sender net debit caps, among other alternatives.

The daylight overdraft issue and the settlement risk it creates can be ascribed to the following two problems. First, a bank's book position can be in balance while its actual funded position is in overdraft because the operations technology often is not capable of actually moving funds as fast as a bank's trading or money desk makes an agreement to move them. A bank may have

This chapter reflects the author's own views and is not necessarily endorsed in any way by the Federal Reserve Board or by the staff of the Federal Reserve System. Comments by Ed Ettin and Jeff Marquardt are acknowledged and appreciated.

purchased funds without yet having received them. In these cases, a large bank's funded position may reflect its book position only after a lag, sometimes lasting as long as thirty minutes. While this problem has definite consequences, it is not the major determinant of the size and number of daylight overdrafts which are observed. A second related but more important cause of daylight overdrafts is the historic lack of any real incentive to conserve on the use of "free" daylight credit. Free goods—goods or services with a zero effective price—are overused and, in addition, institutional practices are developed over time to take advantage of them. A bank that is purchasing funds has not, historically, been given a strong incentive to make sure it receives these funds as soon as it is operationally possible for the sender to send them. This second lag in receiving funds that have been purchased is institutionally, not operationally, determined and results from the fact that daylight overdrafts have been free. This arrangement is not likely to continue, given the current efforts of the Federal Reserve and commercial banks to control the level and growth of daylight overdrafts in the near future. These changes, of course, have implications for the current operation of financial markets and can differentially affect payments participants (Chicago Clearing House Association and McDonough). The likely implications for financial markets of the changes being discussed are noted in the concluding section of this chapter.

The Growth in Large-Dollar Payments

In 1950, total wire transfer payments amounted to a little less than twice that year's GNP.[1] In 1960 and 1970, respectively, wire transfers were almost five and thirteen times GNP. By 1980, GNP was $2.6 trillion, but wire transfers were $116 trillion for the year, or almost forty-five times GNP. Just three years later, wire transfers rose to almost sixty-two times GNP. This extremely rapid rate of growth clearly reflects more than just large-dollar payments to finance the exchange and movement of real goods and services. Although accurate data are not available, the rapid growth in wire transfers seemingly has been due primarily to the parallel growth of new and different types of financial transactions, such as those involved with interbank overnight funding (Federal Funds, Eurodollars, and so forth), funding of bank definitive securities transfers (CDs, bankers' acceptances), trading in U.S. government book-entry securities, and funding foreign exchange transactions.

While the growth of both the Clearing House Interbank Payment System (CHIPS) and FedWire has been rapid, these networks are quite different in other respects. CHIPS serves 134 U.S. domestic and foreign banks through direct electronic connections, whereas FedWire serves 7,738 U.S. banks and other U.S. depository institutions through direct computer links, dial-up terminal connections, and by telephone. All of the 166,000 daily average FedWire transactions, accounting for some $366 billion in daily average dollar flows, reflect payments between U.S. depository institutions. In contrast, around 60 percent of the CHIPS transaction volume of 91,000 a day, which in total accounts for $277 billion in daily average dollar flows, reflects international payments between foreign and domestic banks and between foreign accounts at U.S. banks.[2]

Until quite recently, the rapid growth of wire transfers was viewed as a challenge to be met through the implementation of increased automation by the operations personnel of a commercial bank or a Reserve bank, rather than as a signal to credit officers and auditors that they needed more effectively to monitor, control, and perhaps even limit the daylight risk exposures that have been growing alongside the expansion of the total value of payments. Subsequent developments in payments processing technology for wire transfers have permitted very rapid growth without imposing real-time balance controls or limitations and, in some cases, even without monitoring daylight bank customer and/or interbank balance positions.

The lack of real-time balance limitations on FedWire, a wire transfer network operated by Federal Reserve banks since around 1914, began to manifest itself in the 1960s as Reserve bank operations were being increasingly automated to handle the rising volume of wire transfers (which transfer balances between reserve accounts held at Reserve banks). The extra computer and software costs that would have been necessary to impose real-time monitoring and balance limitations—not permitting a reserve account to go into overdraft would be an example of one such limitation—were judged at that time to be prohibitive. Prior to this time, neither daylight nor overnight overdrafts were thought to be common occurrences, and there was little expectation that problems would develop in the future that would alter the situation. In any case, reserve positions were basically determined at the end of the day by the accounting department, so, with the exception of problem banks, which were closely monitored on a real-time basis, there was little direct observation of banks' daylight balance positions. For purposes of monetary control, the overnight overdraft was thought to be more important, and penalties were (and still are) assessed on banks that incur them. The extent of daylight overdrafts on FedWire was not fully determined until a comprehensive study of their size and incidence was completed in 1979.

Daylight overdrafts on CHIPS, in contrast to those on FedWire, were explicitly part of the system in 1970, when CHIPS began operations. CHIPS participants did not then and do not now transfer good or final funds but rather transfer provisional payments that (today) become final at the end of the day, after settlement occurs. In effect, CHIPS participants have always started out the processing day with a zero balance in their "CHIPS account" and settle the net debit/net credit positions incurred over the day at the close of business. Since the CHIPS account balance starts at zero, just one outgoing-funds transfer by its very nature leads to a net debit or daylight overdraft by the sender. At present, the net position of all the day's gross funds sent and received is settled using a special account at a Reserve bank. The various net debits are paid into this account using (in effect) FedWire transfers, and, once this process is completed, the net credits are paid out until the account is exhausted. Thus, CHIPS provisional-funds transfers are made final through the movement of reserve account balances at Reserve banks.[3] Prior to the Herstadt failure in 1974, CHIPS payments were settled on a next-day basis using reserve accounts. In 1981, however, CHIPS moved to same-day settlement.

The use of reserve account balances for two simultaneous purposes—an instrument of monetary control and a source of good or final funds for settlement—is economically efficient.[4] But other settlement procedures—those using compensating or correspondent balances—are also in use today. These balances are funded and maintained through periodic FedWire or CHIPS transfers and are used to settle the messages sent over the SWIFT and BankWire message transfer networks, which handle a much smaller portion of total U.S. transfer than do CHIPS and FedWire.

Another reason that CHIPS uses reserve balances for settlement is less direct or explicit: it involves the possibility of reduced risk to CHIPS participants in the event of a failure by one of them to settle at the end of the day. Some banks believe that the direct involvement of a Reserve Bank in the CHIPS settlement process may confer more timely access to the discount window in the event of settlement failure. The ability of one CHIPS participant to borrow funds from a Reserve bank if it were otherwise to experience a failure to settle its end-of-day net position confers value on the remaining participants. A discount-window loan would also serve to insulate the payments system and financial markets from the effects of a settlement failure, which are described next. In this instance, systemic risk to the payments system would be absorbed as credit risk by the lending Reserve bank and, ultimately, by the taxpayer. In the following sections, a simulation analysis[5] will be used to demonstrate the possible effects of a settlement failure.

Possible Responses to a Settlement Failure

Pursuant to the CHIPS rules, the inability of a participant to settle its end-of-day net debit position could result in all its transfers, sent and received, being backed out of the settlement (a process termed "unwinding"); a revised settlement position for the remaining participants would then be calculated. In the real world, such an event would occur only after an intensive effort to work out a solution that would allow settlement of all activity *without* unwinding.

Removing the transfers sent and received by a participant would have varying impacts on different participants, depending on their net position with the institution that failed to settle. If an institution sent exactly the same aggregate dollar value of transfers to the failed participant as it received from the failed participant, it would have a net position of zero, and its net position in the settlement would be unaltered. To the extent that an institution received a larger aggregate dollar value of transfers from the failed participant than it sent to same, it would have a net credit balance with that institution, and the removal of all transfers between them would reduce the remaining institution's net credit position in the settlement (or increase its net debit position). Conversely, failure of an institution with which a bank has a net debit position will reduce the bank's net debit position in the settlement or will increase its net credit position.

Because the removal of one institution's payments activity alters the settlement positions of other participants, there is the risk that the failure of one institution can precipitate the failure of others (systemic risk). Systemic risk occurs with a failure to settle on CHIPS (or CHESS), which is a provisional-funds transfer network, but not FedWire (or CashWire).[6] A sender's failure to extinguish its daylight overdraft on FedWire creates credit risk for a Reserve bank. Under Regulation J, Reserve banks provide good and final funds to receivers of FedWire payments. Thus, the failure to "settle" on FedWire cannot affect other bank participants on the network, although the Reserve bank can suffer a financial loss.

A number of factors will affect the degree of systemic risk associated with the default of a participant on its payment obligations on a provisional-wire transfer network such as CHIPS. First, the sources of the shock that causes the bank's default will determine the context in which the default occurs. The more sudden and/or unexpected the shock and resulting default, the less opportunity other institutions will have to reduce their exposure to the failed institution. Second, the number of institutions affected by a shock, the size of the institution(s) that default, and the magnitude of the net positions other institutions have with the defaulting institution(s) will all shape the outcome.

The options available to deal with the shock also bear on its consequences. There are several considerations that will determine the impact of any failure to settle. First, an institution's exposure to the removal from the settlement of another institution's funds transfers to it will depend on the use, if any, it has made or permitted customers to make of the provisional entries representing the funds transferred prior to settlement. With respect to messages received for customers' accounts, the extent to which the bank has permitted the customer to use these balances and the customer's obligation and ability to return any portion of the balance used will determine the impact of the nonsettlement of the transfer. If the customer has not used the funds represented by the transfer or can and does return them, the bank will not be harmed by the nonsettlement of the transfer.[7] Similarly, with respect to funds transfers received for the bank's own account, to the extent that the bank has not relied on them in some fashion, their nonsettlement will not harm it.

If a bank is in a net debit position in the revised settlement, the nonsettlement of funds transferred for which it cannot readily reverse the use it has made or permitted of the funds may present it with a liquidity problem. The resulting need for additional funds to satisfy its revised settlement obligation may be met in one of several ways. Up to some point, an institution will be able to handle the revised settlement obligation from its own resources. For institutions with less than $250 million of capital, the "comfort letter" required by CHIPS also obligates the parent to use its resources to meet the obligations of the subsidiary (although an end-of-day failure may preclude any meaningful exercise of this option). Access to the discount window may, for certain institutions, also provide necessary funds. Finally, it must be remembered that CHIPS is a net-net settlement system, with the activity of the participants being netted with that of their settling participants and settlement occurring first among the settling participants. A settling participant may be willing to settle for one of its associated participants facing a liquidity problem in meeting its revised settlement obligation. All of these factors will determine a participant's ability to meet its revised settlement obligation.

The magnitude of the net position changes that would result from the sudden and unexpected failure of a CHIPS participant can be examined by taking the record of transaction activity for a given day and removing all transfers to and from a particular institution. Using such historical data, it is necessary to assume a precipitous failure of an institution, since there is no way to simulate fully a situation in which other institutions perceive a problem and partially adjust their exposure. However, this problem can be at least partly remedied by removing the transactions to and from a participant in a net credit position for the day studied. The failure of a participant in a net credit position means that other participants have extended the failed institution less gross daylight credit than if it were in a large net debit position during the day and, in this sense, the circumstance is similar to the likely response by network receivers to a questionable participant prior to its relatively unexpected failure to settle.

First Simulation—The Settlement Failure
of a Large Participant

By using the actual record of all transactions for a randomly selected business day during January 1983, the settlement position of all institutions before and after the removal of all payments to and from a large settling participant was calculated. With respect to the associate participants of the settling participant, which were removed, it was assumed that they could find another settling participant or, if necessary, settle directly for themselves at the end of the day. The settling participant selected for the first simulation had a net credit position of $321 million for the day in which it was assumed to fail unexpectedly prior to settlement.

For the first *revised* settlement, twenty-four institutions had settlement obligation that had increased by more than the amount of their capital and ended up in a net debit position. Of these twenty-four, eight had been in a net credit position before the removal of the transactions involving the failed settling participant. Table 8–1 shows the original settlement position of each of these twenty-four institutions (column 1). From this and the revised settlement position (not shown), the magnitude of the settlement position change

Table 8–1
Failure of a Major Settling Participant (Day 1): Institutions with a Net Debit Position in the Revised Settlement and an Increase in Their Net Settlement Obligation Exceeding Their Capital

	Original Net Settlement Position (millions)	Ratio of Position Change to Capital
	(1)	(2)
1.	$ 86.6	22.7
2.	18.5	21.4
3.	− 16.8	1.5
4.	23.1	2.2
5.	− 27.7	4.5
6.	− 28.7	8.2
7.	− 15.2	2.2
8.	− 71.8	1.7
9.	− 15.8	19.1
10.	− 160.7	1.8
11.	3.5	4.2
12.	− 4.4	8.4
13.	− 21.5	15.8
14.	40.8	32.4
15.	− 25.8	7.5
16.	0	12.4
17.	− 9.1	7.1
18.	− 2.7	3.0
19.	2.0	11.1
20.	− 37.8	1.4
21.	− 378.5	2.9
22.	6.6	7.7
23.	− 39.0	12.1
24.	177.3	15.4

was computed, giving the ratio of the settlement position change to the institution's capital (column 2). In revising the settlement, the largest net position erosion was $568 million, which represented 83 percent of that institution's capital (and, since this is less than the institution's capital, this institution is not shown among the twenty-four in table 8–1). Even with this change, however, the institution remained in a substantial net credit position. The largest single net position enhancement was $762 million.

As already noted, there are a number of factors, including the use institutions have made or permitted customers to make of nonsettled transfers, internal resources, the parent's comfort letter, borrowing, and coverage by a settling participant that will influence a participant's ability to meet its revised settlement obligation. Certainly, the interplay of these factors will vary from one participant to another. In order to pursue the settlement revision process to its ultimate conclusion over a number of iterations, the limitations of the study required a standard assumption. For simplicity, the threshold that was used was the same as in table 8–1: namely, if a participant experienced *a position deterioration equal to or exceeding its capital and was in a net debit position in the revised settlement*, then it too was presumed to be unable to settle. This series of iterations—one for each revised settlement—was continued until no participant failed by this definition of an iteration. Thus, for each iteration, a revised net settlement position for all participants was computed after removing any participant that failed, along with all transfers to and from it. Table 8–2 shows the results of this process in the first simulation. Six iterations were required before no participant failed to meet the preceeding criteria. To the extent that institutions on average can sustain settlement position changes in excess of

Table 8–2
Failure of a Major Settling Participant (Day 1)

Iteration	Institutions with a Net Debit Position in the Revised Settlement and an Increase in Their Net Settlement Obligation Exceeding Their Capital	Percentage of the Daily Total Dollar Value of Messages Sent
	(1)	(2)
1	24	15.2
2	12	14.4
3	10	6.2
4	3	2.7
5	1	0.1
6	0	—
Total	50	38.6

their capital, this table overstates the magnitude of the problem which could develop. If, on the other hand, an institution would have withdrawn from a settlement when its revised settlement obligation increased by more than 10 percent of its capital (rather than 100 percent), the impact would be greater. For example, the 10 percent "rule" would make the "total" row in table 8–2 show seventy-three failed institutions (rather than fifty), representing 76.1 percent of the total value of CHIPS messages sent that day (rather than the 38.6 percent).

One of the previously mentioned factors that could facilitate achievement of a settlement is the willingness of a settling participant to represent one of its associated participants despite the latter's having difficulty in meeting its revised settlement obligations. Table 8–3 groups the twenty-four institutions shown in table 8–1, illustrating the first iteration of table 8–2, by their settling participant, showing the aggregate net position change for the associates of each of the ten settling participants who settle for other institutions. (The twelve settling participants who settle only for their own account are not shown.) The net position change for each of the settling participants is also shown. A contrast of columns 2 and 3 illustrates the impact on each settling participant of supporting all of its associate participants. In some cases, the settling participant's net position is considerably worsened by folding in the associate's position with that of the settling participant.

Table 8–3
Failure of a Major Settling Participant (Day 1): Revised Settlement Position After the Failure of a Participant for Institutions that Settle on Behalf of Other Participants and the Increase in Settlement Obligation Due to Associated Participants *(millions of dollars)*

	Settling Participant's Original Net Position	Settling Participant's Revised Net Position	Aggregate Settlement Obligation Increase of Associated Participants
	(1)	(2)	(3)
1.	$ 52.3	$ 13.4	$ −7.4
2.	545.9	284.1	—
3.	147.2	99.6	−95.5
4.	−846.9	−138.8	−57.6
5.	106.9	868.7	−690.6
6.	1,132.8	564.7	−102.3
7.	44.2	347.3	−159.3
8.	22.6	−229.7	—
9.	−549.6	−608.5	—
10.	*	—	−9.6

*Failed settling participant.

Second Simulation with Transactions Data
for a Different Day

To assess the sensitivity of these simulation results to the transaction activity on the particular day used in the first simulation, another day in January 1983 was randomly selected and the simulation analysis repeated. The results of this second simulation are summarized in tables 8–4 through 8–6. Overall, the results are broadly consistent with those for the first simulation examined. Somewhat fewer institutions (sixteen as opposed to twenty-four) experienced an increase in their settlement position obligation that exceeded their capital and were in a net debit position for the revised settlement in the first iteration. In addition, the average ratio of position change to capital was somewhat lower for the second simulation. Two factors may explain these differences. First, the net position of the failed settling participant whose transaction activity was removed from the revised settlement in the second simulation was a very large credit balance. The removal of a settling participant in a large net credit position, compared to a small net credit or a net debit position, was selected to approximate the situation in which at least some adjustment by other participants in their exposures is made prior to the failure by the participant. For the second

Table 8–4
Failure of a Major Settling Participant (Day 2):
Institutions with a Net Debit Position in the
Revised Settlement and an Increase in Their Net
Settlement Obligation Exceeding Their Capital

	Original Net Settlement Position (millions)	*Ratio of Position Change to Capital*
	(1)	(2)
1.	$ 9.1	4.7
2.	– 60.3	13.4
3.	16.6	5.8
4.	5.3	1.2
5.	– 23.0	3.0
6.	13.9	3.5
7.	– 16.6	1.8
8.	58.1	4.3
9.	– 11.0	1.3
10.	0.2	1.5
11.	– 75.4	4.7
12.	– 16.6	1.9
13.	2.0	2.8
14.	– 56.0	3.6
15.	– 91.0	1.2
16.	– 2.6	103.4

Table 8–5
Failure of a Major Settling Participant (Day 2)

Iteration	Institutions with a Net Debit Position in the Revised Settlement and an Increase in Their Net Settlement Obligation Exceeding Their Capital	Percentage of the Daily Total Dollar Value of Messages Sent
	(1)	(2)
1	16	8.7
2	11	9.4
3	12	11.3
4	9	2.1
5	1	0.1
6	0	—
Total	49	31.6

simulation, the net credit position of the settling participant removed was $921 million, roughly three times the same participant's net credit position for the first simulation ($312 million). A second reason could be that the total dollar value of messages sent on the day of the second simulation was significantly lower than on the day of the first simulation. The total value of

Table 8–6
Failure of a Major Settling Participant (Day 2): Revised Settlement Position After the Failure of a Participant for Institutions that Settle on Behalf of Other Participants and the Increase in Settlement Obligation Due to Associated Participants *(millions of dollars)*

	Settling Participant's Original Net Position	Settling Participant's Revised Net Position	Aggregate Settlement Obligation Increase of Associated Participants
	(1)	(2)	(3)
1.	$ 148.9	$ 135.8	—
2.	527.6	453.6	$ −40.9
3.	288.0	266.2	− 13.4
4.	17.3	1,026.0	− 68.8
5.	− 1,076.0	− 686.4	− 151.7
6.	568.9	735.4	− 16.8
7.	− 148.9	− 544.8	− 2.7
8.	− 140.4	− 184.0	—
9.	− 152.2	− 107.7	—
10.	*	—	− 75.0

*Failed settling participant.

messages sent in the first simulation was a fairly typical $255.6 billion. For the second simulation, the total value of messages sent was only $89.4 billion, or about one-third of the earlier simulation.

One surprising fact that emerges in comparing the consequences of a failure of the same participant on two different days is the variability of other institutions affected. In view of the correspondent relationships among institutions, one might expect that those affected by a particular institution's failure would be fairly constant; in fact, there is a fair amount of variation. Of the twenty-four institutions in table 8–1 and the sixteen in table 8–4, there were only five institutions in common in the first iteration. Similarly, of the total of fifty and forty-nine institutions in tables 8–2 and 8–5, respectively, sixteen of the institutions included in table 8–2 are not included in table 8–5. These results suggest that the institutions most likely to be affected by a particular institution's failure cannot be readily identified beforehand. This day-to-day variation in systemic risk exposure means that an institution cannot limit its credit assessment to some small group of participants with which it most frequently deals. Rather, it must carefully monitor all participants in each network and its exposure across multiple networks. It also means that from a supervisory standpoint the consequences of an institution's default on its payments obligations cannot be easily predicted.

Third Simulation: The Settlement Failure of a Large Associated Participant

In addition to analyzing the failure of a major settling participant, the consequences of the failure of a large associated participant on the settlement obligations of other participants were simulated. Tables 8–7 through 8–9 summarize the results obtained upon removing all transfers to and from a selected associated participant (the day studied is the same one considered in tables 8–1 through 8–3). While the number of participants experiencing an increase in their settlement obligation greater than their capital (and in a net debit position for the revised settlement) was somewhat less (thirteen) than observed with the major settling participant (twenty-four) for the first iteration, the impact on the whole network is more similar than might be expected. Overall, forty-nine institutions failed to settle, accounting for 30.8 percent of that day's dollar value of messages sent. This similarity is noteworthy, since the total dollar value of messages sent by this associated participant was only about 16 percent of the total value of messages sent by the settling participant studied in the first simulation.

Repeating the simulation of the failure of a selected associated participant for the same day used in the second simulation resulted, after eight iterations, in the failure of thirty-three institutions accounting for 22.6 percent of

Table 8–7
Failure of a Large Associated Participant (Day 1): Institutions with a Net Debit Position in the Revised Settlement and an Increase in Their Net Settlement Obligation Exceeding Their Capital

	Original Net Settlement Position (millions)	Ratio of Position Change to Capital
	(1)	(2)
1.	$ − 40.5	*
2.	84.5	225.1
3.	− 16.8	2.2
4.	23.1	1.7
5.	− 28.9	1.4
6.	− 380.9	1.6
7.	4.2	2.1
8.	− 257.2	1.4
9.	− 15.8	3.5
10.	21.9	2.3
11.	− 231.4	1.1
12.	− 9.1	15.9
13.	8.7	46.0

*Institution for which capital figure not available from Board of Governors' data.

the total value of messages sent that day. The most significant aspect of this result is that the dollar value of all transfers sent by the associated participant for this second day represented only 0.8 percent of the CHIPS' total for the day.

Table 8–8
Failure of a Large Associated Participant (Day 1)

Iteration	Institutions with a Net Debit Position in the Revised Settlement and an Increase in Their Net Settlement Obligation Exceeding Their Capital	Percentage of the Daily Total Dollar Value of Messages Sent
	(1)	(2)
1	13	11.6
2	18	8.4
3	10	4.9
4	4	3.7
5	2	1.4
6	1	0.4
7	1	0.4
8	0	—
Total	49	30.8

Table 8–9
Failure of a Large Associated Participant (Day 1): Revised Settlement Position After the Failure of a Participant for Institutions that Settle on Behalf of Other Participants and the Increase in Settlement Obligation Due to Associated Participants *(millions of dollars)*

	Settling Participant's Original Net Position	Settling Participant's Revised Net Position	Aggregate Settlement Obligation Increase of Associated Participants
	(1)	(2)	(3)
1.	$ 52.3	$ 42.4	—
2.	311.9	617.6	$ − 19.3
3.	545.9	640.0	− 18.4
4.	147.2	− 4.3	− 225.1
5.	− 846.9	− 573.2	− 25.7
6.	106.9	141.6	—
7.	1,132.8	1,130.1	− 34.4
8.	44.2	− 90.6	− 43.1
9.	22.6	− 29.6	− 28.5
10.	− 549.6	− 580.1	—

Conclusions from the Simulation Exercise

The goal of the preceding simulations was to attempt to illustrate the possible implications for CHIPS participants of an unwinding of an institution's funds transfer activity owing to one institution's sudden and unexpected default on its settlement obligation. As noted, there are a number of factors that will decrease the likelihood of an unwind being necessary. But the simulations do raise serious, if not fundamental, questions about whether settlement revision using CHIPS Rule 13—the ultimate form of credit risk management for some wire transfer networks—is feasible without also disrupting financial markets. More important, the simulations illustrate the dynamic interdependence of institutions that characterizes the payment system. Overall, the simulations indicate that close to half of the participants and one-third of the payment value could be subject to the CHIPS unwind provisions in the event of an unexpected settlement failure of a CHIPS participant. This demonstrates that systemic risk can be significant and that its possible effects on financial markets are substantial enough to constitute a serious problem.

It should be noted that these simulation results are conservative. This is because the "nonsettlement rule" used was (*a*) an institution experiences a reduction in its net credit or an increase in its net debit that exceeds its capital and (*b*) ends up on a net debit position in the revised settlement. Clearly, only (*a*) may be necessary for nonsettlement. An institution may fail if it experiences a reduction in its net credit greater than its capital even if it still has a net credit in the revised settlement. In addition, an institution may decide not to settle its payment obligations that day if it would incur an apparent loss (at least before court action) of something much less than 100 percent of its capital. Thus, in these two important respects, the simulation exercise is clearly on the conservative side and, if anything, probably *understates* the impact of a settlement failure on the payments system and financial markets.

Payments Finality and the Risk of Settlement Failure

Three possible alternatives have been emphasized in discussions concerning the "best" method to control and limit the risks associated with a settlement failure. They are:[8]

1. Bilateral net credit limits set by the payments receiver to enable him to limit his exposure to a single sender;

2. Sender net debit "caps" set by a payments network or adopted voluntarily by senders to limit the exposure of all receivers with a single sender; and

3. Payments finality, where payments received by a bank are made available to the receiving customer without recourse to the customer for losses incurred if the sending bank fails to settle.

Bilateral net credit limits, developed and adopted by the CashWire network, have been subsequently adopted by CHIPS and CHESS. A sender net debit cap has been adopted or proposed by all the individual networks as well. These "caps" have been applied on FedWire as guidelines rather than as limits that cannot be exceeded. On CHIPS, the proposed cap is actually a creative blend of bilateral net credit limits—those applied to the sending institution plus those applied to all participants on the networks—so that, in effect, the CHIPS cap reflects a market determination of a sender's credit risk. Since bilateral net credit limits and sender net debit caps are now well known and have already been adopted (or proposed) on the wire transfer networks, our discussion will now focus on payments finality issues, an area in which there is a considerable difference in views.

Figure 8–1, a schematic representation of a large dollar funds transfer payments flow, will be helpful in understanding the various aspects of the term "payments finality." Using this diagram, we now assume that the sending bank fails prior to end-of-day settlement. What happens next depends on what network was used to send the funds, since different networks have different rules and, as a result, there are different points at which a payments transfer can be considered to be final.

Figure 8–1. Large-Dollar Funds Transfer Payments Flow

Payments Finality and Risk to
Payments Participants

The three questions that follow help determine, first, which of the parties shown in the diagram are at risk if a sender fails to settle and, second, the possible impact of this settlement failure on other (bank, nonbank) payments system participants:[9]

1. Is the sending bank prevented from unilaterally canceling its payment orders and escaping legal liability? (sender finality)
2. Is there some mechanism whereby the network or network participants cover the net debits of any failed sender in order to assure that settlement takes place? (settlement finality)
3. Are customers given irrevocable credit for funds received? (receiver finality)

The answer to the first question is that no payments network permits a sending bank unilaterally to cancel its payment orders. In the case of payment errors, the sender typically must work out an acceptable arrangement with the receiver, and then the receiver returns to the sender the funds it should not have received. Thus, the sending bank is legally liable for the payments it makes, and in this sense, the payments are considered to be final obligations, even though a sender may not be able to settle its payments at the end of the day. With sender failure, however, this type of payments finality, namely sender finality, does not prevent the systemic effects of the sender's failure to settle.[10] While all payment-receiving parties may be made whole over time (in court), the resulting settlement failure may significantly disrupt financial markets in the interim, as demonstrated in the simulation example.

A second aspect of finality involves the receiving bank or the funds transfer network. On two networks (FedWire, CashWire), there is settlement finality since a mechanism exists whereby the network (FedWire) or the participants (CashWire) have adopted loss-sharing arrangements in the event of a sender's failure to settle. On FedWire, all of a failed sender's net debit is covered by Reserve banks, since Regulation J makes individual payments irrevocable when they are received. On CashWire, each receiving participant agrees to cover its particular net credit to the failed sender (which equals, across all receivers, the sender's total net debit).

On CHIPS a different procedure is followed, one that is less certain to assure settlement finality. Settlement could be assured on CHIPS if one participant or a group of participants absorbed the failed sender's net debt, as noted in the simulation example. But if this did not occur, then the emergency settlement provisions of Rule 13 could be used, and the sends and receives of the failed sender would be deleted and a new set of settlement balances would be computed. These deleted payments have sender finality in the sense that the sender is legally obligated to make the payments, but the systemic effects of settlement failure still exist. Put differently, a lack of settlement finality on CHIPS creates systemic risk, but the rules adopted on FedWire and CashWire internalize this risk of loss and prevent systemic risk (at the cost of creating credit risk for Reserve banks and CashWire participants). When Reserve banks (on FedWire) and network participants (on CashWire or on CHIPS) cover the failed sender's net debit, they can attempt to recover these losses from the failed sender. But can they also attempt to recover from their receiving customers any funds received and used by that customer from the failed sender? This depends on the answer to the third question.

Receiving banks are given irrevocable credit and immediate access to funds received over FedWire, and so the funds are considered to be final to both the receiving bank and the receiving customer—thus the term *receiver finality*. Reserve banks absorb all liability for a failed sender's net debit. On CashWire, a similar interpretation is often made but, from a legal point of view, it appears now that receiving customers are *not* in fact required to be given irrevocable credit. It would be fair to say that there remains some confusion on this issue.

On CHIPS the situation is clear. All payments are to be considered provisional by the receiving customer and are final only after settlement at the end of the day. That is, customer access to funds received over CHIPS is typically subject to a credit judgment by the receiving bank and, in the event of a failure to settle, the customer may be required to return the funds. Irrevocable credit is not required to be given to receiving customers on CHIPS. Thus, the payments finality issue, from a systemic risk standpoint, turns on (*a*) settlement finality and (*b*) receiver finality. If receiver finality is assured, as on FedWire, then settlement finality is assured as well. On CashWire, settlement finality exists, but receiver finality is questionable. Even so, it must be concluded that a very serious aspect of systemic risk has been dealt with on CashWire through the adoption of settlement finality. The finality issues most under discussion at present are whether CHIPS should remain a provisional payments network, whether it should move to assure settlement finality, or whether it should provide finality of payments to receiving customers (receiver finality).

Settlement Finality versus Receiver
Finality on CHIPS

There is general agreement that payments finality to receiving customers on CHIPS would impose a very significant increase in the credit risk of many receiving banks. Some banks are not willing to give up recourse to their receiving customer of payments received and used in the case of a sender's failing to settle. Other banks, however, are willing to do so and argue that if such action were taken, receivers would be much more careful in accepting net credits from sending banks. In the latter case, this would probably lower the size of net debits relatively risky senders could send and so reduce the overall likelihood of a settlement failure (and therefore systemic risk) on CHIPS and similar networks.

A number of intermediate alternatives are possible between these two polar positions. For example, it is possible to provide settlement finality by having receiving banks accept (initial) liability for net credits they incur with a failed sender (as now exists on CashWire) but permit 100 percent recourse to receiving customers with a lag of one month for the net payments received. In this situation, customers (after a lag) would be fully liable for the net credit received from the failed sender. This liability could be apportioned among the different receiving customers (i) by taking the ratio of the receiving bank's net credit to gross credit received from the failed sender ($NC/\Sigma_i GC_i$) and applying it to each individual customer's gross credit received from the failed sender (GC_i). More formally, each customer's liability (L_i) becomes:

$$L_i = (NC/\Sigma_i GC_i)(1.00)(GC_i)$$

where there is 100 percent recourse to the customer for the net credit from the failed sender. While the bank provides the funds to assure settlement, this entire amount (NC) is recoverable from its customers (as $\Sigma_i L_i = NC$). One problem with this approach is that the extent of customer liability (L_i) is known only ex post, not ex ante. On the other hand, because $L_i < GC_i$, customers may be better advantaged than they are today under current CHIPS rules, where *all* of the gross payment (GC_i) is a provisional payment.[11] But more important, the payments system would be better insulated against systemic risk than it is today, since one type of settlement finality would then exist on CHIPS.[12]

Another alternative would be to adopt formal loss-sharing arrangements with customers whereby, say, 50 percent of the receiving bank's net credit loss to a failed sender (NC) would be recoverable by recourse to the receiving customer. This is different from the previous alternative, wherein the recoverable amount would be 100 percent (or 1.00 in the formula). Alternatively, if customers were given irrevocable credit on all funds received, as would occur with receiver finality, the percentage would be zero. Still other alternatives could be derived as variants of these two, such as letting the customer determine the recourse liability percentage and, if it is less than 100 percent, assess the customer a fee to compensate for the new credit risk the receiving bank absorbs. This would be similar to the bank's providing "payments finality insurance" to the customer for a fee. Yet another variant would be to set the percentage at zero—giving receiver finality—but protect the receiving bank from loss by requiring that all senders post collateral (which could face a "haircut") with a third party for the average daily value of the total net debit they have incurred over the last three months. Receiving banks would be given a legal right to this collateral in the event of sender failure to offset their losses rather than have full or even partial recourse to the receiving customer. If the size of sender net debits is reduced in the future, through the various methods discussed next, it is likely that settlement finality, and perhaps even receiver finality, will become much more acceptable to all participants on wire transfer networks and may eventually be adopted as a further risk reduction method.

Implications for Financial Markets

Daylight overdrafts basically represent an extension of daylight credit to cover the net debts experienced by certain banks that send a larger value of wire payments than they receive, at least for a number of hours during the day. These overdrafts are typically erased by the end of the day, when the flow of incoming funds rises and eliminates the overdraft, and/or settlement occurs, removing the net debit built up over the day. The proximate cause of funds-transfer daylight overdrafts on the major wire transfer networks (Fed-Wire and CHIPS) concerns the current institutional practices that have evolved in the overnight funds markets. Daylight credit has been free and, as a result, has been "overused" compared to its true value to the user and the risk to the supplier (and/or society as a whole). This is another case of "market failure" wherein the price charged for daylight credit (zero) does not properly reflect its (risk or real resource) cost. Change these incentives, by pricing the daylight credit provided or otherwise limiting the value of credit that can be incurred through bilateral net credit limits or sender net debit caps, and participants will alter their current behavior and reduce daylight overdrafts, or those providing the credit will be more properly compensated for the risk they incur.

Adoption of one or more of four settlement risk reduction alternatives—sender net debit caps, receiver set bilateral net credit limits, settlement or receiver finality, and pricing daylight credit—can significantly affect banks and financial markets in the near future. Such possible effects concern:

1. Changes in the structure and growth of large-dollar wire transfer networks;

2. Shifts in the competitive position among banks, depending on which payments services they specialize in;

3. Improvements in bank monitoring of customer daylight balances and interbank funds transfer positions; and

4. Changes in the institutional structure of financial markets.

Limiting and/or pricing daylight overdrafts can have the effect of reducing the rapid annual volume growth experienced by wire transfer networks and may reduce incentives for new suppliers to enter this market, compared to a situation in which daylight credit is free and few limitations exist.

Pricing and quantitative limitations can also affect the competitive positions of those banks that have been frequent users of daylight credit. Because of the proposed differential treatment of funds-transfer daylight overdrafts and U.S. government book-entry, securities-related daylight overdrafts, which are to be collateralized because of the importance of this market for monetary control, banks that have specialized in securities transactions may be affected less than others. Those banks that have chosen to specialize in third-party funds transfers and/or interbank trading in overnight funds in excess of their need for these funds for their own internal use in asset funding will likely be affected the most. And, of these banks, those in unit banking states have suggested that they would be more significantly constrained than banks in branching states (Chicago Clearing House Association). Unit banks typically rely more heavily on overnight funds than do branching banks, which use core deposits developed internally within their branching network and often incur lower net positions in overnight purchased funds. These differential impacts— by type of payments specialization, by involvement in intraday trading for only trading (not funding) purposes, and by unit or branch organizational structure—will all lead to different costs being experienced and therefore will affect the competitive structure between banks. Of course, over time, the costs associated with risk reduction will be directly passed on to the various internal bank profit centers affected and, subsequently, to banking customers. This shifting process is made easier if a price for daylight overdrafts develops than if only quantitative limitations are adopted (voluntarily by banks or, perhaps, imposed by bank regulators). Pricing, which may result in either case, would lead correspondent banks to reexamine and reprice most or all of their payment services, at times changing their price by more than that attributable to the cost involved in order to practice Ramsey pricing.

Risk reduction will likely lead to important institutional changes in financial markets. These changes concern the development of new procedures and increased reliance on existing methods that reduce the impact of overnight funding on the measurement of daylight overdrafts. Banks that typically purchase overnight funds from the same respondent institutions can attempt to bring these funds in-house, using book-entry procedures or a continuing contract. Alternatively, borrowers could return the *net* value of borrowed overnight funds rather than sending an a.m. return for the gross amount borrowed the previous day with a receipt in the p.m. of the gross amount reborrowed from the same lender. Still other changes may involve a shift from overnight funding to term funds.[13] Depending on the yield curve (which can change significantly on account of changes in interest rate expectations), the extra costs involved with term funds could be positive or negative, but typically are below 50 basis points when they are positive. This could lengthen bank liability structures and decrease the usefulness of liability management as a tool to respond flexibly to unexpected deposit flows and loan takedowns. A related development would be the payment of basis points by borrowers to induce lenders to send borrowed funds earlier than now typically occurs (say, one hour after the amount and rate for that day have been negotiated by phone). Alternatively, borrowers could compensate lenders for delayed return of funds borrowed the previous day. This would provide for a closer matching in time for gross sends and receives and would reduce the duration of daylight overdrafts (and in some cases their amount as well). The basic result here is to provide for a better match between a bank's book position regarding funds purchased and sold with the actual operational position regarding funds received and sent, as noted at the beginning of this chapter.

A more problematical development would be the emergence of an interbank intraday funds market to cover overdraft positions. In effect, this development would be very similar to borrower payment of basis points to lenders to speed up the sending of newly borrowed funds or for the borrower to delay the return of funds previously borrowed. Here the supplier of what would otherwise be intraday funds is the lender himself, rather than some other market participant. The development of a formal and large intraday funds market, it is noted, faces significant operational difficulties, not in negotiating the transfer of intraday funds but in actually transferring these funds in a timely manner.

Lastly, one potentially useful development is already under way, at least for foreign exchange transactions (which, according to knowledgeable bankers, represents a major if not the most important type of funds transfer on CHIPS). This development can be termed "obligation netting prior to the value date." Here, gross payments obligations prior to their value date are netted so that both from a legal, contractual standpoint and from the standpoint of payments flow, only the net position needs to be sent. Today, from a legal standpoint (although, as usual, there is some difference of view), the parties to a foreign exchange contract are liable for the gross values contracted for, even though the net position (for operational simplicity) may be sent on the settlement day (the value date). A group of U.S. banks in New York and London are reportedly considering plans and redesigning the requisite legal contracts necessary to implement this institutional change in the foreign exchange market.

In conclusion, I have attempted to outline briefly how historical technological advances in the ability to process large-dollar payments more rapidly have permitted a truly exceptional growth in this payments volume. The ability of commercial banks and Reserve banks to transfer funds has expanded so fast that, until quite recently, the credit and systemic risks associated with these payments flows were not well understood. Using simulation analysis, I have attempted to illustrate the possible degree of risk involved, especially to the continued smooth operation of the payments system and financial markets. Among the various "solutions" to this problem now being discussed (and in some cases being implemented), I have focused on the issue of payments finality in an attempt to develop some possible compromises between the two polar positions that usually emerge in discussions. In my judgment, it seems possible to move significantly toward reducing systemic risk without adopting the polar position of receiver finality that is typically put forth. Settlement finality would suffice. Lastly, considering the risk reduction alternatives that are most likely to exist in the near future, I have outlined their possible effects on the institutional structure and operation of financial markets. I do not believe that these markets will be disrupted; rather, I am convinced that many relatively low-cost institutional changes are available with which to reduce measured daylight overdrafts and systemic risk involved. The successful implementation of these alternatives should reduce the market failure that has been shown to exist in this case through the provision of free daylight overdraft credit even though the risks and real resource costs involved with a settlement failure are nonzero.

Notes

1. Wire transfer payments, as used here, are the sum of the dollar value of payments made over the FedWire and CHIPS wire transfer networks. This effectively captures close to 100 percent of wire transfer payments, because the two other remaining networks (CashWire, CHESS) are small. Message transfer networks, such as SWIFT and BankWire, are not included herein because they do not transfer funds—only messages about funds—that are to be transferred between accounts at the *same* bank. FedWire, CHIPS, CashWire, and CHESS, in contrast, seek to transfer funds between banks.

2. CashWire and CHESS represent much smaller networks, with thirty and six participants, respectively. Together, they process about 1,000 transfers a day, totaling on average less than $1 billion.

3. The CashWire and CHESS networks also use an arrangement similar to the one used by CHIPS in settling its payments at the end of the day.

4. Reserve balances are also a source of revenues to the U.S. Treasury, since no interest is paid on them. The payment or nonpayment of interest on reserves does not affect their use as a settlement medium.

5. This simulation analysis was performed jointly by Jim Lyon (Federal Reserve Bank of Minneapolis), Jack Walton (Federal Reserve Board), and the author.

6. A failure to settle on CashWire has effects that actually seem to lie between CHIPS and FedWire, as is explained in the discussion of payments finality.

7. The customer, and perhaps a wider circle of the nonbanking economy, could be adversely affected, however.

8. Other risk reduction alternatives have been suggested but they have not, to date, been the main focus of attention. They have concerned collateralization of daylight overdrafts, the purchase of settlement insurance from a private firm, charging a fee for daylight overdrafts, and rolling settlement whereby a large-dollar network settles more than once each day (see also Humphrey 1984 and other sources not cited here).

9. Jeff Marquardt originally suggested these questions.

10. Rule 13 on CHIPS does, however, permit a *group* decision by the New York Clearing House to cancel all sender obligations when an *unwind* has been attempted but does not lead to settlement. In either case, disruption of financial markets would occur.

11. While court action following a settlement failure may achieve the same result, namely, that a customer using provisional funds may only have to return his share of the receiving-bank-incurred net credit loss from the failed sender, this result is not certain and the customer often has not signed an explicit legal agreement to that effect.

12. Some systemic risk would still remain if the real sector and, to some degree, financial markets were disrupted as customers hastily liquidated assets to repay receiving banks for their immediate provision of funds to ensure settlement finality. But this remaining systemic risk could be controlled to a large degree if customers' legal agreements stipulated some time period—say, one month—in which repayment could be arranged in a more orderly fashion.

13. Term federal funds and, in some states, continuing contract federal funds are subject to regulatory loan limits on sellers of these funds. These limits are 15 percent of the seller's capital when funds are loaned to a single borrower, or 25 percent to a single borrower if these loans are collateralized. Overnight federal funds are not subject to lending limits. Thus, the shift from overnight to term or continuing contracts may also involve a greater diversification of funds sold across borrowers than now occurs for overnight funding.

References

Association of Reserve City Bankers, *Risks in Electronic Payments Systems,* Washington, D.C. (October 1983).

———— . *The Final Report of the Risk Control Task Force,* Payments System Committee, Washington, D.C. (October 1984).

Chicago Clearing House Association, *Daylight Overdrafts,* Chicago (1984).

Frankel, Allen, and Jeffrey Marquardt, "Payments Systems: Theory and Policy," working paper, International Division, Board of Governors of the Federal Reserve System, Washington, D.C. (January 1984).

Humphrey, David B., *The U.S. Payments System: Costs, Pricing, Competition and Risk,* Salomon Brothers Center for the Study of Financial Institutions, New York University, Monograph Series in Finance and Economics, vols. 1 and 2, chap. 8 (1984).

McDonough, William, "Daylight Overdrafts: One Perspective," *The Bankers Magazine* (September/October 1984):74–78.

Rosborough, Bruce, and Michael Urkowitz, "Meeting the Challenges of Risk Management," *Journal of Commercial Bank Lending* (September 1983):2–9.

Smoot, Richard L., "Billion-Dollar Overdrafts: A Payments Risk Challenge," Federal Reserve Bank of Philadelphia *Business Review* (January/February 1985):3–13.

Stevens, Edward J., "Risk in Large-Dollar Transfer Systems," Federal Reserve Bank of Cleveland *Economic Review* (Fall 1984):2–16.

9

Controlling Risk on Large-Dollar Wire Transfer Systems

William C. Dudley

T he problem of daylight overdrafts—consolidated intraday, net debit positions on a wire transfer payment system—has come to the attention of banks and regulators only in the past few years. With payment volume growing much faster than bank capital and reserve balances at the Federal Reserve, the magnitude and frequency of daylight overdrafts have increased dramatically. Currently, at certain times of the day, the daylight overdraft position of a bank may exceed its capital by as much as four or five times.

The growth in daylight overdraft volume has caused observers to ask: What are the consequences of such extensions of intraday credit? And what happens if, at the end of the day, a bank cannot cover its overdraft position and make good on its promises to pay that it made earlier in the day? Because the answers to these questions have not always been reassuring, regulators and the private wire networks have started to look for the means to ensure that banks will adequately manage the risks associated with daylight overdrafts and to minimize the effect of such a failure to settle.

The Federal Reserve has taken the lead in encouraging private wire transfer networks and payments system participants to focus upon the implicit and explicit risks associated with daylight overdraft exposures. A May 1985 memo by the staff of the Board of Governors that discusses risk reduction on wire transfer payment systems briefly outlines Federal Reserve involvement in this area:

The opinions expressed in this chapter are those of the author alone and do not necessarily reflect the views, opinions, or policies of Morgan Guaranty Trust Company. The author gratefully acknowledges the helpful comments and suggestions made by Douglas Harris, James Johnson, Stuart Schweitzer, and Caroline Shapiro of Morgan Guaranty Trust Company, David Humphrey of the Board of Governors of the Federal Reserve System, and Lawrence White of the Graduate School of Business Administration, New York University. The author also thanks Roland Bullard of Philadelphia National Bank, James Byrne and Lawrence Uhlick of Morgan Guaranty Trust Company, Anthony Cluff of the Association of Reserve City Bankers, and Edward Ettin of the Board of Governors of the Federal Reserve System for educating the author about the issues associated with controlling risk on large-dollar wire transfer systems.

The Board began its review of daylight overdraft risks in 1979. In 1981, when the Board approved same day settlement services for CHIPS [Clearinghouse Interbank Payments System] in order to eliminate the overnight risks then associated with that large dollar net settlement network, the Board publicly indicated its intention to reduce daylight overdrafts. In 1982, the Board adopted a policy of *ex post* monitoring of daylight overdrafts on Fedwire and counseling of those institutions with Fedwire overdrafts in excess of 50 percent of their primary capital. The same year, the Board approved provision of settlement services to Bankwire for its Cashwire service, but required that network to impose a 50 percent of capital sender net debit cap on its participants until the Board had an opportunity to consider risk issues more fully. At that time a moratorium on settlement services was announced. . . . In March 1984, the Board requested public comment on various options to reduce risk on large dollar transfer systems.[1]

In May 1985, the Board of Governors issued a statement of its policy to control and reduce the risks associated with depository institution participation on large-dollar wire transfer systems.

Institutional arrangements that affect the timing of payment and receipt are one major cause of daylight overdrafts. For example, in the case of an institution that funds a significant portion of its assets with overnight money (for example, Fed Funds), it generally returns yesterday's overnight money in the morning and receives today's overnight money in the afternoon by institutional arrangement. In the interim period when it does not have any overnight money, it may run a daylight overdraft. A second cause is the stochastic pattern of the timing of payment and receipt. Even if two sides of a transaction are executed at the same time, payment may not arrive at the same time that the disbursement is made. For example, suppose a bank engages in a foreign currency (German marks) swap. It buys DM in the spot market with dollars and simultaneously sells a three-month forward DM contract for dollars. If it pays for the DM on the spot market before receiving payment on the three-month forward contract, it might run a daylight overdraft. On private wire networks, daylight overdrafts are inevitable because there are typically no positive working balances to serve as a buffer against differences in the timing of payments. For example, whoever makes the first payment of the day on CHIPS must be, at least temporarily, in an overdraft position.[2]

This chapter focuses on the daylight overdraft problem on CHIPS, the major private wire transfer system. CHIPS currently has more than 130 participants and a daily payment volume of more than $275 billion. Unlike Fedwire, in which all payments are final once received, CHIPS payments are provisional. Payments received during the day are essentially a promise to pay. At the end of the day, each member of CHIPS settles its net debit position with the clearinghouse either directly, if it is a settling participant, or indirectly through a settling participant, if it is a nonsettling participant.[3] If an institution has a positive net position with another institution—the dollar value of payments it received during the day was greater than the dollar value of payments it sent—this position is netted against any net debit position the institution may have generated with other institutions. If the participant's overall net position is positive at the end of the day, it simply waits for payment. If the institution's overall net position is negative, it makes payment in this amount. Since the total value of payments sent on CHIPS must equal the total value of payments received, the payments of participants in a net debit position equal the positive balances of those participants in a net credit position. Once settlement occurs, the payments are disbursed by debiting and crediting the Federal Reserve accounts of settling banks via Fedwire.

If settlement does not occur at the normal 5:45 p.m. time—because a nonsettling bank or settling bank fails to cover its net debit position—CHIPS rules dictate a series of steps to effect settlement. First, participants can be given more time to settle. Second, if settlement still has not occurred, all transactions between the CHIPS participant that is unable to settle and other CHIPS participants are deleted. This means that the net debit and net credit positions are recalculated for all participants that are initially able to settle as if none of the payments received or sent by the participant that has failed to settle were ever made.[4] The deletion of payments changes the net positions of the other participants, with some participants being made better off and others worse off, depending on their net position with the participant that failed to settle. For those participants that were in a net debit position with the participant that failed to settle, either their overall net debit position falls or their overall net credit position increases. For those participants in a net credit position with the failed participant, either their overall net debit position increases or their overall net credit position falls. While those institutions that were in a net debit position with the failed participant improve their position, for the system as a whole, the *collective* net debit position of all participants other than the institution that failed to settle must worsen, because the failure to settle can occur only if a participant is in an overall net debit position. The total sum of all payments received minus payments sent becomes negative when the payments of the institution in an overall net debit position are deleted. After a participant fails to settle and deletion occurs, settlement can then proceed only if those participants with greater overall net debit positions can obtain additional funds to settle. If some of these participants are unable to settle, the process is repeated. Deletion of payments occurs and new net debit and net credit positions are calculated. Since the collective net debit position grows larger as more participants are unable to settle, the risk increases that still more participants will be unable to settle. As a result, the entire payments system may grind to a halt. As the Federal Reserve staff put it:

The Board's major concern has been this *systemic* risk, i.e., the potential cumulative impact on the liquidity and solvency of a large number of institutions resulting from a failure by one institution to settle its net debit position on a private network, and the resultant implications for the stability of the banking system, for the firms dependent on the functioning of the payments mechanism, and for the operations of financial markets generally.[5]

In the case of a settlement failure, a bank which does settle that is in a net credit position with the bank or banks that fail to settle may suffer loss. In the case of bank-to-bank transactions, the bank can seek recovery from the bank that has failed to settle. In the case of transactions that have been executed on behalf of customers, the bank also has recourse to its customers that received provisional credit for funds transfers received from the institution that failed to settle. Thus, as long as the customers have the funds in the bank or elsewhere, the bank has another method of recovering the net credit balance it is owed. However, because the customers typically are allowed use of provisionally credited wire transfer payments, the funds may no longer be in the bank. In this case, the bank's ability to recover its funds depends on its ability to obtain the funds from its customers.

This systemic risk that a single settlement failure could lead to multiple settlement failures is considered by most observers to be the major risk posed by daylight overdrafts. If daylight overdrafts were lower, it would presumably be easier for institutions to settle after the deletion of payments that would result from the failure of one bank to settle.

The Nature of the Daylight Overdraft Problem

If one could be certain that settlement failure would never occur and that the extensions of intraday credit in the form of daylight overdrafts would not affect bank behavior, one could conclude that daylight overdrafts were not a problem. No systemic risk from settlement failure would exist, nor would the existence of large overdrafts affect the safety and soundness of banks. Thus, the seriousness of the daylight overdraft problem depends on the risk of settlement failure and the response of banks to this risk.

The risk of settlement failure (even assuming that the Federal Reserve will not try to intervene to prevent such a failure) is very low. For settlement failure to occur, a bank must be unable to obtain the funds necessary to settle its position, and for this to happen, an institution would have to fail suddenly, because if it were solvent it could obtain funds either through the discount window or from other banks. Such a failure of a bank during the day would be an unprecedented event. Failure of this sort could probably occur only if significant losses due to fraud or theft were uncovered during the day.

It might be argued that settlement failure will never occur, as the Federal Reserve will always advance funds to ensure settlement.[6] If the Federal Reserve postpones the failure by opening up the discount window, the settlement risk would be transferred to the Federal Reserve and other creditors of the bank. CHIPS participants would receive their payments, but the Federal Reserve would be exposed to the amount of its discount window loan. In this case, the systemic risk due to payments system failure would be averted, but there would still be the risk of systemic collapse, owing to the effect of losses suffered by other creditors of the failed bank.

At first blush, it might appear that the Federal Reserve should always act to avert settlement failure. Since settlement failure has never occurred, its consequences are unknown. It is unlikely that the consequences will be more favorable than those resulting from the Federal Reserve averting the settlement failure and bearing (along with the failed bank's other creditors) the exposure to loss. In fact, one can argue that the consequences of allowing settlement failure would be far more severe: The effects of a bank failure would be magnified. The other participants would be owed the net debit position of the failed bank. They, in turn, would need funds to settle. A severe liquidity crisis could develop that could generate its own set of losses. The integrity of the payments mechanism could also be impaired. Some believe that if a CHIPS settlement failure ever occurred, CHIPS would no longer be a viable payments system.

The difficulty with following such a policy course is that if banks know that the Federal Reserve will always advance funds to ensure that settlement will occur, they will have no incentive to monitor their net credit positions with other banks. By allowing weaker banks to run very large net debit positions, such behavior may increase the probability of systemic collapse if settlement failure occurs.

The proper course for the Federal Reserve depends on three factors:

The current assessment of banks concerning the likelihood that the Federal Reserve will allow settlement failure.

How this assessment influences bank policy concerning overdrafts.

How such changes in bank policy affect the probability of bank failure and the magnitude of such failure when it occurs.

If banks currently believe that the Federal Reserve would allow a major settlement failure to occur, they would protect themselves against the risk of settlement failure, and the daylight overdraft problem would already be partially solved. Unfortunately for the Federal Reserve, the opposite is probably the case. After reviewing the history of regulatory intervention to prevent financial market disruption, most participants probably believe that the likelihood of the Federal Reserve's allowing a large settlement failure to occur is very small.

As long as this assessment does not influence bank behavior, there is little difficulty. Most likely, however, an increase in the risk (real or perceived) of settlement failure does influence the net credit positions a bank is willing to extend on an intraday basis. Thus, a perception that the Federal Reserve will not permit settlement failures may lead to a less stringent attitude toward daylight overdraft exposures.

To prevent this outcome, one could argue that the Federal Reserve should permit a settlement failure, in order to get banks to take the risks seriously.[7] If banks were convinced that the Federal Reserve would allow a settlement failure to occur, they would no doubt monitor their net credit positions more closely.

Even if such a policy did force banks to reduce their net credit exposures, it is not clear that such a reduction would serve any useful purpose. There is value in getting banks to recognize the risks inherent in daylight overdrafts only if such recognition causes banks to behave in a manner that reduces the probability of failure or the expected size of such a failure. To illustrate this point, suppose banks knew that the Federal Reserve would allow settlement failure to occur. They might then reduce their net credit exposures with institutions that they deemed weaker credits. If this change did not affect the likelihood of failure or pattern of growth of these institutions, the reduction in net credit limits would not change the total exposure of the banking system and its customers to loss. The only thing that would be changed in the case of a settlement failure is that the participants on CHIPS that had reduced their limits would suffer smaller losses. The total loss borne by the financial system and the failed bank's customers, collectively, would be unaltered.

Only if the reduction in limits causes the bank to change its behavior in a manner that reduces its probability of failure or the size of failure would a reduction in limits lead to a reduction in overall risk. Thus, the best that can be said for the Federal Reserve's allowing settlement failure to occur is that it would provide incentives for banks to discipline weaker credits by reducing their exposures. With lower net debit limits, weaker credits would face higher costs and would have some incentive to remedy their deficiencies to avoid the lower net debit constraints.

The preceding conclusion does not mean that managing the risks associated with daylight overdrafts is inappropriate; doing so can make the banking system more sound. Such actions have value, however, not because they reduce the risk of settlement failure (the Federal Reserve can already solve this problem) but because they force banks with poor operating controls or poor credit quality to improve in these areas, thereby reducing the likelihood that these institutions will ultimately fail.

The Federal Reserve also has the option of following an intermediate course. It might allow the problem institution to fail to settle and then extend liquidity to all other participants in order to effect settlement. In this case, banks with net debit exposures would be exposed to loss but the systemic aspects of payments system collapse would be averted. The failure by a bank to settle would have consequences that differed little from those associated with any other bank failure. To the extent that losses caused some of these creditors to fail, the systemic risk of financial collapse would not be averted. But such a risk exists in the case of any bank failure.

In theory, this sort of intervention might not work under existing rules. If, after deletion of the failed bank's payments, a bank had a significantly higher net debit position, it would have the right under Rule 13 to decide not to settle, even if the Federal Reserve loaned it the necessary funds. Thus, the extension of liquidity by the Federal Reserve might not prevent systemic collapse. In practice, it is likely that any institution would settle if it could. Failure to settle would mean that all the payments executed during the day on behalf of its customers would be unwound, and the consequences of such treatment would be severe for the bank's competitive position.

The Federal Reserve could base its initial decision whether to allow a settlement failure on whether the bank involved was solvent. A solvent bank that was unable to settle would be extended credit; otherwise, settlement failure would be permitted. The systemic aspects of settlement failure would be averted by having the Federal Reserve provide funds to allow settlement to occur at this point. Such a policy would force banks to monitor their daylight overdraft exposures because there would be some risk of loss without forcing the banking system to bear the costs associated with the Federal Reserve's failing to fulfil its lender-of-last-resort function.

What Price for Intraday Credit?

To the extent that there is a risk of loss, intraday credit is underpriced. A bank running a daylight overdraft does not have to compensate the bank in the net credit position for this intraday loan. To date, the failure of the market to price this credit probably reflects three factors at work. First, bankers probably believe that the Federal Reserve will always intervene to prevent settlement failure. As long as the Federal Reserve will in fact do this, there is no direct risk to the banks and, thus, no reason to price extensions of intraday credit. Second, the risk of sudden failure is very low. In the case of banks that are large enough to be CHIPS participants, failure seldom occurs quickly. Instead, funds run off, the Federal Reserve opens the discount window, and the institution's problems are more closely investigated. During this time interval, banks would naturally reduce their intraday exposures to the problem bank; for example, major banks closely monitored their intraday positions with Continental Illinois National Bank and Trust Company during its liquidity crisis. Third, because intraday exposures are generated as a result of payments, those banks typically have not focused on the issue from a credit perspective. One of the Federal Reserve's goals in this area is simply to force senior management to focus on the fact that they are extending credit to many institutions during the day.

Because intraday credit currently is free, banks run higher overdraft positions than they otherwise would. The solution to the problem would seem to be either to develop a price for intraday credit or to eliminate the risk of loss. In the first case, creditors would be compensated for the risks they absorb; the problem is determining the correct price. Since failure to settle has never occurred, there is no actuarial basis for calculating a price. Moreover, the price would have to depend on the size of the exposure and the credit quality of the borrower. Largely for these reasons, the Board of Governors announced that it had tentatively rejected this option when it asked for comments on daylight overdrafts in March 1984.

The second solution is to eliminate the risk of loss. This could be done simply enough by requiring daylight overdrafts to be collateralized. In effect, this would result in a price for daylight overdrafts to the extent that pledged collateral had value elsewhere. The advantage of the collateral approach is that the effective price would vary by the quality of the credit. The opportunity cost to sound banks of pledging collateral would be less than for shaky institutions. The problem with requiring banks to pledge collateral is that this might not be the best use of such collateral.

The Federal Reserve also rejected this option in March 1984, at least for daylight overdrafts arising from transactions not involving government securities transactions. It argued that collateralization was not an acceptable solution because it "would shift risk to the deposit insurance funds, it could not provide liquidity for settlement, and to the extent that collateral was defined broadly, would not serve as an effective constraint."[8]

It is difficult to see how the Federal Reserve concludes that collateralization is undesirable on the basis of these arguments. First, to the extent that daylight overdraft exposures are reduced by any means, some risk will be shifted to the deposit insurance funds and other bank creditors. Second, only the Federal Reserve can ultimately provide the liquidity for settlement. The collateral would merely serve to protect the participant (be it a bank or the Federal Reserve itself) in the net credit position. In the case of a private wire transfer system, to obtain a discount window loan so that it could settle, a bank would have to pledge collateral with the Federal Reserve. Third, to the extent collateral is broadly defined, this would only reduce the effective cost of running daylight overdrafts, not eliminate it. The Board of Governor's conclusion seems based, in part, on a concern that the effective cost of collateralization and, hence, of generating daylight overdraft exposures would be so low that the volume of daylight overdrafts would not be reduced. The Federal Reserve could increase the cost by simply defining collateral more narrowly.

To date, the methods of enforcing discipline upon banks with respect to daylight overdrafts have been confined to quantity limits. These limits take three forms:

Bilateral net credit limits. These limits restrict the maximum amount of daylight overdraft exposure an institution can have with any other single institution.

System net debit sender caps. These limits restrict the overall net debit position an institution can have with respect to all other institutions in a system.

Cross-system net debit sender caps. These limits restrict the overall net debit position an institution can have with respect to all other institutions on all the wire transfer payment systems on which it operates.

The logic behind these three types of limits is that systemic risk arises not just from the magnitude of exposures between institutions but also from the total exposure of all the banks in the system and the total exposure of all banks across all systems. When deletion occurs, the total change in the net debit or credit position of a single bank is determined by its net debit or credit position with the bank that failed to settle. But the systemic risk depends, in part, on the total number of institutions that suffer a significant deterioration in their net debit positions. System net debit sender caps and cross-system net debit sender caps help ensure that the impact of a settlement failure will be limited. And cross-system net debit sender caps help ensure that new private wire transfer systems will not be started simply because debit caps on existing private networks and Fedwire have become binding.

Although such quantity limits have been endorsed by the Federal Reserve, there is some question whether these limits make good sense. With quantity limits, the price of daylight overdrafts is essentially positive for banks above the limit and zero for banks below the limit. But the risk of settlement failure and the consequences of settlement failure are present for both types of institutions.

The work that has been done to date suggests that the degree of systemic risk is not closely related to the size of the net debit position of the institution that fails to settle. In fact, one of the Federal Reserve's simulation results (see chapter 8) assumes settlement failure of an institution in a net credit position (an unlikely event, as the institution could settle by doing nothing). This particular simulation indicates that in an unwind a lot of other banks would be unable to settle as well. This suggests that there should also be a price for smaller levels of daylight overdrafts.

If quantity limits are used, the next quesiton is, What type of limits? Should limits be based upon average daily overdrafts, peak daily overdrafts, or an average of peak daily exposures? The Federal Reserve has endorsed dual cross-system net debit sender caps: one cap would be placed on a bank's maximum daily daylight overdraft position, and a lower cap would be placed on the average of the maximum daily overdraft position over the reserve maintenance period.[9]

Given the assumption that the Federal Reserve will always intervene to prevent systemic collapse, the risk exposure that is created when settlement failure occurs is the dollar value of the net debit position at the end of the day. If a firm has failed during the day, this position will equal the net debit position at the time of failure. Thus, average exposures would seem to be more indicative of the risk than peak exposures.

An additional problem with quantity limits such as bilateral credit limits and net debit sender caps is that if these limits are strictly enforced, payments will be rejected by the system.[10] Such rejections drive up costs. Because the timing of receipts of payments cannot be forecast with certainty and because a bank's overdraft position can change by billions of dollars in minutes, a bank could have a "bad run," not receive payments as soon as expected, and find itself up against a daily limit. With averaging, the bank at least has some advance warning that it is approaching the limit and can adjust its behavior accordingly.

One proposal that would address this problem is to allow banks intraday overline facilities at the Federal Reserve. Under such a facility, a bank could borrow from the Federal Reserve for part of the day. The Federal Reserve staff has concluded that the need for an intraday credit facility has not yet been demonstrated. The Federal Reserve has suggested that an advisory group of bank and thrift representatives evaluate the need for such a facility in the future.

Probably the major reason that quantity limits have been utilized is that they are the easiest to administer. The use of any sort of pricing mechanism requires decisions as to the appropriate unit of time as well as the appropriate price. If a $600 million overdraft is outstanding for one minute, should this cost the same as a $10 million overdraft that is outstanding for sixty minutes?

A related question is whether all daylight overdrafts should be treated identically. Is the daylight overdraft that arises from a government securities transaction somehow different from the overdraft that arises from a foreign exchange transaction? And is an overdraft transaction arising from the bank's own business (for example, the sale of Fed Funds) different from an overdraft created by a customer's actions?

To date, the Federal Reserve has divided overdrafts into two groups: overdrafts arising from government securities transactions are exempted from bilateral credit and cap limits, whereas overdrafts arising from all other types of transactions are not. The Federal Reserve has simply allowed banks to remove all government securities transactions in calculating their net debit or credit position. Currently, the Federal Reserve is evaluating a proposal that would give a depository institution three options concerning treatment of book-entry government securities transactions. An institution could:

1. Treat these overdrafts just like any other type of overdraft.
2. Collateralize such overdrafts with definitive securities.
3. Collateralize such overdrafts with book-entry securities the institution could warrant that it could pledge.

It is difficult to follow the logic of either the Federal Reserve's current procedures or its most recent proposal. Why should there be limits on certain types of transactions that generate overdrafts but not on others? Or why should collaterization be permitted for certain types of overdrafts but not for others? Conceptually, the risk in a daylight overdraft depends on the credit quality of the party generating the overdraft, not on the instrument or product the payment is used for.

Other Alternatives for Reducing Overdraft Exposures

A number of other plans have been proposed as methods to reduce or price daylight overdrafts. Some of these plans have been rejected by the Federal Reserve, and others are still under study. One type of plan opts to reduce the time frame over which daylight overdrafts are outstanding. (Although many of these proposals were developed to apply to Fedwire, they could, in principle, be adopted to CHIPS.) Two proposals of this nature are rolling settlement (which was rejected by the Federal Reserve in 1984) and the Fed Funds settlement window (which is still under consideration). The rolling settlement proposal suggests replacing a single settlement at the close of the day with multiple settlement times during the day. With multiple settlements, the dollar value of daylight overdrafts would be reduced because banks would be forced to reduce their accumulated overdraft positions to zero several times each day. The problem with rolling settlement is that it would require firms to come up with the funds to settle during the day, which would necessitate large changes in the Fed Funds market and other money markets.

The Fed Funds settlement window proposal attempts to reduce the volume of daylight overdrafts that result from one type of transaction, the purchase and sale of overnight Fed Funds. Currently, large money-center banks that are net purchasers of Fed Funds usually return previously purchased funds in the morning and receive new, overnight money in the afternoon. During this period, depending on other payment activity, daylight overdrafts may develop. This proposal would reduce the time period between return and repurchase of Fed Funds through mutual agreement. For example, rather than Fed Funds being returned at 9:00 a.m. and new funds being received at 3:00 p.m., both sides of the transaction—the return of funds purchased the previous day and this day's purchase—would be required (with some exceptions) to occur within a shorter time interval (such as 11:00 a.m. to noon).

While this proposal is feasible, it is not clear that it would reduce daylight overdrafts by very much. The average exposure would be cut, but the peak exposure would not be greatly affected. If the peak currently occurred within the time period of the window, it probably would remain unchanged. More important, it is not clear why a bank cannot arrange time periods for return and purchase itself; why should a window have to be established by regulatory fiat?

The most innovative new approach to managing the risks inherent in daylight overdrafts is the latest CHIPS proposal for a CHIPS sender net debit cap. Under this proposal, an institution's cap would depend on the sum of the bilateral credit limits extended to it by other participants. Bilateral credits would be tied directly to caps. As bilaterals were raised or lowered to reflect changes in credit quality and risk, an institution's cap would change as well. Thus, the cap would be set by the same market judgments that are used to set the bilateral credit limits instead of being imposed as some fixed percentage of capital. If the quality of an institution deteriorated markedly, the bilateral credit limits that other banks extended to it would be lowered, and thus, its overall ability to run daylight overdrafts would be reduced as well.

The proposals with the widest-ranging implications are those that would make payments on CHIPS final rather than provisional, as they are today. Most proposals of this nature would require that the depository institution receiving payments guarantee these payments to its customers. Currently, such payments are provisional and, as mentioned previously, the bank has recourse to its customers in the case of an unwind if these payments are deleted. Advocates of such "receiver guarantees" argue that if banks did not have recourse to their customers, banks would have to bear the whole risk of settlement failure. In this case, banks would adopt much more stringent credit limits, and the dollar volume of daylight overdrafts would fall as a result.

Whether a system of receiver guarantees is a good idea depends on whether it is the lowest-cost method for controlling daylight overdraft exposures and reducing systemic risk. A preliminary analysis suggests that the costs of this system are sufficiently high that this is not likely to be the case. There are two significant costs that would be generated by a system of receiver guarantees. First, receiver guarantees would concentrate risk. Thus, *ceteris paribus*, these guarantees would increase systemic risk. There would be a greater likelihood that a settlement failure by a single bank would cause the settlement failure of another bank for a given volume of daylight overdrafts. Put another way, daylight overdrafts would have to be reduced by a greater amount with receiver guarantees in place to achieve the same reduction in systemic risk. This indicates that receiver guarantees are an inefficient method of reducing systemic risk. Second, a system of receiver guarantees would result in a significant change in the legal relationships among the sending bank, the receiving bank, and its customers. Currently, a bank that receives a payment over CHIPS acts as an agent for its customer. Under receiver guarantees, it would be forced to assume the risk as if it were a principal to the transaction.

Such a change in legal relationships would generate significant costs if a settlement failure were ever to occur. Under receiver guarantees, it is not even clear what the rights and obligations of the parties to the transaction would be. As Morgan Guaranty Trust Company noted in its comment letter to the Federal Reserve:

> Finally, such a change would result in a dramatic shift in the legal relationships between CHIPS participants and such participants and their customers, and it is questionable whether such a shift can be accomplished without a change in applicable law.[11]

First National Bank of Maryland raised similar concerns to the Board about the feasibility of receiver guarantees:

> Since there is very little case history and virtually no law governing such issues, some bankers have privately indicated that if faced with a large loss due to a settlement failure they might disregard any existing receiver guarantees, charge the beneficiary and let the issue be resolved in court.[12]

Receiver guarantees are a type of insurance. So far banks have not experienced a demand for this insurance from their customers, and thus, it is unclear why such insurance should be mandated by regulation.

A system of receiver guarantees would probably cause a reduction of daylight overdraft volume. But, at the same time, it would impose an additional cost on banks. Banks, in turn, would pass these costs on to their customers, and the customers would be forced to pay for a product for which they evidently have no desire. One reason that receiver guarantees are not currently offered may be that as the size of the exposure grows, both banks and bank customers are increasingly risk-averse to exposure to loss. Thus, the current system of sharing the risk may be appropriate. In fact, if banks were forced to bear the entire risk, market failure might occur: The risks might be so great for very large transfers that the receiving bank would be unwilling to bear the risk at any price.

Conclusion

The Federal Reserve, banks, and the private wire transfer networks have made great strides in coming to grips with the daylight overdraft problem in the past two years. The underlying problem has been less the risk itself of settlement failure than the effect on bank behavior of the knowledge that the Federal Reserve would prevent a settlement failure. Banks have not had to worry very much about their credit exposures resulting from other banks' daylight overdrafts because the Federal Reserve has been present to reduce (if not eliminate) the risk of settlement failure. This has had the consequence, in turn, of allowing banks of poorer credit quality or without good operational controls in place to run larger overdrafts than otherwise would have been the case. As a result, these institutions did not have the proper incentives to remedy their problems. Today, banks have a much greater awareness of the implicit credit decision made when a bank allows another bank to be in a net debit position. Banks restrict their exposures and, thus, place pressure on poorer-quality institutions to improve their performance.

The next step of the process of managing the risks associated with daylight overdrafts should be to substitute some sort of pricing mechanism for the strict quantity levels that have been adopted to date. Collateralization or an overdraft line of credit supplied by the Federal Reserve are two possible methods.

Drastic measures such as receiver guarantees or racheting down the quantity limits to zero are inappropriate because the costs of such actions would far outweigh the benefits. Overdrafts, just like other extensions of credit, are beneficial in many ways. They allow the payments mechanism to function efficiently.

Notes

1. Federal Reserve Board of Governors, staff memo, 1985, 16.
2. For Fedwire, reserve balances at the Federal Reserve serve as working balances; thus, in theory at least, daylight overdrafts are not inevitable on Fedwire.
3. Nonsettling banks receive and send payments during the day just as settling banks do. The major difference is that for nonsettling banks, final settlement must be executed through one of the settling banks.
4. The paying bank that cannot settle is still liable for payments that have been deleted.
5. Federal Reserve staff memo, 15.
6. Although the Federal Reserve cannot lend directly to Edge Act and Agreement Corporations of domestic or foreign banks under the terms of the Monetary Control Act because these types of entities are not considered to be depository institutions, it is unlikely that this lack of authority would present a meaningful obstacle in preventing settlement failure. As noted on page 78 of the 1985 Board of Governors staff memo: "Staff believes that a parent bank likely would cover the overdrafts of its Edge Act or Agreement Corporation subsidiary because failure of a bank subsidiary would seriously injure the bank itself." The Federal Reserve could assist by opening the discount window to the parent company, which would then loan the funds to the

troubled Edge Act or Agreement Corporation. In the long run, this potential problem will probably be dealt with by having the parent company act as the agent for the Edge Act or Agreement Corporation on CHIPS.

7. Ideally, the Federal Reserve could announce that it would allow a settlement failure, get banks to take the risks seriously, and then prevent a settlement failure from actually occurring. Of course, such a plan could probably work only once, at best, and it would not work at all if the banks did not believe the Federal Reserve's announcement.

8. Federal Reserve staff memo, 19.

9. The size of each cap would be a multiple of capital determined by an institution's evaluation of its creditworthiness, operational policies and procedures, and credit policies and procedures.

10. This would not generally be true for cross-system debit caps because these caps will be monitored on an ex post basis.

11. Morgan Guaranty Trust Company comment letter to the Federal Reserve Board of Governors staff, 1985, B24–B25.

12. First National Bank of Maryland comment letter to the Federal Reserve Board of Governors staff, 1985, B25.

References

Association of Reserve City Bankers, *Risks in Electronic Payments Systems*, Washington, D.C. (October 1983).

——— . *The Final Report of the Risk Control Task Force*, Payments System Committee, Washington, D.C. (October 1984).

Board of Governors of the Federal Reserve System, Press Release (17 May 1985).

——— . Staff, "Reducing Risk on Large Dollar Transfer Systems," Washington, D.C. (May 1985).

Humphrey, David B., *The U.S. Payments System: Costs, Pricing, Competition and Risk*, Salomon Brothers Center for the Study of Financial Institutions, New York University, Monograph Series in Finance and Economics, vols. 1 and 2, chap. 8 (1984).

McDonough, William, "Daylight Overdrafts: One Perspective," *Bankers Magazine* (September/October 1984):74–78.

Smoot, Richard L., "Billion-Dollar Overdrafts: A Payment Risk Challenge," Federal Reserve Bank of Philadelphia *Business Review* (January/February 1985):3–13.

Stevens, Edward J., "Risk in Large-Dollar Transfer Systems," Federal Reserve Bank of Cleveland *Economic Review* (Fall 1984):2–16.

10
Technology and Bank Monitoring

Gregory F. Udell

T he impact of technology on the banking industry has been profound. To most observers, it has been a positive force in providing financial institutions with the ability to offer a more responsive and cost-effective product. The impact of technology on monitoring bank risk may not be so positive, however. Technology has provided immediate and inexpensive access to new domestic and global markets. For some institutions, lower transactions costs provide the impetus to improve diversification, which may in turn improve the safety and soundness of the banking system. On the other hand, low-cost access to speculative markets may provide the incentive for a risk-taking management quickly to change the risk characteristics of the institution without detection by bank regulators. Technology may provide its own solution, however, if it offers regulators a cost-effective mechanism with which to monitor bank activity continuously. This chapter will examine the role of technology in designing an optimal monitoring policy. The term *bank* will be used in a generic sense to refer to both banks and savings and loan associations, unless otherwise specified.

It will be useful to develop a working definition of technology at the outset of our discussion. Ours is a broad definition that encompasses physical technology, financial technology, and financial innovation. Physical technology has provided financial institutions with extensive information and delivery systems that have dramatically changed the industry's profile at both the retail and wholesale levels. Banks have improved their ability to price component services at marginal cost. In addition, banks have the ability to search across international markets and quickly redeploy financial resources. Financial technology has provided banks with powerful new decision-making tools. For example, sophisticated GAP and Duration-GAP models have significantly improved bank management of interest rate risk; discriminant analysis techniques have been applied in credit evaluation; and valuation models have been used in pricing traded securities. Many of these same tools are equally adaptable to the task of monitoring bank risk.

Financial innovation implies the development of new financial products in response to emerging market need. This process can be viewed as somewhat independent of the method and science necessary to create those products. In practice, however, financial innovation is not so easily separable from technology. No doubt the introduction of new products such as negotiable CDs, money market deposit accounts, and brokered CDs are much more the artifact of a changing regulatory environment than any improvement in technology. Nevertheless, the pricing and delivery of these products are closely linked to a technological environment that has become much more competitive in the sense that consumers of these products can search across sellers at low transaction cost. Another example of financial innovation that affects monitoring problem is bank access to new and existing "speculative" markets. These markets can provide huge benefits to bank risk management. For example, interest-rate futures markets provide at low transactions costs a convenient mechanism to manage interest-rate risk. Similarly, for some time banks have actively used forward currency markets to manage exchange rate risk. However, in the absence of sufficient constraints, these markets also provide the opportunity to assume significant risk if the bank so chooses.

In order to analyze the relationship between technology and bank monitoring, it is important to understand the role of bank monitoring within the regulatory process. In the following section I discuss the purpose of bank monitoring from both a historical and theoretical point of view. I argue that the primary beneficiary of bank monitoring is the insurer (the FDIC or the FSLIC). Next, I discuss deposit insurance and suggested reforms of the present system, and I examine the impact that technology has had on the mechanics of monitoring as well as the challenges that technology has created. Because current technology does not permit cost-effective continuous monitoring, it is imperative that the deposit insurance contract be designed in such a way that perverse incentives are minimized without unduly constraining private decision making. Finally, I propose deposit insurance reform within the constraints of existing technology.

The Purpose of Bank Monitoring

Historically, the principal method of bank monitoring has been the bank examination. These examinations are conducted periodically by bank regulators and consist not only of a review of the bank's books and records but, in addition, an evaluation of the assets, liabilities, procedures, and policies. In his 1973 study of bank examinations, Benston stated "the principal reason for examining banks in the past, and indeed in the present, is the prevention of bank failure as a result of poor management and/or dishonesty."[1] The history of such examinations in the United States can be traced to the New

York Safety Fund in 1829.[2] With the creation of the National Banking System in 1863, the use of examinations became more widespread, since the Comptroller of the Currency was required to examine national banks chartered by that office. By 1931 every state had created an official supervisory authority with responsibility for examining state-chartered banks. Today, bank examinations are conducted by the FDIC, the Comptroller of the Currency, and the Federal Reserve Board, as well as by state authorities.

For whose benefit is bank monitoring (specifically bank examinations) conducted? Benston lists six reasons that may have originally shaped our examination philosophy but are *no longer* valid considerations: (1) maintenance of currency, (2) protection of small depositors, (3) bank examination and monetary policy, (4) bank failure and community disruption, (5) bank failures and the economy in general, and (6) bank runs. He argues that bank examinations play no role in any of these functions.

There has been little disagreement with Benston with respect to the first four reasons. Maintenance of currency is the sole responsibility of the Treasury and the Federal Reserve and has nothing to do with bank examination. FDIC deposit insurance eliminated (2) as a problem. There is little evidence to support the contention that bank examinations play any role in monetary policy. The FDIC's management of bank failures has minimized problems created by (4). In the vast majority of cases, the FDIC has arranged the merger of insolvent banks with solvent banks under what is called a "purchase and assumption," rather than under a "payout" plan in which the bank is liquidated (and all uninsured depositors share with FDIC in losses not covered by the proceeds from liquidation of the bank). Under a purchase and assumption, depositors in effect have their accounts transferred to the assuming bank without loss. The FDIC compensates the assuming bank with value equivalent to the deposits less a premium paid by the assuming bank. The net effect has been to provide virtually 100 percent insurance coverage. Recently the FDIC has modified its procedures in some cases by arranging mergers that do not indemnify all uninsured depositors. However, the feasibility of continuing a policy of selective incomplete insurance in light of recent events (that is, Continental Bank, Financial Corporation of America [FCA], and the Ohio and Maryland crises) is quite problematic.

With respect to (5), it has been argued that bank failures in the early 1930s caused a reduction of the money supply and availability of credit, which in turn exacerbated the severity of the depression. The evidence, however, seems to support a counterargument that emphasizes the culpability of the Federal Reserve's discount window policy—specifically the fact that the Fed allowed a precipitous reduction in the money supply.[3]

With respect to (6), prior to 1934 bank panics were a major problem in the United States and were particularly acute in the banking crisis of 1893 and in the early 1930s.[4] The creation of FDIC (and FSLIC) deposit insurance (along with the management of bank failures according to the policies described previously) and the Federal Reserve discount window policy have eliminated bank panics, although not individual bank runs. Horvitz, for example, has argued that bank examinations do not play a role in reassuring the public as to the safety of deposits. Instead, "deposit insurance (now) plays that role."[5] It should be noted that we have, indeed, witnessed in the last dozen years some rather sizable individual bank runs (for example, Franklin National Bank, $1.7 billion; First Pennsylvania, $925 million; Continental Illinois, $15 billion; and FCA, $7 billion). These individual bank runs have not, however, precipitated bank panics in the form of concomitant runs on solvent banks.

Aharony and Swary empirically examined the sufficiency of the regulatory safety net by using capital market data to test for evidence of a "contagion effect" caused by large bank failure. A contagion effect occurs if the failure of a single bank causes a loss of public confidence in the banking system as a whole. Aharony and Swary indirectly measured this effect by examining bank stock returns during three large bank failures (Franklin National Bank, United States National Bank of San Diego, and Hamilton National Bank). They were unable to confirm the existence of such an effect with respect to the three largest bank failures prior to the 1980s; but Swary conducted a similar study with respect to Continental Illinois and found positive evidence of a contagion effect.

The issue of whether a contagion effect still exists may have important implications in designing the optimal bank monitoring policy. If the current safety net provided by deposit insurance and the discount window policy has completely eliminated the possibility of a bank panic, then the role of bank monitoring is limited to protecting the insurer. If, on the other hand, the nature of the monitoring policy (or failure to execute properly that policy) in and of itself can influence the presence of stability in the system, then that policy should be considered part of the safety net. Goodman and Shaffer, for instance, make a similar argument by emphasizing the importance of bank examinations in addition to the other two mechanisms (that is, the discount window and deposit insurance) in "safeguarding the banking industry from destabilizing influences." This latter view implies a dual purpose for bank monitoring: protection of the insurer *and* stability of the banking industry. Ascribing this dual role would support a higher marginal social benefit from expenditures on monitoring activity than the single-purpose view (which is that the purpose of bank examinations is limited to protecting the insurer). Much can be learned from the events of 1984 in resolving this issue. Swary suggests that the presence of a contagion effect could partially have resulted from uncertainty regarding regulator behavior in handling the Continental crisis because of its unprecedented dimension. To the extent that that uncertainty is now resolved, the presence of a contagion effect may not materialize in the future. This in turn leaves protection of the insurer as the primary benefit of bank monitoring. A good test of this hypothesis would be to replicate the Swary test with respect to the bank run on FCA (an S&L roughly comparable in size to Continental), which occurred just after the Continental crisis.

It is possible that there exist other beneficiaries of bank monitoring. Benston points out that stockholders, employees, and private insurance companies "have the same desire to avoid insolvency and defalcation in banks that they have for any other enterprise in which they have similar interests." A great deal of information about management performance, for instance, may be generated from the bank examination process. That process typically concludes with a meeting with members of the board and bank senior management in which this information is conveyed. In an agency theoretic sense (à la Jensen and Meckling) this information may promote the design of improved managerial contracts that minimize related agency costs. Moreover, to the extent that the regulator is not compensated for the production of this information, it represents a free good to the beneficiaries.

Deposit Insurance

All things considered, it seems prudent to adopt the view that the primary beneficiary of bank monitoring is the insuring agency. Therefore, the optimal monitoring policy will be one that is directed toward protecting the insurance fund. However, the design of such a policy must be viewed within the context of the deposit insurance contract as a whole. In other words, a discussion of the optimal monitoring policy is inseparable from the whole issue of deposit insurance reform.

As part of the Garn-St Germain Act of 1982, Congress required the Federal Home Loan Bank Board (FHLBB, the parent organization of the FSLIC) and the FDIC to conduct studies on the present insurance system and to recommend changes for the future.[6] Campbell and Horvitz in their appraisal of those studies point out that underlying each is the premise that the Depository Institutions Act of 1980 and the Garn-St Germain Act of 1982 have seriously impaired the ability of regulators to control risk taking. Three areas of reform were considered by the studies: risk-adjusted premiums, increased reliance on uninsured creditors, and private deposit insurance. Both the FHLBB study and the FDIC study argue that insurance reform should include the first two. The FHLBB argued that increased private participation in deposit insurance is both possible and desirable (although the FHLBB did not provide a specific format for coinsurance). The FDIC study was neutral on the subject of private insurance.

Events that have taken place since these reports were submitted to Congress on April 15, 1983, have raised serious questions about increased reliance on uninsured creditors and implementation of private insurance. In the Continental Illinois case, the FDIC was forced to cover all depositor exposure. Nearly the same assurance was provided by the FHLBB with respect to FCA. These actions, in combination with subsequent policy pronouncements, have explicitly promised complete coverage for the country's largest institutions.[7] In light of these actions and the crises in Ohio and Maryland, it may be difficult for the depository agencies to pursue a new bank failure policy in which uninsured depositors are exposed. In other words, there is considerable doubt about whether anything other than complete insurance (that is, 100 percent explicity or de facto coverage) is feasible.

With respect to private insurance, the Ohio and Maryland crises raise serious questions about the ability of nonfederal insurance funds to tolerate significant unsystematic risk. It appears that, among other problems, the Ohio and Maryland funds were just not big enough to diversify away the unsystematic risk associated with the failure of one of their insured institutions. Moreover, the ability to cover large unsystematic risk would seem to confirm the widely held view that private insurance has no role to play in managing *systematic* risk. (If a private fund cannot tolerate the effects of a securities fraud on one institution, for instance, it surely cannot handle the effects of systemwide shocks such as LDC debt, plummeting oil prices, or rapidly increasing interest rates.)

The probable net effect of this situation is to leave risk-related premiums as the only reform still on the table. The case in favor of risk-related premiums stems from allocative inefficiencies that are imbedded in the current system in which all institutions are charged exactly the same premium per dollar of deposits. As Pyle points out, "Insurer insolvency per se is not the major reason for concern about the deposit insurance system." Even with a single flat fee the fund can be protected if *on average* all institutions pay premiums consistent with fund solvency. In fact, a number of studies have concluded that deposit insurance premiums are excessive. For example, Scott and Mayer reached that conclusion using historical failure rates. In a much more recent paper, Marcus and Shaked, using a contingent claims approach, also concluded that deposit insurance was overpriced. Specifically, Marcus and Shaked adopted the approach offered by Merton (who suggested the analogy between deposit insurance and a put option) in order to value deposit insurance offered in 1979 and 1980. It remains to be seen whether a similar conclusion about FDIC insurance can be reached with respect to pricing in subsequent years. Moreover, there can be little doubt based on current market value that the FSLIC reserve is underfunded—and this underfunding was a consequence of the enormous systematic risk to which the savings and loan industry was exposed and which was not embedded in past FSLIC premiums.

The issue of overpricing notwithstanding, the case for risk-related premiums is primarily based on the perverse incentives inherent in the current contract. Specifically, flat rate premiums fail to take into account differences in risk across institutions. The failure to price insurance based on individual risk provides an incentive for the insured to risk-shift on the insurer (the "moral hazard problem"). This incentive for excessive risk taking stems from the asymmetry of payoffs related to asset value fluctuations: the insurance fund (the de facto creditor, given 100 percent coverage) absorbs most of the losses and participates in none of the gains from riskier investments, given a fixed rate contract.[8]

The moral hazard problem has received considerable attention in the recent banking literature. The argument that risk-related premiums provide the solution is a powerful one. To the extent that the insurance premium accurately reflects the ex ante riskiness of an institution, deposit insurance can be priced as a fair game. This in turn will minimize distortion in private decision making. Nevertheless, risk-related premiums have not been uniformly embraced as a solution. For example, i Costa and Greenbaum argue that the stringent informational requirements of a risk-sensitive pricing scheme more than offset its advantages. Along similar lines, Flannery and Protopapadakis emphasize that advocates of risk-related premiums fail to recognize that both risk-related premiums and restrictive regulations require the *same* amount of information. Moreover, in their view there is little reason to suggest that "information available to bank insurers can be utilized more effectively with a risk-sensitive premium than with the current arrangement (or vice versa)."[9]

Pyle makes a persuasive case that focusing on just the riskiness of a bank in valuing deposit insurance may be misdirected. He develops a richer version of the Merton options model to examine the sensitivity of the insurer's liability to both asset risk and the insolvency ratio (that is, the closure rule) used by the regulator. Pyle defines the insolvency ratio "as the ratio of the market value of assets to the face value of deposits below which a bank will be declared insolvent."[10] He demonstrates that the insurer's liability is significantly more sensitive to the insolvency ratio than to the riskiness of the bank's assets. This result is not so surprising from a theoretical point of view when one notes that the insolvency ratio is equivalent to the exercise price of the option. The policy implications of this conclusion, however, are impressive. The current practice of closing a bank only when the market value of its assets is less than or equal to the par value of its deposits (given 100 percent de facto insurance) results in closing banks who *on average* have a negative market value. An extreme interpretation of this relationship suggests imposing a policy that includes the closure of some solvent institutions in order to minimize the average loss to the insurer. It should be noted that the Pyle model does not take into account the cost of bank closure. It is, therefore, not clear whether the inclusion of closure costs would change the overall results.[11] It should also be noted that the imposition of a tighter closure role does not eliminate the risk-shifting incentive (unless an extreme closure rule is imposed that closes firms on average with zero market value); rather, it reduces the profits from risk shifting. Moreover, the closure rule by itself does not address the dynamics of the risk-shifting incentive. As a bank's market value deteriorates, the incentive to risk-shift accelerates because at some point only the riskiest of strategies provides any possibility of restoring a positive market value.

Horvitz and Bennett suggest that by adopting a stronger closure policy, bank regulators can entirely eliminate the subsidy to risk taking. Both emphasize the distinction between bank failure and the risk of loss to the insurer by noting that all insurer losses can be avoided if banks are closed when their net worth just becomes negative. Horvitz, in fact, states that the "true role of bank examination is the prompt detection of insolvency, not its prevention." Implicit in their recommendations is the assumption that the insurer can monitor continuously the condition of the bank. We address that subject next.

The Effects of Technology on Monitoring

The relationship between technology and bank monitoring can be reduced to two issues. First, does technology provide the prospect of cost-effective continuous monitoring? If it does, then (following the Horvitz argument) the problem of risk shifting disappears, the FDIC contract ceases to be an insurance contract, and the FDIC closes financial institutions before their market value becomes negative. If, however, continuous monitoring is not feasible, then the challenge is to design an improved deposit insurance contract that minimizes the ill effects of risk shifting.

The Prospects for Continuous Monitoring

The feasibility of continuous monitoring depends on two conditions: first, the regulator must have the ability to monitor fluctuations in asset value continuously; and second, fluctuations in bank asset value must be continuous. These conditions are much more likely to be met with respect to that portion of the bank portfolio composed of publicly traded securities than that portion that is not publicly traded (that portion that represents private securities).

The technology necessary to monitor continuously the value of the securities portfolio of a financial institution is available today. Banks are no doubt adopting this technology for the securities held in their trading account. These securities are in fact marked-to-market for accounting purposes. However, those securities that are held in the investment portfolio are not marked-to-market. Nevertheless, from a technological point of view it would clearly be feasible to monitor the value of all publicly traded securities (both in the trading account and in the investment account). This suggests the possibility of developing a system that interfaces with that of the regulator. Such a system would, therefore, simultaneously report the market value of the bank's entire securities position to its own management and to the regulator. This type of system is clearly feasible, although much of the technology is not now in place. Moreover, it remains to be seen whether the costs of such a system are justified by the benefits. In great part the value of those benefits depend on the extent of the risk-shifting problem, a subject to which we will return in the next section.

The second issue of whether changes in the value of the securities portfolio follows a continuous process is somewhat problematic. Clearly, large discontinuous changes in interest rates have violated this assumption. Nevertheless, the exposure of the insurance fund to such changes, with respect to the securities portfolio, is probably manageable (for example, via the closure rule or via premium adjustment).

The feasibility of continuous monitoring of the nontraded assets of a portfolio is quite a different matter. Private loans represent a major part of the asset portfolio of a commercial bank, and credit risk represents a major portion of a bank's total risk. Both conditions necessary for continuous monitoring are clearly violated. Credit evaluation, particularly with respect to commercial loans, is an expensive and labor-intensive endeavor. Moreover, credit information is not revealed continuously, particularly for those borrowers whose liabilities are not traded in the capital markets. Nevertheless, two phenomena working in opposite directions are worth mentioning. First, the rapid securitization of the residential mortgage market has significantly increased the portion of the portfolio that is traded in the capital markets. This securitization is likely to extend into other portions of the portfolio as well. Second, some banks are actively engaging in "loan selling," which in many respects creates a traded security out of a commercial loan.[12] This activity, however, is generally limited to the securities of large borrowers with strong credit ratings.

Technology and Risk Shifting

A number of researchers have expressed concern that the creation of new markets has increased the ability of banks to assume great risk quickly. The regulatory response has often been to constrain bank exposure in order to minimize excessive risk taking. Such constraints, however, run the risk of limiting the very great benefits that these markets can provide in terms of risk management. Nevertheless, market technology can clearly be a double-edged sword, as in the case of brokered CDs. On the one hand, brokered CDs provide small banks with access to national markets, which were once the sole domain of large banks. Moreover, investors can now shop in a much deeper national market. On the other hand, for a small risk-neutral (or risk-taking) bank that wants to take advantage of deposit insurance pricing by assuming excessive risk, the brokered CD market provides an excellent opportunity to leverage that strategy without waiting for an increased local deposit base.

Technology in the broadest sense seems to have significantly increased the ability of bank regulators to measure bank risk. The same techniques that have been developed to assist bank asset and liability managers are available to regulators to monitor interest rate sensitivity.[13] In addition, regulators now have at their disposal a growing resource of academic literature on pricing insurer exposure. This work adapts financial modeling based on options pricing to the task of setting deposit insurance premiums.[14] Some of this research suggests using standard contingent claims valuation techniques and stock return data to measure bank risk.[15] Other researchers, however, point out that there are limitations to this technique, not the least of which is the assumption of constant volatility of bank asset returns.[16]

Financial technology has also been adapted to measure commercial loan risk. Techniques such as the Z-score and Zeta™ analysis have been developed that provide an objective standard based on statistical multivariate techniques.[17] These techniques are particularly useful and cost-effective when used in a loan review program. This fact also makes them adaptable to bank monitoring.

Technology and Risk-Related Premiums

The techniques we have described, in combination with more conventional regulatory analysis such as the CAMEL system, would certainly provide sufficient information to develop some sort of risk premium schedule. The real issue is how closely premiums can be tied to risk. On this point there does not seem to be general agreement. The FHLBB report seems much more enthusiastic about the adoption of risk-related premiums than does the FDIC report. To some extent, this can probably be explained by the fact that savings and loan exposure has historically been primarily interest-rate risk. Indeed, the FHLBB emphasizes the applicability of duration-based techniques in measuring interest-rate exposure.

The FDIC position, on the other hand, emphasizes the comparative difficulty in measuring credit risk as opposed to interest-rate risk. But the FDIC's report included several additional reservations about risk-related premiums. The FDIC report noted that not all banks are examined with the same frequency or at the same time. Moreover, the FDIC noted along with many others that for the most part, the premiums paid under a risk-related system would not be that different across risk types. These and other factors led the FDIC to conclude that a pricing system "with premiums closely tied to risk is simply not feasible."[18] Consequently, the FDIC report recommended only a limited use of a system of risk-related premiums.

All factors considered, the feasibility of a risk-related premium probably lies somewhere between the FHLBB position and the FDIC position. Nevertheless, such a system must adequately address the problems suggested in the FDIC report. One of the most difficult of those is the problem of lags in setting rates. The FDIC report recommends the use of call report information in that respect instead of the CAMEL system. However, it is not at all clear that the call report is sufficiently robust to reflect the menu of financial instruments and markets with which a bank can virtually instantaneously assume risk (including a variety of off-balance sheet instruments). It is clearly not up to the task of measuring credit risk. Moreover, a system that relies on measuring ex ante risk only one day per month gives a risk-taking bank the remaining twenty-nine days to choose its own risk-return strategy.

A Proposal for Deposit Insurance Reform

In the absence of cost-effective, continuous bank monitoring, the challenge in deposit insurance reform is to design a new contract that minimizes excessive risk taking in a cost-effective way. This section outlines a proposal for a new deposit insurance contract within the constraints of the monitoring technology currently in use. The proposal entails offering a deposit insurance contract that encourages financial institutions to reveal their risk characteristics truthfully by choosing their own risk-related premium from a schedule offered by the insurer. The schedule offered could be along the lines of the risk premium categories proposed by the FHLBB or the FDIC. However, in order to provide the incentive for the insured to choose the correct premium, this proposal relies heavily on a fundamental reform in the way bank examinations are conducted.

Before discussing the proposal itself, some comments about the nature of the problem this proposal attempts to address are in order. While there has been extensive discussion about the presence of the moral hazard (risk-shifting) problem under the current deposit contract, there has been virtually no serious research concerning its magnitude. As a result, some serious questions remain unanswered. One question seems most vexing: If the perverse incentives inherent in a flat rate insurance premium system encourage risk shifting, then why do we not observe risk-shifting by all banks?[19] In the absence of an efficient monitor, the agency theoretic paradigm of Jensen and Meckling tells us that all firms will in fact risk-shift and, therefore, rational creditors will price their debt contracts accordingly. The purpose of this chapter is not quite so ambitious as to offer an equilibrium solution in which only some firms risk-shift; this task is made doubly difficult by the lack of a well-defined theory of the banking firm. Instead, I offer some observations.

Banks have had access for some time to highly speculative markets. However, it does not appear that banks in general are assuming excessive risk in these markets. For instance, Grammatikos, Saunders, and Swary analyzed the returns and risks of U.S. bank foreign currency activities and concluded that "despite . . . relatively poor performance [of foreign currency activities], the risk of ruin or failure for a 'representative bank' was found to be approximately zero when judged in comparison to the capital funds available to large money-center banks to cushion such losses." Nevertheless, it does appear that some bank failures are the result of deliberate ex ante excessive risk taking (while other bank failures appear instead to be much more the result of ex post bad luck or mismanagement). Moreover, there appears to be a pattern (albeit imperfect) to those banks that fall into this category: they tend to be owner-managed (at least to the extent that one individual controls the destiny of the institution and has a significant ownership interest); and, the owner/manager does not appear to be particularly risk averse.

A disturbing feature of this profile is that it is not limited to small institutions. Three cases illustrate this point. The United American Bank of Knoxville, Tennessee, which failed in 1983, was controlled by Jake Butcher. There is little doubt that the primary reason this bank failed was that much of its $800 million loan portfolio was invested in the Knoxville World's Fair, and ex post the fair failed. Nevertheless, there is also little doubt that the lack of loan portfolio diversification evidenced significant ex ante risk. Moreover, the evidence of massive insider lending abuse suggests that, ex ante, Jake Butcher probably had a high expected rate of return on his investment.

Empire Savings and Loan of Mesquite, Texas, was run by Spencer H. Blain, Jr., who owned 60 percent of its stock. This case is of interest not only because of its high risk loan portfolio (concentrated in condominium loans whose appraised values were artificially inflated using land "flips"), but because it also dramatically demonstrated how market technology can influence the course of financial events. In the twelve months prior to its failure, it grew from $30 million in assets to $320 million through the use of brokered CDs.

Because of its size, the most disturbing example is Financial Corporation of America. Through merger and acquisition, as well as through tapping capital markets, Charles Knapp took a $900 million institution as of 1978 and transformed it into the largest thrift in the country, with assets of $32.7 billion in 1984. Unlike most S&Ls, however, the emerging financial giant did not bring to the early 1980s a legacy of mismatched assets and liabilities. Instead, Knapp invested heavily in fixed rate assets financed by short-term liabilities and embarked on this strategy *after* 1980. When interest rates failed to fall in 1983 and 1984, the institution's solvency became a serious issue and eventually led to a $7 billion run in the third quarter of 1984. The 1983 10K report showed that 73 percent of its assets were invested in long term (more than five years) fixed rate securities and 91 percent of its liabilities had a maturity of less than one year. The evidence is quite clear that on an ex ante basis, FCA was assuming a huge interest-rate risk.

Although these three cases appear to fit a common profile, it is difficult to extract from them a well-defined theory. What is clear, however, is that the managers in each case pursued high-risk strategies ex ante. Moreover, the convexity of the shareholder profit function offered them the opportunity to enjoy all of the gains from excessive risk taking (had their investments succeeded) while forcing most of the losses on the insurer. However, it is not at all clear that such behavior is endemic. Quite the contrary, the FDIC's conclusion (shared by many) that the difference in risk premiums across banks would be very small suggests just the opposite. Consequently, it seems prudent that deposit insurance reform recognize the distinct possibility that abuse is quite selective.

The proposal outlined here relies in part on a combination of a risk-related premium system and a restructuring of the bank examination procedure. Current risk-related premium proposals[20] require the insurer to set the institution's rates based on information obtained by the insurer; these rates will then be adjusted as the insurer acquires new information. The proposal offered here, however, requires the bank to set the insurance rate based on all of the information the bank has at its own disposal. The bank would be given a risk premium schedule based on risk categories (which could be consistent with either the FHLBB or FDIC proposals). The bank would then report its own risk category by choosing the appropriate risk premium consistent with its own risk characteristics. In comparison with current proposals, this arrangement would have the distinct advantage of avoiding lags in setting rate premiums. If the bank wished to change its risk category, it would merely announce the change to the insurer and immediately begin paying a new rate. Of course, an incentive mechanism to encourage the bank to reveal its ex ante riskiness truthfully would be critical.

An incentive mechanism that would produce the desired result (that is, one that would encourage banks to choose their risk premium correctly) would either have to force bank shareholders to share in the FDIC's losses from risk shifting or would have to impose sufficient penalties on the *upside* such that the benefits from risk shifting would be eliminated. Either solution would destroy the convexity of the shareholder profit function and thus would destroy the incentive to risk-shift. I assume that the former alternative is not possible; in other words, it is not possible to create a contract in which bank stockholders can be made to share in the losses beyond their equity interest in the bank.[21] This leaves the necessity of devising a system in which those banks that lied about their ex ante risk characteristics forfeit the profits from their risk taking when they occur. The key element in such a system is the method of bank examination.

Currently, we examine banks to determine their condition *as of the date of the examination*. Under current risk-related premium proposals, this information could be used to set the insurance premium based on the ex ante risk characteristics of the institution *on that date*. However, because bank assets and liabilities are composed solely of financial instruments, there is very little cause for the *period of evaluation* to be confined to *the date of the examination*. Suppose counterfactually, for instance, that interest rates had fallen during the last two quarters of 1983, and suppose that FCA was examined on December 31, 1983. Suppose further that the examination of the bank's condition as of that date showed a substantial profit for the six-month period ended thereon (which would have been the case for FCA if interest rates had fallen during the last half of 1983). The bank examiners would then evaluate the portfolio composition retroactively—say, back to June 30, 1983. In other words, on December 31, 1983, the examiners would analyze the risk composition of FCA up to six months earlier to see whether its current profits were the result of unreported risk taking. What they would have found (if interest rates had gone down during the last six months of 1983) is that the profits enjoyed by FCA during the last two quarters of 1983 were the result of an earlier mismatching of asset and liability maturities. As long as FCA had honestly informed the regulators about the extent of that mismatching by having chosen *during the six months ended December 31, 1983*, a rate premium consistent with the level of interest-rate risk, then the results of the examination would merely confirm the accuracy of the premium. However, if FCA on June 30, 1983, had chosen a lower rate than that to which it was entitled based on its ex ante risk exposure, then the insurer would extract a penalty. In order to insure incentive compatibility, the size of the penalty should bear some relationship to the difference between the profits that the bank realized ex post and the profits that the bank would have realized ex post had it in fact assumed the risk it claimed. For a risk-neutral bank, the penalty ought to exceed the expected profits from risk shifting.[22]

In the preceding example, risk taking was in the form of maturity mismatching. However, the concept of examining ex ante risk ex post is equally applicable to examining the loan portfolio. Specifically, the bank examiner asks to see the credit files on the bank's commercial loan customers and evaluates the riskiness of the borrowers as of an earlier date (the *evaluation date*). The examiner then compares the riskiness of the loan portfolio as of the evaluation date with the risk reported on the evaluation date (the risk reported to the regulator through the bank's selection of the risk premium). The bank examiner must be careful, however, to confine the risk evaluation of commercial loans to information available to the bank as of the date of evaluation. More than anything else, this proposal requires that one embrace the notion that risk is fundamentally an ex ante proposition. However, this proposal does have the added virtue that ex post outcomes could be used to determine the probability of examination. If a bank reports huge profits that seem inconsistent with the reported ex ante risk, this could be used to trigger an examination. Another feature of this proposal is that it treats the problem of dynamic risk shifting: the ever increasing incentive for a deteriorating bank to take on additional increments of risk with increased deterioration. This risk dynamic could also be unraveled by an ex post–ex ante evaluation.

In order for such a proposal to work, banks would have to have confidence that ex ante risk was being correctly assessed. Great caution would have to be taken to insure that high ex post return not be automatically related to high ex ante risk. This proposal is not intended to be a windfall profits tax. In fact, quite to the contrary, in a rational expectations framework we should not see any penalties assessed at all because banks would be encouraged to reveal honestly their own risk. While ex post return might be used to determine the frequency of examination and even the period of evaluation, it should play absolutely no role in the evaluation itself. This proposal would be perfectly consistent with the broad risk categories proposed by the FDIC, which would seem to have the least risk of misspecification. Moreover, the broad category approach seems most consistent with the selective abuse of the current contract and would have the least effect on the large percentage of banks that do not appear to be risk shifting.

Conclusion

This chapter examined the dual impact of technology on the problem of monitoring bank risk. On the one hand, technology has provided banks with new opportunities to increase risk, while on the other hand, it offers regulators improved techniques with which to monitor that risk. Technology, however, does not appear to offer in the near future the luxury of cost-effective continuous monitoring. Consequently, the optimal monitoring policy must be part of a deposit insurance contract that minimizes the incentive to exploit the insurer. This is critical, because the primary beneficiaries of an improved monitoring policy are the insurance funds. A proposal is offered, consistent with current technological constraints, that offers the prospect of significantly limiting the moral hazard problem without concomitantly affecting private decision making. A major part of this proposal involves redefining the monitoring procedure so that bank examinations focus (ex post) on evaluating ex ante risk.

Notes

1. Benston (1973), 11.
2. See Benston (1973) for an interesting discussion of the history of the role of bank examination in the United States.
3. See, for example, Warburton (1966).

4. See Benston (1973) and Merrick and Saunders (1985) for a more detailed description.

5. See Horvitz (1980). See also Kreps and Wacht (1971), Black, Miller, and Posner (1978), and Flannery and Protopapadakis (1984) for similar conclusions.

6. The National Credit Union Administration, the third depository insurance agency, also submitted a report.

7. The FDIC announced that its deposit insurance would explicitly cover 100 percent of all deposits in the country's eleven largest commercial banks.

8. This problem arises in any shareholder-bondholder contracting situation in which risk levels chosen by shareholders cannot be perfectly observed by the creditors (see Jensen and Meckling [1976]; Galai and Masulis [1976]).

9. Flannery and Protopapadakis (1984), 7.

10. Pyle (1984), 10.

11. The effect of closure costs would depend on its functional specification. If, for instance, closure costs are positively related to the excess of the par value of deposits over the market value of the bank's assets, then its effect might be ambiguous.

12. Bankers Trust, for example, has become well-known for its loan-selling activities.

13. It should be noted, however, that the same information-systems limitations that constrain bank managers also constrain bank regulators. Very few banks have an integrated asset and liability system in which the maturity structures of assets and of liabilities are all entered (including commercial loans). This makes it very difficult for banks to adopt a sophisticated duration-based system, for instance, should they desire to do so.

14. See Merton (1977) and McCulloch (1984), for example.

15. See Marcus and Shaked (1984) and Pennachi (1983), for example.

16. See Merrick and Saunders (1985) for a good discussion of the problems involved.

17. See Altman (1968, 1983) and Altman, Haldeman, and Narayanan (1977), respectively.

18. See FDIC (1983), II–9. Other objections raised by the FDIC to a premium structure closely tied to risk included the potential distortion of incentives if risk is incorrectly measured, the inherently subjective nature of the evaluation of credit risk, and the possibility that banks would be less forthright during the examination process if bank examiners were using the examination results to determine the premium. The last two objections led the FDIC to recommend using call report data in lieu of the CAMEL system to set the premiums.

19. In the Keeton (1984) model, all banks do, in fact, risk-shift on the FDIC. But because all banks are homogeneous (that is, all banks are risk-neutral and have the same investment opportunity set), the FDIC can price deposit insurance such that the contract correctly anticipates the level of risk shifting. In equilibrium, however, all banks choose a level of investment that is socially suboptimal by choosing a portfolio that does not maximize expected return.

20. See, for example, Kane (1983) and the FHLBB and FDIC proposals.

21. One possibility is to impose personal liability on the shareholders. Such arrangements were not uncommon in British and American banking prior to the twentieth century. A less drastic alternative is to encourage bank regulators actively to use their

right to remove management that is engaging in excessive risk taking. In a sense, this right is an ex post penalty that can be used by the regulator to encourage bank management to reveal ex ante characteristics. Bennett (1984) makes a strong case that this right should be exercised more often.

22. The penalty would also have to take into account the probability of being evaluated on any given date.

References

Aharony, Joseph, and Itzhak Swary. "Contagion Effects of Bank Failures: Evidence from Capital Markets." *Journal of Business* 56 (September 1983):305–21.

Altman, Edward I. "Commercial Bank Lending: Process, Credit Scoring and Costs of Errors in Lending." *Journal of Financial & Quantitative Analysis* (November 1980):813–32.

———. "Financial Ratios, Discriminant Analysis and the Prediction of Corporate Bankruptcy." *Journal of Finance* (September 1968):589–619.

Altman, Edward I., Robert Haldeman, and P. Narayanan. "ZETA Analysis: A New Model to Identify Bankruptcy Risk of Corporations." *Journal of Banking and Finance* (June 1977):29–54.

Bennett, Barbara A. "Bank Regulation and Deposit Insurance: Controlling the FDIC's Losses." *Economic Review*. Federal Reserve Bank of San Francisco (Spring 1984):16–30.

Benston, George J. "Bank Examination." *The Bulletin*. no. 89–90. New York University Graduate School of Business Administration Institute of Finance (May 1973).

Black, Fisher, Merton Miller, and Richard A Posner. "An Approach to the Regulation of Bank Holding Companies." *Journal of Business* 51 (July 1978):379–411.

Campbell, Tim, and Paul M. Horvitz. "Reform of the Deposit Insurance System: An Appraisal of the FHLBB and FDIC Studies Mandated by the Garn-St Germain Act of 1982." Paper presented at the Western Economic Association meeting (July 1983).

Federal Deposit Insurance Corporation. *Deposit Insurance in a Changing Environment*. FDIC:Washington, D.C. (April 1983).

Federal Home Loan Bank Board. *Agenda For Reform*. FHLBB:Washington, D.C. (March 1983).

Flannery, Mark J., and Aris A. Protopapadakis. "Risk Sensitive Deposit Insurance Premia: Some Practical Issues." *Business Review*. Federal Reserve Bank of Philadelphia (September/October 1984):3–10.

Galai, Dan, and Ronald W. Masulis. "The Option Pricing Model and the Risk Factor of Stock." *Journal of Financial Economics* (January 1976):53–81.

Goodman, Laurie S., and Sherrill Shaffer. "The Economics of Deposit Insurance: A Critical Evaluation of Proposed Reforms." *Yale Journal of Regulation* 1 (1984): 145–62.

Grammatikos, Theoharry, Anthony Saunders, and Itzhak Swary. "Returns and Risks of U.S. Foreign Currency Activities." Working Paper no. 337, Salomon Brothers Center for the Study of Financial Institutions. New York University Graduate School of Business Administration (January 1985).

Horvitz, Paul M. "The Case Against Risk-Related Deposit Insurance Premiums." *Housing Finance Review* 2 (July 1983):253–63.

——— . "A Reconsideration of the Role of Bank Examination." *Journal of Money, Credit and Banking* 12 (November 1980):654–59.

i Costa, Ricart, and Stuart I. Greenbaum. "Pricing Deposit Insurance." Banking Research Center Working Paper, Northwestern University (1983).

Jensen, Michael, and William Meckling. "Theory of the Firm: Managerial Behavior, Agency Costs and Ownership Structures." *Journal of Financial Economics* 3 (October 1976):305–60.

Kane, Edward J. "A Six-Point Program for Deposit Insurance Reform." *Housing Finance Review* 2 (July 1983):269–78.

Keeton, William R. "Deposit Insurance and the Deregulation of Deposit Rates." *Economic Review*. Federal Reserve Bank of Kansas City (April 1984):28–46.

Kreps, Clifton H., and Richard F. Wacht. "A More Conservative Role for Deposit Insurance." *Journal of Finance* 26 (May 1971):605–14.

Marcus, Alan, and Israel Shaked. "The Valuation of FDIC Deposit Insurance Using Option Pricing Estimates." *Journal of Money, Credit and Banking* 16 (November 1984):446–60.

McCulloch, J. Huston. "Interest Sensitive Deposit Insurance Premia: Stable ACH Estimates." *Journal of Banking Finance* (Forthcoming 1985).

Merrick, John J., and Anthony Saunders. "Bank Regulation and Monetary Policy." Working Paper no. 314, Salomon Brothers Center for the Study of Financial Institutions. New York University Graduate School of Business Administration (January 1985).

Merton, Robert C. "An Analytic Derivation of the Cost of Deposit Insurance and Loan Guarantees. An Application of Modern Option Pricing Theory." *Journal of Banking and Finance* 1 (June 1977):3–11.

Pennachi, George G. "Valuing Variable and Fixed Rate Deposit Insurance for Intermediaries Subject to Interest Rate Risk." Working Paper, Massachusetts Institute of Technology (December 1983).

Pyle, David H. "Deregulation and Deposit Insurance Reform." *Economic Review*. Federal Reserve Bank of San Francisco (Spring 1984):5–15.

Scott, Kenneth G., and Thomas Mayer. "Risk and Regulation in Banking. Some Proposals for Federal Deposit Insurance Reform." *Stanford Law Review* (May 1971):537–82.

Swary, Itzhak. "Continental Illinois Crisis: An Empirical Analysis of Regulatory Behavior." Working Paper, New York University Graduate School of Business Administration (Jaunary 1985).

Warburton, Clark. "Has Bank Supervision Been in Conflict with Monetary Policy?" In *Depression, Inflation and Monetary Policy*, 317–26. Reprinted from *Review of Economics and Statistics* 34 (February 1952):69–74.

Comment

Jarl G. Kallberg
Kenneth L. Parkinson

T he basic issues raised by Gregory Udell, David Humphrey, and William Dudley concern attempts to (1) reduce the risk inherent in the present financial and payments systems, (2) apportion logically (through regulation, pricing or other strategies) the remaining risk, and (3) achieve these two aims within the technological and other constraints present. While they focus on two specific aspects of this risk—deposit insurance (Udell) and daylight overdrafts (Humphrey and Dudley)—the strategies adopted by regulators, financial institutions, *and* the private sector have extremely broad implications. In a climate of regulatory uncertainty and intensifying competition from the "nonbank" sector in the financial services area, risk reduction strategies have to be carefully analyzed not only for their economic rationale and their impact on the stability of the financial sector, but also for the incentives they will create to bypass existing (more regulated) channels.

Deposit Insurance

Udell's chapter represents a modern financial theory perspective on the issue of bank monitoring, especially the question of deposit insurance. There are a number of important directions typified by this chapter; it is representative of a vital new area in banking research that is attempting to bring to bear on banking questions some of the machinery created by contemporary theorists in finance and economics. Among those areas that hold the most promise for banking research are signaling, agency, contracting, and contingent claims analysis; these are treated in Udell's work.

In addition to his perspective on the connections between the existing literature and contemporary problems, one of the most interesting contributions in this chapter is his proposal for a more flexible and voluntary form of deposit insurance. It has long been evident that the existing form of deposit insurance has created perverse incentives; but the selection of plausible alternatives that are consistent with bank monitoring technology has proven somewhat elusive.

Udell then goes on to discuss a form of retroactive monitoring by bank examiners to monitor consistency of stated and actual risk attitudes. His approach offers a pragmatic solution to the monitoring problem. Given the asymmetries of information and the costs of monitoring, this type of signaling approach has been shown to be valid in related theoretical spheres. (As we shall see in the next section, this philosophy of voluntary compliance and ex post monitoring is already being tested by the Federal Reserve in the daylight overdraft area.)

While Udell carries out the important task of establishing an economic and pragmatic basis for a superior insurance contract, a logical progression of this work would include a more formal analysis of the optimality of the type of insurance contract he proposes. There is an active economic literature that treats the design of optimal insurance contracts and incentive contracting.[1] The typical approach is to formulate the optimal contracting problem in a calculus of variations (or optimal control) framework, possibly introducing incentive-compatibility as a constraint.[2]

In these models the type of contract proposed by Udell does not arise. (In the next section another aspect of this will be examined.) There are a number of reasons for this. In the first place, as Udell observes: "It is not possible to create a contract in which bank stockholders can be made to share in the losses beyond their equity interest in the bank." Second, the microeconomic settings of these references do not have the richness required for an adequate modeling of the diverse risks faced by a deposit-taking financial institution. For example, the standard insurance contracting or principal-agent problems are based on a rather simplistic framework that would require considerable extension. However, enough similarities exist to suggest that these economic paradigms can be useful in Udell's setting as well.

While it is easy to carp about the modeling inadequacies (as for example has been done with respect to contingent claims analysis [option pricing] of the rationality of deposit insurance), the directions suggested by this strand of research offer interesting opportunities to tackle questions of great practical significance.

Daylight Overdrafts

The daylight overdraft issue has captured the imagination of a large number of participants in the financial sector. The scope of this problem and an analysis of the effectiveness of some of the proposed solutions, as described by Humphrey and Dudley, is clearly warranted. The Federal Reserve memorandum issued on May 6, 1985, gives the following statistics on the volume of daylight overdrafts:

Total daylight overdrafts average $110 to $120 billion per day. About $30 to $40 billion is the result of book-entry U.S. government and agency security transfers over Fedwire. . . . $80 to $90 billion represents cross-system funds only overdrafts. . . . Over a typical two-week period, between 4,000 and 4,500 institutions incur a daylight overdraft; on any given day, about 1,600 to 1,700 institutions are in overdraft.

The discussion in both of these papers (unfortunately) largely limits itself to overdrafts on the CHIPS network. While the conclusions of Humphrey's simulation unambiguously point out that the unwinding solution causes an enormous impact throughout the entire CHIPS system, the failure of one of the CHIPS banks is far less likely than the failure of a participant on one of the other funds transfer networks. The repercussions of this latter failure are as yet unknown. By focusing on failures on the CHIPS system, Humphrey may be overstating the impact.

The current technology seems to prohibit a number of the potential solutions to this problem as presented by Dudley. The suggestion of interest charged by the hour is intriguing but realistically probably five years from being within the technical capabilities of most financial institutions. The solutions that seem to allow market forces to play a larger role are likely to be the most successful. Examples are the CHIPS proposal tying caps to net credit limits and (to link with the previous section) insurance strategies that tie premiums to risk.

To a large extent, risk remains a function of the current regulatory structure and market practices. Many observers believe that the major portion of the volume of daylight overdrafts is related to Federal Funds, foreign exchange, and government securities transactions. This indicates that the problem arises mainly from the structure of the overnight interbank borrowing market and foreign exchange transactions, not from corporate transfers. Similarly, structural changes in the Fed Funds market, such as a separate settlement procedure or a greater movement to term Fed Funds (perhaps through something similar to a master note arrangement), could help mitigate the problems without interfering with the payments system to the degree that other procedures will. In the foreign exchange area, certain financial institutions are utilizing netting strategies to reduce the number of transfers. It is clear that the interaction of all of these strategies, both regulated and voluntary, will be required to reduce the risk effectively. Regulation, and the threat of regulation, spur the utilization of market risk reduction strategies.

The connections between Udell's discussion of the deposit insurance and the daylight overdraft issue are not as vague as they initially appear. Consider the following excerpt from the Federal Reserve Board's statement on guidelines for daylight overdrafts, issued on May 6, 1985:

Individual institutions would be asked voluntarily to establish a limit on their intra-day overdraft positions across all wire systems.
— The board of directors of each institution would establish the institution's own cap classification based on Federal Reserve guidelines.
— A specific sender net debit cap would be associated with each cap classification.
— The cap would apply, with some exceptions, to each institution, not to the consolidated entity.
— Agency examiners would review the risk classification file of each institution as part of the examination process, reporting views to the institution's board of directors.
— Monitoring would be *ex post*, except (on Fedwire) for problem institutions.

A number of parallels are quickly seen between this proposal and Udell's proposal for deposit insurance. The problems that he raises with respect to truthful signaling apply here as well. In addition, the proposed ex post monitoring will be carried out semiannually. Is this interval sufficiently short to allow effective control of deteriorating institutions?

A Corporate Perspective

Through all of the discussion on daylight overdrafts and risk in the payments system, the corporate viewpoint seems to have been given the back seat. At times it seems as if the payments system were strictly a bank matter rather than a service that the banks provide for their customers. The regulators have shown little interest in discussing the impact that risk reduction measures may have on corporations; the banks have been little better.

A number of the risk reduction strategies have the potential to disrupt greatly the existing corporate cash management function. This will occur, for example, if the Federal Reserve carries out its threats to reject transactions ("Fedwire overdrafts of institutions that Reserve banks believe will expose them to excessive risk would be subject to real-time monitoring that would permit rejection of funds transfers and would pend book-entry transfers that would cause the Reserve bank to incur unacceptable risk exposure."[3]) or to increase its monitoring of the automated clearinghouse system (". . . staff recommends that ACH transactions be included in the ex post monitoring of daylight overdrafts in such a way as to neutralize any benefit from using the ACH mechanism for circumventing the risk controls applied to wire transfer networks. . . ."[4]) so as to reduce its usage for corporate cash concentration. One effect will be that corporations will be scrutinizing banks far more carefully to see how these regulatory impediments affect the banks' ability to provide the types of services that corporations require. This will exacerbate the problems that certain banks may have because of more stringent controls placed upon them owing to their risk.

Another important and largely overlooked impact of the risk reduction measures now being contemplated is the acceleration in the development of ways to bypass existing regulated systems. From the regulator's point of view, this may not be undesirable; from the banks' perspective, it can be. To take but one example, corporations are actively developing industry-specific payments systems. While this type of intercorporate netting arrangement has existed for more than a decade in the petroleum industry (Petroclear) and the airlines, other industries—automotive, chemical, grocery, and insurance—have recently taken the initiative. These systems will reduce these industries' dependence on established banking systems and will reduce the volume of transactions that flow through these regulated channels.

Notes

1. See, for example, Mossin (1968), Raviv (1979), Brennan and Solanki (1981), John and Kalay (1985), and references therein.
2. For an excellent example of the technical development, see Gelfand and Fomin (1962).
3. Federal Reserve Board, Memorandum on Daylight Overdrafts, 6 May 1985.
4. Ibid.

References

Brennan, M., and Rav Solanki. "Optimal Portfolio Insurance." *Journal of Financial and Quantitative Analysis* 16 (September 1981).

Federal Reserve Board. Memorandum on Daylight Overdrafts. 6 May 1985.

Gelfand, I., and V. Fomin. *Calculus of Variations* (Englewood Cliffs, N.J.: Prentice-Hall, 1962).

John, Kose, and Avner Kalay, "Informational Content of Optimal Debt Contracts." In *Recent Advances in Corporate Finance*, edited by E.I. Altman and M.G. Subrahmanyam. (Homewood, Ill.: Richard D. Irwin, 1985).

Mossin, Jan. "Aspects of Rational Insurance Purchasing." *Journal of Political Economy* 76 (July/August 1968).

Raviv, A. "The Design of an Optimal Insurance Policy." *American Economic Review* 69 (March 1979).

Comment

Frederick S. Hammer

No great professional or academic insight is required to conclude that modern technology has had a profound impact on the way banks, and financial markets in general, do business. What is less clear is the precise nature of the impact and the extent to which the financial system has been exposed to increased risk. Two of the previous chapters examine a specific risk induced by technology—the risk of settlement failure arising from daylight overdrafts occurring as a result of wire transfers. A third chapter deals with risk taking by bank management in the context of deposit insurance, arguing that the current system of federal deposit insurance encourages risk shifting by creating perverse incentives for banks.

Daylight overdrafts have only recently become the focus for professional and academic concern. As David Humphrey has pointed out, wire transfers rose from thirteen times GNP in 1970 to sixty-two times GNP in 1983. One result of this explosive growth has been a dramatic increase in the incidence and size of overdrafts in a bank's clearing account (or reserve balance) during the business day. There are a number of reasons for daylight overdrafts: the complexity of the modern payments system virtually guarantees that a bank, acting as agent, may have to send money before it receives good funds; to do otherwise would risk inducing gridlock in the payments system and, perhaps more important from the bank's point of view, risk losing a valued customer, a risk exploited by many users—as the E.F. Hutton case illustrates. Overdrafts also arise from securities transactions and from the structure of the Federal Funds market itself. Nor is the problem confined to large, money-center banks. My own institution, PSFS, occasionally incurs daylight overdrafts as do other, smaller regional institutions.

What is far from clear is the extent of the risk posed and what, if anything, should be done about it. There appears to be some agreement that daylight overdrafts create risk in the payments system. Overdrafts are, after all, a loan and represent an extension of credit. Should an institution fail during the business day and be unable to settle its obligations, the possibility of a systemic failure arises. If the payment system in question is the FedWire, the

Federal Reserve is at risk directly for the unsettled net debit. This effectively prevents systemic failure through payments finality, but could impede the orderly execution of monetary policy. The failure of a private system, such as CHIPS, to settle presents a more problematic set of circumstances. Here the stream of payments during the day is only provisional until net settlement is made at 5:45 p.m. Under CHIPS rules, settlement failure could result in unwinding all the failed bank's transactions during a day, a procedure that could cause settlement problems for other banks.

Although there has never been a settlement failure on a wire transfer system, most parties agree that something ought to be done to reduce the perceived risks. Many "solutions" have been proposed both by banks and regulators. Not surprisingly, banks tend to opt for voluntary action to restructure payments flows while still allowing for flexibility in reducing daylight overdraft exposure. As William Dudley points out, the costs of any regulatory scheme would not be fairly apportioned and might not, in the event, accurately reflect each bank's contribution to the risk of the system as a whole. If I understand his proposal correctly, he favors a method of tying bilateral credit agreements to caps, thereby lowering systemic risk and providing an incentive for banks to lower the level of their daylight overdraft position. He argues that receiver guarantees would actually increase systemic risk by concentrating it. He also points out that receiver guarantees would change the legal relationships involved in a wire transfer by making the bank a principal to the transaction rather than an agent. Regulators, while sensitive to the issues of costs and risk concentration, feel that some feasibly administered set of regulations is necessary to ensure the safety and soundness of the payments and financial system.

Among the more common proposals, some of which have been implemented on a trial basis, are bilateral credit agreements, net debit caps, cross-system debit caps, settlement finality (for private wire systems), and receiver finality. Although there is no consensus, it seems likely that quantity limits—debit caps in some form—will be the most likely outcome in the near future, simply because they are the easiest to administer. As Gregory Udell argues, continuous bank monitoring, while probably feasible to a limited extent, would not be cost-effective. The lack of continuous monitoring would act in favor of a regulatory scheme that placed ex-ante restrictions on individual banks through either net-debit caps or cross-system caps.

Moving from settlement risk to risk in general, Professor Udell examines the current framework of deposit insurance in light of today's increasingly sophisticated technology. Technology is here broadly defined to include not only physical technology but also financial technology and financial innovation. He argues that technology has increased the amount and kind of risk a bank can take, but at the same time has provided increasingly effective tools for risk management. Applying the same logic to the problem of bank monitoring by regulators, he argues that the primary beneficiary of bank monitoring is the insurer (FDIC or FSLIC). Given that a bank cannot be monitored on a "real-time" basis, he argues that the current deposit insurance contract must be revised in such a way as to minimize the "perverse" incentives for risk taking without unduly constraining private decision making.

Despite the somewhat technical nature of the issues at hand, there is no question that whatever the outcome of the debates over regulatory policy and technology, the financial system in the United States will change in many profound and perhaps unexpected ways. These changes will affect not only banks and their regulators, but also both business and consumers.

Part IV
Overview

11

Technology and the Clearing Function

Marc L. Berman

Much of the discussion in the previous chapters is focused on the use of technology as a surveillance tool in our financial marketplaces and the fact that the existence of technology has in fact created a variety of new products and opportunities that create new potential for regulatory problems and financial risk to the system. Coming from the clearance and settlement side of the financial service industry, I and my organization (The Options Clearing Corporation) are interested in using the technology that exists today for protecting the financial services industry. The previous chapters do not consider, to any significant degree, the way in which technology can be used in that way.

Banks, brokerage firms, commodity brokers, and insurance companies are all interrelated parts of the financial services industry, and there have been numerous examples over the past two or three years indicating that the regulatory distinctions between these industries are being eliminated or at the very least are becoming more murky. We have seen this type of erosion taking place with the implementation of the Shad/Johnson accord (resolving a jurisdictional dispute between the CFTC and the Securities and Exchange Commission), the erosion of the Glass-Steagall Act in terms of the ability of banks to get into various securities-related functions, the erosion of the Bank Holding Company Act, the phenomenon of the nonbank bank, and the participation in the business of banking by entities that are normally considered part of a different industry.

We have seen over the past year or two a tremendous increase in financial service industry systems exposures: the potential for a large money-center bank to fail and not be rescued by federal authorities, and the exposure resulting from the utilization by participants in the financial services industry of repurchase agreements in a manner designed to provide quick rewards to participants in that marketplace either through dramatically increased returns on investments (in the case of purchasers of government securities subject to repurchase with a high rate of return) or by the massive financing of government securities by brokers engaged in the repo business as agents with minimal capitalization. A phenomenon similar to that of repos occurs in the stock loan business for firms with minimal amounts of capital who do not mark-to-the-market their positions on a continuing basis and who do not have sufficient capital to meet cash flow requirements to pay mark-to-the-market payments to stock lenders who do mark-to-the-market the positions of the borrowers. We have seen also the potential for failure of firms resulting from the failure to police the margin accounts of their customers for concentrations and their failure to meet maintenance margin calls. Recently we witnessed the failure of a commodities firm, which resulted in a loss to a commodities clearinghouse of approximately 10 million dollars of its guarantee fund, because individuals were allowed to overtrade by establishing positions with little or no margin.

What all this indicates to me is that technology is not being utilized today to its potential in a manner to prevent the risks that I have just described. Inadequate funding, lack of competition, and (in some cases) political turf protection have caused technology to lag behind its potential. This is unfortunate for the financial community as a whole. At The Options Clearing Corporation (OCC) and its subsidiary, The Intermarket Clearing Corporation (ICC), we are using technology to protect ourselves against many of the risks that I have described. I strongly believe that further strides can be made in this area by using technology to implement the concepts of cross-margining of options and futures positions and that the common clearing of futures and options positions can be beneficial to reducing overall systems risks. We do not believe that the implementation of these concepts needs to inhibit the ability of competing exchanges and boards of trade to develop unique systems that enhance the attractiveness of their market over others. Roger Rutz has suggested that neither the OCC nor the National Securities Clearing Corporation (NSCC) was a common clearing agency for multiple marketplaces. He argued that OCC is not a common clearing organization because it does not perform the trade-matching function but rather relies on each exchange to perform that function itself. It is precisely because we do recognize that exchanges can gather greater market share by providing better, more efficient, and more effective facilities than other exchanges for processing transactions as they occur that the exchanges have elected to develop different systems for performing such functions. We have not required the Chicago Board Options Exchange to adopt the Philadelphia Stock Exchange's locked-in trade-matching system. Each exchange believes it derives advantages from its own system and that various systems must differ in order to meet the needs of different marketplaces.

However, once the process of trade comparison is completed, it is counterproductive to force matched trades to be settled through a multitude of different clearing entities requiring firms that participate in numerous markets to receive multiple and different types of reports of transactions and to settle the transactions through numerous money settlements. It is also unnecessary to require a firm to pay margin at one clearing corporation when it has a position at another clearing corporation that completely offsets the risk, or to expose both clearing entities to the risk that fixed dollar margin levels will be inadequate when the hedged position carried at the other entity will move in tandem with the position of the other entity and will provide complete protection. It is unfortunate that the technical systems and the regulatory environment do not easily permit both positions to be maintained at a single entity, thereby reducing risk to all system participants who may have to finance losses through their guarantee fund deposits. These problems and risks could be minimized by common clearing and cross-margining. Another advantage of common clearing is that it allows for the establishment of both the quality and quantity of margin independently of marketing considerations by exchanges and boards of trade.

Common clearing has also been criticized on the grounds that clearing entities have fiduciary obligations to their members and that members of a clearing organization that deal primarily in derivative products in the bond market do not necessarily want to expose themselves to the risks associated with persons trading in derivative products in the gold and silver market. While this may be a legitimate concern, it can be dealt with appropriately. One solution that has been implemented is the establishment of separate clearing funds for separate product lines. If the clearing fund for each product line is adequate to cover the potential risks of firm failures from dealing in that product line, limited exposure would exist for participants in the clearing entity who participate solely in the other product lines. While there may be some theoretical limitations to this approach in the event that the individual product line clearing fund is inadequate, thereby requiring the use of unrelated funds or the net worth of the clearing entity as a backup, we think the practical risk of that happening is insignificant.

In conclusion, I would hope that in the future technology will be utilized as much as a risk reduction mechanism as it has been used in the past to develop the new or unique products that have resulted in significant exposures to the financial services industry.

12
Technology and New Regulatory Challenges in Futures Markets

Franklin R. Edwards

Technology and the regulation of financial markets are related in three ways: First, advances in technology frequently result in new products and services being offered by banks and other financial service firms, which present regulators with new problems and challenges. The development of money market mutual funds by securities firms as a competitive alternative to bank savings deposits is an example. There, regulators were faced with the challenge of how to change Regulation Q and with having to deal with the effects of such a change in our diverse financial institutions. An example in futures markets is twenty-four-hour trading through international clearing arrangements.

Second, technological advance may create new opportunities and pressures for a change in the institutional structure of financial markets. It may make existing institutional arrangements inefficient compared to new ones, and it can create internal and external pressure to change existing institutions. For example, advances in communications, information, and data-processing capabilities will very likely increase the size of the "minimum efficient" bank or financial service firm. The result will be an increased demand by banks to become larger, both through acquisition and by more extensive geographical operations. Thus, bank regulators must reexamine existing merger and branching policies to determine whether other approaches might be preferable. A similar kind of development relevant to futures markets is the controversy about whether automated trading is a more efficient trading alternative to the current open-outcry, auction market, floor-trading system used by futures exchanges.

Third, advances in technology may permit regulators to expand and/or improve their supervisory roles. Such opportunities, however, confront them with two questions: Do the benefits of adopting this technology (or of forcing industry to adopt it) justify the costs involved? And, will adopting the new technology expand regulatory involvement beyond desirable boundaries? For example, it is easy to conceive of surveillance systems that would infringe to too great an extent on the privacy of individuals. Another example may be "variable premium" deposit insurance. The ability to institute such a system depends on the capability of regulators to monitor the risk exposures of insured banks accurately and in a timely fashion. This requires both the insured and the insurer to have sophisticated computer and information processing systems.

A more obvious example, and one being hotly debated today in the futures industry, is the "one-minute time-stamping" of futures trades. Presently, executed futures trades are bracketed into thirty-minute intervals, which often makes it difficult to reconstruct a time-sequential audit trail within that thirty-minute period. Going from thirty-minute to one-minute bracketing of trades, however, would necessitate using a higher-cost technology than that which is now employed by organized futures exchanges. Should regulation (or the CFTC) require exchanges to adopt this higher cost technology? Do the likely benefits exceed the costs?

Analysis of Specific Regulatory Issues

In the remainder of this chapter, I will discuss three current issues related to futures markets that I believe demonstrate the interplay between technology and regulation. These issues are complex enough to demonstrate the kinds of difficulties that regulators encounter in deciding how to respond to technological change.

Centralized Clearing

There are eleven clearing associations in the United States that clear for eleven exchanges. Each is an entirely separate organization. Clearing associations process and "clear" all trades made on affiliated exchanges, and they act as guarantors vis-à-vis clearing members. Thus, they serve as an information and data-processing entity and in a fiduciary capacity as insurer of futures trades. Each has its own rules and regulations and carries out its responsibilities in its own unique way.[1]

Futures Commission Merchants (FCMs) that trade for their customers and for themselves on many different exchanges must clear through different clearing associations. In addition, since each clearing association has its own staff, computers, and so forth, there is clearly some duplication of resources and effort.

Advances in technology, and the growth of futures trading, have intensified the demands of FCMs for centralized clearing—one institution that would clear and guarantee all trades, regardless which exchange it is executed on. This arrangement, they argue, will reduce direct clearing costs (because of economies of scale), and more important, will reduce the overhead expenses of FCMs by simplifying back-office procedures and by reducing their required personnel.

While the cost savings that might result from centralized clearing have not been clearly demonstrated, intuition suggests that they exist. There are undoubtedly some economies of scale and scope in data processing, especially with respect to the smaller clearing associations. If there is any doubt, this could seemingly be verified by comparing the clearing costs per trade at the Chicago Board of Trade (the largest of the associations) with unit costs at the smaller clearing associations (such as the New York Mercantile Exchange). Surprisingly, such a study has never been done either by the industry or by regulators, and sufficient cost data have not been made public to permit academicians to examine the question. Perhaps these data should be made available.

Whether there are economies in performing the fiduciary or guarantor function of clearing associations is another important issue. To the extent that the price volatilities of different futures contracts are largely unrelated and, therefore, independent probabilities exist of trader default on different contracts, a consolidation of clearing associations may reduce each clearing member's risk by spreading the default risk among more traders and clearing members. It is analogous to the insurance principle of the Law of Large Numbers: as the number of exposure units increases, the more certain it is that actual loss experience will equal probable loss experience. This, too, is a subject that has not received the attention it deserves.

In addition, with a fully consolidated clearing operation, there will be better information on the overall positions of traders. This will enable clearing associations to monitor more accurately their risk exposures. Finally, when associations take an action to reduce their risk, such as raising margin levels, they may affect other clearing associations. Centralization would be able to internalize these interdependencies.

Assuming there are benefits associated with centralization, why would the market on its own fail to bring it about? Why is this a regulatory issue? If benefits exist, exchanges and their affiliated clearing associations should see them and want to consolidate and merge their operations. Indeed, a freely competitive market would seemingly require this result. This has not happened. What we have instead is many clearing associations, some many times larger than others. The reason, I expect, is not the lack of competition, but rather the perception on the part of most clearing associations that clearing costs are a minor aspect of the products (contracts) sold (traded) by exchanges. More specifically, an advantage in clearing costs is not seen as significant enough to alter the distribution of traders among the different exchanges. (While the direct costs of trading—commissions and so forth—would go down, these costs are already quite low. The "price" elasticity of demand for futures trading might indeed be small.)

This view, however, fails to consider the costs that are imposed on large FCMs in having to deal with disparate clearing systems. These costs do not show up as clearing associations costs—they would not be reflected in a cost study of economies of scale in clearing. Thus, centralized clearing may result in significant indirect cost savings for large FCMs. These savings may not accrue to smaller clearing members because they may deal with only one or two exchanges.

An alternative view of why centralized clearing has not occurred is the political one. The decision to merge clearing operations must be made by all clearing members, or by their representative member committees. Members have heterogeneous interests, so membership composition, and therefore committee membership, may not be reflective of aggregate dollar interests. Voting influence does not always equal dollar benefits. Further, centralization will undoubtedly diminish the political influence of some members and increase that of others. It is likely that large FCMs will gain relative to others, since they have representatives at most exchanges and clearing associations. Thus, given the nature of competition in futures markets, and given the governing structure of exchanges, it seems at least possible that centralized clearing will not occur on its own, even if it were true that it would result in a net social benefit.

Is this the kind of situation that calls for direct intervention by regulators? Mandating centralization according to a specified institutional structure is not an attractive remedy. Regulators are seldom in a position to judge which organizational structure is best. Moreover, once this scheme is enunciated, regulators are apt to defend it, however inappropriate it may be. The danger that we will end up with a worse institutional structure than we have now is not an insignificant one.

A further risk in the current environment is that large FCMs, out of frustration, will turn to regulators and to Congress for a remedy. If their voting power at exchanges is not commensurate to their economic resources, they may find politics a more fruitful avenue to pursue. They may be more successful in transforming economic power into political power. History has shown, however, that the outcome of the political process is highly uncertain.

A better alternative, I believe, is for regulators to find a way to make the market work better through competition. When the existing institutional structure of a market is inefficient, the usual market response is new entry. Even the threat of such entry will give all clearing members an incentive to make their system as efficient as possible. Just how this might be accomplished is not obvious.

The recent announcement by the New York Futures Exchange that it would begin clearing all trades through the Options Clearing Corporation (which already provides centralized clearing for all options trading in the United States) suggests a possible answer. However, there is little reason to think that other futures exchanges will also do this.

Another approach might be for regulators to endorse a form of centralized clearing that could achieve some of the benefits of centralization without significantly interfering with the ability of present exchange members to control their own destinies. In particular, there could be an integration of back-office clearing and processing functions, while independent clearing entities were still maintained with respect to the guarantor and risk management functions. Harmonization of rules and regulations would, of course, be the ultimate objective. Further, it seems clear that if such an approach is taken, the small New York clearing associations should be the prime candidates for centralization. To the extent that economies of scale and scope exist, significant benefits would be realized by consolidating the smaller associations.

Off-Exchange Trading

Technological advances and more intense competition have renewed the interest of FCMs in conducting off-exchange trading, which has rekindled the controversy over "leverage dealing." Sections 4h and 4b of the original 1922 Commodity Exchange Act (CEA) sought to limit (or ban) off-exchange futures trading.[2] Nevertheless, an over-the-counter futures market still exists today in the United States, albeit in a limited fashion—the result of a bizarre mixture of historical quirk, effective lobbying, regulatory indecision, and congressional ambivalence. Ironically, despite the history of public scandals associated with such dealing and the repeated attempts by public officials to deal with them, there exists today a sharp (and growing) disagreement in the futures industry over what policy to adopt toward off-exchange trading. Should leverage contracts and all other off-exchange trading be banned, or should such trading be encouraged and fostered under a regulatory aegis similar to the one currently applied to organized exchange trading?

The so-called leverage issue is part of a much larger issue: off-exchange trading. Leverage transactions themselves are not capable of precise definition. The CEA nowhere defines leverage, except to say that it is what is commonly known in the trade as "leverage." A leverage contract is a variable mixture of a futures and forward contract. It is standardized like a futures contract with margins, "offset capability," and other such characteristics, but the price of the contract is determined by bilateral negotiation with the leverage dealer. Noticeably absent is any guarantee of the kind given by clearing associations. Its attractiveness to speculators is that it may provide them with a "futures" contract not available on an organized exchange, or, possibly, one at a lower effective cost (like lower margins).

Two other kinds of over-the-counter futures trading are conceptually possible: "block-trading" and over-the-counter dealing in futures contracts very similar to those already traded on organized exchanges. While such transactions would now seem to be illegal under sections 4, 4b, and 4h of the CEA, it is not clear that these provisions prohibit the trading of a "privately created" futures contract "by or through a member of a contract market." What distinguishes an exchange-created futures contract from a privately created one is unclear. Thus, the present law is ambiguous enough to allow regulators either to encourage or to thwart off-exchange "futures" trading. In doing so they will be making a decision about the wisdom of either encouraging or discouraging competition.

There are sound arguments on both sides of the issue, but decisions must still be made. Further, I believe that we will see a significant increase in off-exchange trading in future years if nothing is done to prevent it.

The argument in support of banning off-exchange trading is a straightforward one. The organized futures exchange is the creation of regulation (and especially of self-regulation), and the concept of granting exchanges a "contract monopoly" is well established. Forcing all trading to go through the auction markets of organized exchanges was considered a vital aspect of these markets, to enhance liquidity and to provide a more efficient price discovery mechanism. In some sense, trading in a futures contract may be considered a "natural" monopoly: the more trading that is done through a centralized market, the better and more efficient is the market. Trading costs per unit are lower. Even if futures markets are not natural monopolies, they are clearly subject to extensive economies of scale. There have been few historical cases of two exchanges successfully trading the same contract. One exchange eventually captures all of the trading. Thus, by banning off-exchange trading and forcing all activity through the designated contract market, full market efficiency was sought. (The same outcome, arguably, should be achieved by permitting the free interplay of competitive market forces!)

Once an exchange is successfully trading a futures contract, there are incentives for firms to trade (or deal in) the same contract—or a close subsitute for it—off the exchange. By "free-riding" on the exchange, off-exchange dealers can offer much the same product at a lower cost. They can utilize the price setting done by exchanges and can take advantage of the goodwill and public image that exchanges pay dearly to achieve and maintain, while at the same time avoiding the costs of belonging to an exchange.[3] To the extent that business is diverted from exchanges, they are harmed.

Further, off-exchange trading may continue for a long time, even if it is inferior to exchange-traded contracts. Many customers may not value what the exchange has to offer until a crisis occurs. The situation is similar to the current problems we are having in the United States with savings and loan associations and their alternative deposit insurance systems. Many depositors, given the choice between federal or state-backed deposit insurance, chose to put their money where the interest rate was highest, notwithstanding the difference in bankruptcy risk. Now that their funds are in jeopardy, of course, they are only too aware of the distinction. Thus, regulation banning off-exchange trading can be viewed either as an efficiency-enhancing strategy (to centralize trading) or as an attempt to protect (in a paternalistic way) unwary traders.

The argument against banning off-exchange trading is "consumer sovereignty" and competition. Some traders may wish to use off-exchange contracts because these contracts provide them with a preferable bundle of characteristics. They may, for example, prefer a lower margin contract despite the greater risk that their FCM will become insolvent. Banning off-exchange dealing would deprive traders of their ability to choose among alternatives, reducing their freedom of choice, and (it could be argued) their welfare.

Off-exchange trading also may be an important competitive force in keeping organized futures exchanges efficient. For example, if exchanges, because of their contract monopolies, failed to adopt efficient institutional structures (perhaps a new advance in technology), off-exchange dealers may adopt these technologies and divert trading from exchanges. In other words, "entry" into the industry will occur—the classic competitive force. This may provide exchanges with a greater incentive to maintain efficiency and to improve their products. Although it is true that, even without permitting off-exchange dealing, new entry can take place through the organization of a new exchange, this is clearly a higher-cost competitive alternative. As such, it is not as effective a competitive threat as is off-exchange dealing.

The final aspect of this debate is the claim that off-exchange trading has proven to be a haven for crooks and swindlers. History seems to give this argument credence. There have been repeated episodes of fraud by off-exchange dealers, which has been a source of embarrassment for organized exchanges. Exchanges feel, quite justifiably, that off-exchange trading scandals tarnish the integrity and reputation of organized futures trading. Traders and the public in general cannot distinguish among legitimate and crooked brokers and dealers, and often confuse off-exchange trading with trading on an organized exchange. There may, therefore, be a negative externality associated with off-exchange dealing that harms exchanges.

If off-exchange trading is permitted, it may be necessary to subject off-exchange dealers to protective regulations similar to those that protect customers who trade on organized exchanges. Alternatively, off-exchange trading might be limited to "high quality" dealers, although this limitation risks giving some monopoly power to these dealers. Finally, if traders could be made aware of the risks associated with off-exchange trading and could be alerted to the differences among dealers, the market itself would solve the problem.

One-Minute Time-Stamping

The desire to introduce a technology capable of creating a better audit trail for futures trading stems from a concern that floor traders may sometimes take advantage of their customers.[4] Floor traders can and often do trade for themselves as well as their customers (so-called dual trading). Thus, it is possible that, knowing the customers' orders that they are holding for later execution, they will trade ahead of their customers for their own benefit. For example, if they are holding large buy orders for their customers, they might buy for themselves, knowing that if prices do not rise they can always sell their positon "back" to their own customers without loss.

There are, of course, regulations that prohibit such trading abuses,[5] but without a good time-and-sales record it is difficult to monitor trading and to enforce these regulations. It is the responsibility of the CFTC to assure that an adequate trading record is made available.[6]

The argument, therefore, in favor of imposing a one-minute time-stamping rule on futures exchanges is that it will largely eliminate floor trading abuses, making futures trading fairer for "outside" traders. This will, arguably, improve the public's image of futures markets, increase trader participation, and enhance market liquidity.

The argument against adopting one-minute time-stamping is threefold. First, the exchanges claim that the technology required to keep such a record, especially for highly active trading pits, is either unavailable or exorbitantly expensive (and the costs will have to be passed on to traders). Second, even with the best available technology, there will be extensive trading congestion in active pits. Order execution will be slower. As a result, the average size of trade on the floor will increase, which in turn will result in larger bid-ask spreads. This will increase trading costs, reducing trader participation in futures markets. Third, the incidence of trading abuses is actually low—too low to justify the costs involved in eliminating them. There already exists time-sequential data on price changes for futures contracts, which, when combined with the thirty-minute bracketed time-and-sales records, provide an audit trail capable of detecting most trading abuses. Thus, the benefits of creating a better audit trail are small in comparison to the costs. Overall, the result would be higher trading costs with less trader participation in futures market and poorer market liquidity.

It is, of course, difficult to distinguish these arguments from the alternative view that exchanges (and, in particular, floor traders) do not want to relinquish the advantages that dual trading gives them. If they really do take advantage of customers, a better audit trail will reduce their earnings. Indeed, the seat values of exchanges might even fall.

Regulators are the ones left to sort out truth from fiction, to determine true costs and benefits. This is not a simple task. They must, for example, weigh the highly uncertain and intangible benefits of greater fairness for all traders, or even the perception (if not the reality) of greater fairness. They must assess likely costs and make inferences about unobservable price elasticities of demand, and, perhaps most important of all, they must determine whether there is a "market failure," and, if so, why? Finally, if they decide to intervene, they must determine the best way to go about it. One can only hope that they are the beneficiaries of divine guidance.

Notes

1. For a description of these rules and regulations, see F.R. Edwards, "The Clearing Association in Futures Markets," *Journal of Futures Markets,* 3, no. 4 (Winter 1983):369–92.

2. 7 U.S.C., sec. 6h; CCH Rep., sec. 11, 1567–68.

3. In addition, off-exchange dealers may themselves use organized exchanges to hedge their own net risk exposures.

4. As an example of how futures markets are sometimes perceived as unfair, see "Amateur Speculators in Commodities Face Pros Holding the Aces," *Wall Street Journal,* 16 February 1984.

5. See CFTC Regulation 155.2; 17 C.F.R. 155.2; CCH Rep. 3182, 3201.

6. See 7 U.S.C. 6j(1); CCH Rep. 1131, 1568; and 17 C.F.R. 1.35(g); CCH Rep. 2164, at 2177–78.

13
The Interface between Technology and Regulation in Banking

Laurie S. Goodman

At the present time, banks are buying, selling, and trading products that no one would have dreamed of a decade ago—zero coupon bonds, mortgage products, interest rate swaps, interest rate caps, futures and options. Combinations of these products, such as the right to buy an option in the future, can be customized. These products are the result of two trends: an increase in the volatility of interest rates and the advances in computer technology. Computer technology has made changes in the way risks are evaluated and managed and in the scale and scope of trading activities. These trends and their implications for regulation are the subjects of this chapter.

Computer technology has allowed financial institutions to unbundle the inherent claims in a financial instrument; each of those claims can then be traded individually. In order to unbundle the claims, a firm must have the ability to keep track of each one separately. Moreover, a firm must have the ability to estimate and hedge, if desired, the risk inherent in the total position. Neither of these actions would be possible in the absence of technological advances. Computer technology has also allowed for the development of economies of scope in the provision of risk management services. For example, real-time arbitrage systems allow financial institutions to profit from small, nonsynchronous movements in prices in different markets, thereby keeping market prices in line.

There are two regulatory consequences of the advancement in computer technology. First, it is contributing to the erosion of the separation between commercial and investment banking activities. Banks are under regulatory pressure to increase capital/asset ratios, and, consequently, they are searching for ways to earn additional income without taking on additional assets. The search for new sources of income, in conjunction with the increased emphasis on trading and economies of scope inherent in many types of computer-based systems, has spurred the desire of banks to become further involved in activities that were, until recently, the province of the investment bankers.

The second implication for the regulatory front is the need for a supervisory system that is less asset-based and that gives increased attention to internal risk guidelines. This supervisory system must also be fully aware of the off-balance sheet activities in which banks actively participate.

Computer Technology and the Unbundling of Risks

When one is asked to name an instrument whose claims have been unbundled, the first example that comes to mind is coupon stripping—the creation of zero coupon Treasury bonds. In a stripped bond, the coupons are each peeled off and sold separately. Thus, the first coupon to be received six months hence may sell for $95 or so, while the coupon to be received in ten years would sell for $36. The February 1988 claim, no matter which Treasury bond it was stripped off of, would be a homogeneous commodity. The price of each claim could then be viewed as the price of money to be received on that date. Bonds can be evaluated against these pure prices to determine which are cheap and which are rich, and price discrepancies can then be corrected.

When one thinks of an option, one usually conceptualizes an instrument with an asymmetric payoff structure. When reduced to its essence, however, an option is merely a continuously readjusted combination of the underlying security and a risk-free investment. This holds true for both over-the-counter and exchange-traded options. Thus, technology has made it possible to estimate, as well as hedge, the exposure arising from option writing.

A product that has attracted a great deal of attention in the past year or eighteen months is interest rate agreements. In these agreements, the financial institution selling the service agrees that when rates go above the prespecified ceiling, it will pay the buyer the difference between current interest rates and the ceiling rate. The buyer has purchased a series of put options, and the seller must evaluate the risk accordingly. In order to reduce the cost of this product to the buyer, slight variants of this service are offered; in a floor-ceiling, the seller agrees that if rates go above the ceiling, it will compensate the buyer for the difference between the ceiling rate and the current rate. If rates go below a certain prespecified floor, the institution selling the product will be compensated by the buyer for the difference between current rates and the floor rate. The financial institution offering the product has essentially written a series of put options and bought a series of call options.

In a textbook interest rate or currency swap, there is no risk to the institution that arranges the transaction; there is one party who has borrowed floating and wants to receive fixed or wants to borrow in one currency and receive proceeds in another currency. The arranger finds another institution to take the offsetting position and subsequently collects a fee. In the real world, however, a counterparty cannot always be found on the spot for a given transaction; the arranger may want to assume the risk for a period of time while a counterparty is being located. Moreover, in many transactions the amount to be swapped is nonconstant over time. A single swap is then linked with several counterparties so that the arranger can minimize its interest rate or currency risk. This generally takes time to organize, and the arranger must take some interim risk.

Conventional mortgage securities are bonds with a declining balance and a prepayment option. The prepayment option is a complex call option. Adjustable rate mortgages are floating rate instruments with a variety of options attached (most typically yearly caps and lifetime caps).

The ability to evaluate, at least approximately, the risk of each component of a complex instrument allows the institution to decide what risk to maintain and what risk to sell off. Of the risk that is carried, it must be decided what to hedge and what not to hedge. For example, Citicorp Investment Bank recently concluded a mortgage pass-through deal consisting of Citibank's own adjustable rate mortgages with the caps removed. A determination was made that as a unit, the capped mortgages were priced low: selling uncapped mortgages and hedging the option risk was a more profitable course of action.

Several previous chapters have discussed how technology has spurred trading which, in turn, has spurred securitization of instruments that were never before securitized. In the mortgage area, everything from traditional single-family homes to commercial property can now be traded. Technology played an important additional role in this process in that it allowed for the unbundling of the origination and servicing roles from actually holding the mortgage in portfolio. Given current computer technology, servicing is a profitable activity in and of itself. Prior to the existence of this technology, no institution wanted to service mortgages it did not own. The trend toward mortgage securitization and sales blurs the distinction between commercial and investment banking, as shall be discussed later.

Economies of Scope in Computer Technology

As earlier chapters have already extensively pointed out, computers aid market makers in unbundling claims. Once this is done, the computer does not care that an instrument is a government security or a corporate bond, a bank-eligible municipal bond or a bank-ineligible municipal bond. Thus, computer technology is providing economies of scope, particularly involving a number of activities in which banks cannot currently compete. This places increased pressure on Glass-Steagall restrictions.

Arbitrage—the setting up of a truly riskless position—and basis trading—the setting up of an almost riskless position by being long one security and short another—are crucially dependent on being able quickly to detect and act on small discrepancies in prices. This is greatly aided by having real-time prices in a usable form on a computer. Once one has these prices, it is a simple matter to write software to spot securities that are out of line relative to combinations of other securities with the same series of basic claims. For example, one can always create a current coupon Treasury security using a combination of a high coupon bond and a zero coupon bond, where all three have the same final maturity. A four-year 10 percent par bond will pay coupons of $5 per semiannual period. A 12 percent premium bond will pay coupons of $6 per $100 face. By buying $80 face of the 12 percent bond and $20 of the four-year zero, one can exactly replicate the cash flows from the par bond. Testing numerous combinations will allow the detection of situations where it is profitable to be long the combination of the high coupon bond and the zero coupon bond and short the par bond.

Similarly, in option trading, if the implied volatility is out of line on the December 70 call option relative to the December 68 call option, this would suggest a profitable opportunity to buy the low volatility option and to sell a properly weighted amount of the high volatility option. The position holder can only be favorably affected by a realignment of the implied volatilities.

While all issues are not identical in the corporate and municipal market, historical patterns may indicate that bond X trades within 3 basis points of bond Y. If this spread widens to 6 basis points, it would indicate a good basis trade. In the municipal market, this opportunity cannot be utilized if a bank can trade X but not Y. In the corporate market, where a bank cannot trade X or Y, it would be impossible to take advantage of this discrepancy.

In addition to arbitrage and basis trading, there are a number of other areas in which computers provide economies of scope. Many pension funds and money managers are interested in dedicated and immunized portfolios; these portfolios generally allow highly rated corporate bonds. When such bonds are included, the portfolio can be purchased more cheaply than a portfolio of government securities alone. Thus, the restriction that commercial banks cannot sell corporate bonds limits the ability of these institutions to compete in the area of dedicated and immunized portfolios.

Defeasing a portfolio in the least costly manner is a similar type of linear programming problem. A defeasance problem is, technically speaking, an after-tax dedication with before-tax constraints. The rules on defeasing a portfolio are such that government securities must be used. However, defeasance to remove debt from a firm's balance sheet requires a review of other alternatives, such as repurchasing the debt and performing debt-equity swaps. Commercial banks cannot participate fully in these activities and hence receive relatively little of the defeasance business.[1]

In a similar vein, banks can securitize their own mortgages in the form of mortgage-backed bonds or collateralized mortgage obligations (CMOs). In so doing, they are acting merely as agents for the distribution of their own paper.

The software for these structured transactions is complicated and expensive to develop initially. Consequently, it is natural to want to underwrite mortgage bonds based on mortgages originated by others.

Many municipal bonds are sold with a number of put options and other features attached. The expertise involved in the development of pricing for housing and health care bonds is little different than for other types of revenue bonds.

Implications for Regulation

Technology and the resultant increase in trading have created the need for a different type of bank supervisory structure. The current supervisory structure looks at the balance sheet of the bank at a single point in time. This is appropriate for financial institutions that buy assets and hold them in portfolio. A number of different ratios are used to spot problem banks, including capital/asset ratios, liquidity ratios, and ratios to measure credit quality. The present bank supervisory system is known as CAMEL—the initials of the key elements of the examination process (capital, assets, management, earnings, and liquidity). Indeed three of the five components of this system (capital, assets, and liquidity) are predicated on a fairly static portfolio. Recently, increased attention has been given to some off-balance sheet items, including futures, options, and standby letters of credit. These, too, are monitored only at a single point in time.

The current approach poses a fundamental problem in that if the portfolio is actively traded, a snapshot one day may differ considerably from that of another day. The regulators take some account of that by looking at a bank's own mechanism for monitoring interest-rate risk, credit risk, and sovereign risk within the confines of the bank examination process. Further emphasis on internal risk management, including the development of formal measures to quantify the interest and credit risk, are important.

Note that this approach is greatly at odds with Gregory Udell's proposal discussed earlier in this book. His proposal is that the supervisor should look at the balance sheet at several points in time to make sure the bank has claimed a correct risk premium. This, too, works for banks with assets that are fairly constant over time; it does not work for a bank with a dynamically managed portfolio.

Although we are a long way from portfolios devoid of stable assets, the major banks are moving in that direction. The current debate over capital adequacy standards, the role of liquidity, and concerns over credit quality will become less important. Business-type ratios—such as earnings, what the demand for various services will be, and where the resources of the institution are deployed—will become more important. Earnings and earnings volatility should be stressed more in the future.

Pressure on Glass-Steagall

Computer technology, by creating economies of scope, has also increased the importance to banks of breaking down Glass-Steagall restrictions. Further, it has blurred the distinction between lending and underwriting; indeed, this may create a social benefit by providing increased competition in these services, thereby lowering costs.

As commercial banks clamor to provide investment banking services, investment banks quite justifiably note that banks will have quite a comparative advantage in the provision of many services because of deposit insurance. In this regard, there are two possible courses of action. The first is to retain the distinction between commercial and investment banks. Commercial banks would obtain expanded powers but would still be prohibited entirely from participating in the equity market, and perhaps limits would be placed on underwriting corporate debt. The range of investment banking activities would remain unchanged.

The second possible course of action, which represents a more radical departure from the status quo, is to allow both banks and investment banks to be composed of two entities: (*a*) "deposit taking asset holding entities" and (*b*) underwriting/trading entities. Only the former would be insured, with rules limiting risk exposure. The ability of the trading entity to obtain funds from the deposit-taking entity in the event the former falls on hard times must be greatly circumscribed. Any commercial or investment bank could have either one or both entities.

At this time my sympathies lie with the first approach. Nevertheless, I think it is important to recognize that the movement of commercial banks into investment banking must be implemented with an eye toward the fact that commercial banks have deposit insurance, which has certain advantages and certain costs. Wholesale expansion of banks into investment banking activities would require some decisions as to what the scope of deposit insurance ought to be.

Note

1. The only exception to this was in the area of instantaneous defeasances—a corporation issues debt in the Euromarket at below government rates and buys U.S. government securities to defease it. U.S. banks can, of course, underwrite debt in the Euromarket. In October 1984 the Financial Accounting Standards Board (FASB) ruled that instantaneous defeasance is no longer allowed.

14
Technology and the Regulation of Financial Markets

Edward J. Kane

The first three sections of this book are constructed such that chapters are presented by a high-ranking federal agency employee, an industry representative, and an academic. Exemplifying the nostrum that what we see depends partly on where we sit, in the securities and futures sections the industry and government-agency chapters focus on issues of broad regulatory strategy and occupy two nearly contradictory positions. The alternative positions personify the distinction between proactive and reactive regulation that Cox and Kohn discuss in their chapter.

On the one hand, the industry-based chapters emphasize that regulatory lags in responding to new technological opportunities and other problems tend to be longer for government regulators than for self-regulatory organizations and that governmental actions tend to be relatively less well adapted as well. The authors of these chapters portray government regulation as predominantly reactive and at least occasionally unnecessarily wasteful and unfair.

On the other hand, the government-based chapters paint a proud record of federal-agency concern for building state-of-the-art information and clearing systems. These chapters' authors emphasize instances in which government regulators have formulated proactive policy strategies aimed at promoting two laudable ideals:

1. real-time, systemwide (that is, intermarket, interregional, and even international) electronic execution and reporting of trades;

2. automated surveillance of clearing and settlement transactions.

Such policies look toward generating the best possible data bases and systems of data-base management that modern technology can permit.

I am going to argue that government regulators' proclivity for constructing high-tech data bases is rooted in bureaucratic politics (including a need to resort to implicit compensation) and has more than a little in common with the Pentagon's advocacy of Star Wars systems of missile defense. Differences in the incentive systems under which governmental and self-regulatory bodies function make proactive efforts to build a state-of-the-art information system fully consistent with a tendency for government regulators to be relatively more reactive than self-regulatory organizations in most other endeavors. Critical differences exist in the *objective functions* and *constraints* under which government and private entities operate, particularly:

1. in the criteria by which agency performance is judged and its budget determined;

2. in the extent to which highly skilled personnel can exact the market value of their services in the form of monetary compensation.

Economic Explanation of Proactive Attitudes toward Information and Clearing Systems

To my mind, the typical government agency's proactive efforts to promote state-of-the-art reporting and execution systems reflect the *absence of profitability constraints* on the technology it uses and the ease with which it can cite the mere existence of high-tech information and clearing systems as turf-protecting and budget-enhancing evidence to politicians and voters that it is doing a swell job. It also reflects the substitution of career-enhancing investment in enriched (even *unique*) job experience for monetary compensation of government employees. Opportunities to construct and operate state-of-the-art information and clearing systems overcome salary compression for high-level staff and technical personnel in that they enable management to disguise implicit employee compensation as expenditures on capital equipment. These expenditures increase the value of employees' human capital in ways that can be realized in subsequent employment. Over the past thirty years, one can observe job enrichment substituting for current salary in state-university funding of chaired professorships and in technological decisions made by federal agencies as diverse as the armed forces, the FBI, and the Federal Reserve System.

Economic Explanation of Differential Response Lags

Explaining the tendency of government agencies to be relatively more reactive and maladapted in the administrative use they make of information collected by their high-tech systems takes a bit more effort. In particular, it requires me to appeal to the "regulatory dialectic," a conception that underscores the inherent conflict between attempts to regulate and attempts of regulated parties to lessen the burden of whatever regulations apply to them.

The Regulatory Dialectic

Regulation consists of setting *rules* on someone else's behavior. Such rules seek either to *forbid* or to *compel* particular kinds of behavior. Regulations would not be needed in the first place unless a notable portion of the designated regulatees (the regulated parties) and at least some of their customers did not prefer to engage in alternative behaviors.

Because regulatees are asked to act against their own or their customers' interests, regulators must monitor and enforce compliance by penalizing disobedient regulatees. The divergent interests of financial regulators and their regulatees may be analyzed by viewing them as engaged in a *game within a game*: like a football cornerback's efforts to keep wide receivers from breaking open deep down the field. The principal game is the production and delivery of financial services. The subgame involves regulator-regulatee-customer jostling for position or dominance. Both games are multisided.

The object of regulatory surveillance is to make regulatees and their customers obey the *spirit* of politically determined rules so that the financial system achieves various ostensible and hidden goals: macroeconomic stability, economic efficiency, system integrity, equity, and wealth redistribution. The object of regulatees and their customers is economic maximization. Utility and profit maximization requires regulatees to search out loopholes in the fabric of regulation that they can use to reduce the net burdens that particular regulations ultimately thrust upon them. A regulatee's regulatory burden may be viewed as the logical equivalent of an income tax, since regulators use the force of law either to take potential main-game profits away from regulatees or to drive up the effective charges for delivering their services to customers.

Regulation and regulatee circumvention or avoidance behavior are as inseparable as Siamese twins. It is instructive to view the printed text of each Congressional statute and each regulatory restriction as containing both rules and loopholes. The difference between them is that rules are printed in large boldface type, while loopholes are encoded in an alien alphabet and set in small and very faint letters that cannot be recognized without detective and decoding skills and magnifying devices or exceptionally sharp vision.

The regulatory dialectic describes the interaction between regulators and what we may call loophole prospectors and loophole miners. Dialectic is merely a fancy philosophical term for a process of ongoing conflict and conflict resolution between opposing ideas (that is, assertable propositions) and the logical, physical, political, or economic forces associated with them. Dialectical outcomes are those governed by the push and pull of opposing forces.

Dialectical thinking is associated with Hegel (1770–1831, an almost-exact contemporary of Beethoven), who named the opposing ideas, the *thesis* and *antithesis*, and called the idea that develops to resolve their conflict the *synthesis.* The key insight that distinguishes dialectical thinking from equilibrium thinking is the notion of an evolutionary sequence of creative actions and responses. Each synthesis becomes a fresh thesis in a new three-part dialectic. According to this view, the evolution of thinking on any issue is driven by a *three-stage cycle* in which every idea that resolves a given conflict is immediately confronted with a contradictory proposition, so that the cycle is perpetually renewed. Evolution takes the form of an infinite sequence: Thesis—Antithesis—Synthesis (Thesis)—Antithesis—Synthesis (Thesis). . . .

When it is applied to the regulatory scene, the thesis and antithesis may be identified with *regulation* and *avoidance* and the third stage with *reregulation*. (I want to emphasize that I did not say *de*regulation. Deregulation is almost always misadvertised. Deregulation—that is, the complete removal of rules—is a pure or platonic form of reregulation that is almost never observed in the real world.) In the dialectical view, all regulation becomes synthetic *re*-regulation. Every new rule is merely the latest response to the continuing collision of economic and political pressure.

The dialectical view portrays regulation as a game of strategy with sequential moves. In responding to changes in technology or regulation, individual moves are generally freer and executed more quickly for regulated players and whatever less regulated competitors exist than they are for the regulators themselves. Finally, moves are generally freer and responses quicker for self-regulators than for government regulatory agencies.

To analyze the interaction of technology and regulation, it is useful to distinguish between sequences according to whether regulators or regulatees make the first move. Two basic sequences may be distinguished:

1. regulation-avoidance-reregulation;
2. avoidance-reregulation-avoidance.

For an illustration of each of these archetypal sequences, we may look at the U.S. driving public's response to the 1973 adoption of the 55 miles-per-hour highway speed limit. By 1985, this regulation has led to the installation of 4 million radar detectors on private cars and trucks. In turn, the spread of radar detectors fed a demand by enforcement personnel for a new radar system that could make nearly instantaneous reads (that is, establish a vehicle's speed before its driver can slow down in response to a detector's warning buzz) and could calibrate a vehicle's speed from behind. Such a system is now available and is known as the Hawk radar unit. In effect, the technological advances that perfected avoidance over the past decade are now being used to improve regulatory enforcement. But, by making existing radar detectors obsolete, this potentially successful act of reregulation creates a demand for more sensitive and multidirectional radar detectors. As this illustration suggests, opportunities for avoidance and reregulation benefit those who manufacture equipment for players on either side of the game.

Differences in Motivation and Adaptive Efficiency of Government Agencies and Self-Regulatory Organizations

Reoptimization is not a continuous process. Lags exist between the moves made by regulators and regulatees and by private and governmental players. To complete the perspective, we may attribute the existence and relative lengths of response lags to an underlying difference in the adaptive efficiency of private firms and government bureaus.

We call the lag that exists between regulation and avoidance the *avoidance lag*. This lag reflects: (1) the tendency for profitable innovations to lag behind the technical advances or inventions that make them feasible, and (2) the tendency for less regulated competitors to try to take advantage of restrictions on regulated firms' ability to compete by developing differentially regulated substitutes for regulated products. Career choices made in deciding to work for either a government agency, a self-regulatory agency, a regulated firm, or a less regulated (and nontraditional) player may themselves reflect a broad self-sorting of personnel hired by different players that accords roughly with their preexisting levels of adaptive efficiency.

We call the lag between avoidance and reregulation the *regulatory lag*. Theory and observation indicate that the regulatory lag tends to exceed the avoidance lag. Differences in the time it takes to size up avoidance opportunities created by technological change reflect differences in the degree of competitive pressure felt by government regulators, private regulators, regulatees, and less regulated competitors.

Differences in group and individual motivation may be described as differences in profit incentives between members of what we may call the regulatee cartel and firms operating outside the cartel and differences between profit and bureaucratic incentives. When new avoidance opportunities develop, the push and pull of competing political pressures on government regulators disposes them toward inaction. Government regulators tend to be reactive rather than proactive in their response to emerging avoidance opportunities. This tendency reflects the typically short horizon (and generally advanced age) of agency heads and the prevalence of *blame avoidance* and *blame dispersion* as motive forces in bureaucratic behavior. Concern for covering agency and staff-member rear ends tends to delay regulatory action until it seems relatively riskless politically. The cost of delay is smaller for government regulators than for regulatees and private regulators because survival of their bureaus and their own jobs is seldom truly at stake.

Agency interest in building protections against outside criticism leads to:

1. A narrower range of monetary rewards and punishments for employees. Limits on speed of promotion and range of available strategies are stricter in government than in private enterprise.

2. Differences in information flows about changing opportunities in regulated markets. Private operatives have greater incentives to track changing avoidance opportunities.

3. Differences in the costs of entry into new activities and particularly in the costs of exit from old ones. Duplicate regulatory functions and overlapping administrative boundaries provide opportunities for the entry and exit of regulatees. Regulated firms (especially new entrants into regulated and substitute markets) shrink the domains (and therefore the budget resources) of regulators whose response to the evolving needs of the marketplace proves shortsighted or inflexible. However, in the battle for regulatory turf and budgetary funds, agency entry and exit are subject to direct Congressional interference. A government agency's political clout and the occurrence of scandals or crisis may undo competitively induced losses in an agency's turf. The second or January 1984 Accord between the SEC and CFTC illustrates a bureaucratic surrender of regulatory market share. Effectively, the SEC forced the CFTC politically to give up ground it had won economically over the previous decade by authorizing futures substitutes for ordinary securities, ground which the CFTC thought it had consolidated in an earlier 1983 accord.

Financial regulatory rivalry embraces not only the CFTC, the SEC, and federal deposit–institution regulators but also their counterparts in the individual states and various private and quasi-private regulatory cooperatives. From a political perspective, multiple regulators develop as a way of formally providing ongoing protection for the interests of diverse political constituencies. But from an economic perspective, competition resulting from overlaps in regulatory responsibility establishes an evolutionary mechanism for adapting regulatory structures over time to technological and regulation-induced innovation. I believe that competition between governmental regulatory agencies and self-regulatory cooperatives produces more efficient regulatory structures over time than administratively streamlined monopoly regulation would.

A Summary View of Effects of Technological Change on Opportunities for Avoidance and Reregulation

Regulation is a multiopponent game like tag, rather than a two-sided game like tennis. The main players are specialized regulators, regulatees, their customers, less regulated competitors and their regulators, and evolving political coalitions for and against particular regulatory schemes. The behavior of regulators and regulatees must be viewed as jointly conditioned. Each needs to anticipate the reaction of players on other sides of the regulation. The regulatory dialectic differs from the usual legislative or political-science model precisely in that it anticipates that strategic countermoves occur in response to every regulatory adjustment.

The great strength of a dialectical vision is the evolutionary perspective it gives us for confronting and interpreting change. About the interaction of technology and regulation, the dialectic tells us three things:

1. In the face of exogenous changes in technology and risks, no permanent equilibrium is possible. Every apparent regulatory equilibrium contains the seeds of its own future destruction.

2. The current regulatory problems facing any set of regulatees and regulators is shaped by the detailed history of their prior conflicts.

3. As in a chess game, myopia on either side tends to be punished severely. Good regulatory players are those who can discipline themselves to plan several moves ahead.

The benefits and costs of innovation differ between government and private regulators and between regulators and regulatees. If I may be permitted to exaggerate slightly for the purpose of emphasis:

1. Detailed technological changes are viewed at least potentially as friends by the management and staff of most regulatees and less regulated competitors and by their customers as well. Learning about new processes and products promises to improve profit performance, customer service, and job opportunities for employees. Innovation typically improves the capitalized value of the lifetime compensation anticipated by managers, stockholders, and employees of well-managed private firms in both the short and long runs.

2. Agency technical staffs and managers of self-regulatory organizations (who are urged to protect mainstream industry interests) have career interests that closely parallel those of their industry counterparts. However, technological change tends to be viewed as an enemy by top government regulators, particularly when they are nearing retirement age. Dealing with new processes and products promises to complicate the job of managing a government agency in the short run without suitably increasing the monetary rewards a typical agency head can earn over either the short run or the longer haul. Unlike the still relatively young Charles Cox, most of these managers prefer job simplification to job enrichment.

Conference Participants

Molly G. Bayley, Executive Director, Commodity Futures Trading Commission

Marc L. Berman, Executive Vice President, Options Clearing Corp.

Charles C. Cox, Commissioner, Securities and Exchange Commission

William C. Dudley, Associate Economist, Morgan Guaranty Trust Co.

Franklin R. Edwards, Professor, Columbia University

Stephen Figlewski, Associate Professor of Finance, New York University

Laurie S. Goodman, Vice President, Citibank

Frederick S. Hammer, President, PSFS

David B. Humphrey, Assistant Director, Research and Statistics Division, Board of Governors of the Federal Reserve System

Edward J. Kane, Everett D. Reese Professor of Banking and Monetary Economics, The Ohio State University

Jarl G. Kallberg, Associate Professor of Finance, New York University

Bruce A. Kohn, Counsel to Commissioner Cox, Securities and Exchange Commission

David Marcus, Senior Vice President, New York Stock Exchange

Terrence F. Martell, Senior Vice President, COMEX

Charles B. McQuade, President, Securities Industry Automation Corp.

Henry F. Minnerop, Partner, Brown, Wood, Ivey, Mitchell & Petty

Kenneth L. Parkinson, Editor, *Cash Management*

Todd E. Petzel, Chief Economist, Coffee, Sugar, & Cocoa Exchange, Inc.

Roger D. Rutz, President, Chicago Board of Trade Clearing Corp.

Anthony Saunders, Associate Professor of Finance, New York University

Richard O. Scribner, Executive Vice President, American Stock Exchange

Robert A. Schwartz, Professor of Economics and Finance, New York University

Seymour Smidt, Nicholas H. Noyes Professor of Economics and Finance, Cornell University

Lee B. Spencer, Jr., Partner, Gibson, Dunn & Crutcher

Hans R. Stoll, Walker Professor of Finance, Vanderbilt University

Gregory F. Udell, Assistant Professor of Finance, New York University

Lawrence J. White, Professor of Economics, New York University

Robert J. Woldow, Senior Vice President, National Securities Clearing Corp.

About the Editors

Anthony Saunders is associate professor of finance at the New York University Graduate School of Business Administration. During 1984–85 he was acting director of the Salomon Brothers Center for the Study of Financial Institutions at NYU. He received his B.S. (1971), his M.S. (1972), and his Ph.D. (1981) from the London School of Economics. He is the author of *Sovereign Debt and Optional Default Decisions* (with J. Khoury and R. Glick, Lexington Books, forthcoming) and *The Role of the Capital Market in Financial Development* (with K. John and A. Khanna, forthcoming). He has published articles in leading finance and economics journals. He has been the editor of the *Salomon Brothers Center Monograph Series in Finance and Economics* since 1984.

Lawrence J. White is professor of economics at the New York University Graduate School of Business Administration. During 1982–83 he was on leave to serve as director of the Economic Policy Office, Antitrust Division, U.S. Department of Justice. He received his B.A. (1964) from Harvard University, his M.Sc. (1965) from the London School of Economics, and his Ph.D. (1969) from Harvard University. He is the author of *The Automobile Industry Since 1945* (1971), *Industrial Concentration and Economic Power in Pakistan* (1974), *Reforming Regulation: Processes and Problems* (1981), *The Regulation of Air Pollutant Emissions from Motor Vehicles* (1982), *The Public Library in the 1980s: The Problems of Choice* (1983), and articles in leading economics journals. He is coeditor of two conference volumes, *Deregulation of the Banking and Securities Industries* (1979) and *Mergers and Acquisitions: Current Problems in Perspective* (1982), published by Lexington Books. He also served on the senior staff of the President's Council of Economic Advisers during 1978–79. He is currently the North American editor of the *Journal of Industrial Economics*.

DATE DUE

MAY 2 8 '88			

DEMCO 38-297